Essays on the Internment of Italian Canadians

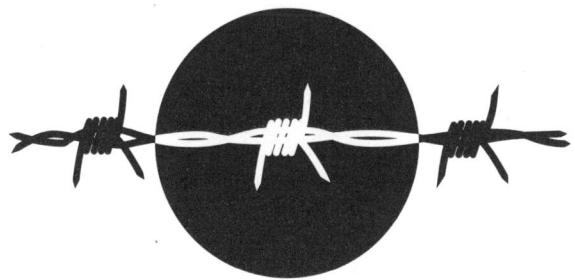

Edited by Licia Canton, Domenic Cusmano, Michael Mirolla, Jim Zucchero

GUERNICA
TORONTO • BUFFALO • BERKELEY • LANCASTER (U.K.)
2012

Copyright © 2012, the Editors, the Authors, Translators,
Association of Italian Canadian Writers,
Columbus Centre, Accenti Magazine, and Guernica Editions Inc.
All rights reserved. The use of any part of this publication,
reproduced, transmitted in any form or by any means, electronic,
mechanical, photocopying, recording or otherwise stored in a
retrieval system, without the prior consent of the publisher is an
infringement of the copyright law.

Michael Mirolla, series editor
Licia Canton, editor
Domenic Cusmano, editor
Jim Zucchero, editor
Guernica Editions Inc.
David Moratto, book designer
P.O. Box 117, Station P, Toronto (ON), Canada M5S 2S6
2250 Military Road, Tonawanda, N.Y. 14150-6000 U.S.A.

Distributors:
University of Toronto Press Distribution,
5201 Dufferin Street, Toronto (ON), Canada M3H 5T8
Gazelle Book Services, White Cross Mills, High Town, Lancaster LA1 4XS U.K.
Small Press Distribution, 1341 Seventh St., Berkeley, CA 94710-1409 U.S.A.

First edition.
Printed in Canada.

Legal Deposit – First Quarter
Library of Congress Catalog Card Number: 2012930744
Library and Archives Canada Cataloguing in Publication

Beyond barbed wire : essays on the internment
of Italian Canadians / edited by Licia Canton ... [et al.].

(Essential essays series ; 61)
Includes bibliographical references.
Issued also in electronic formats.
ISBN 978-1-55071-391-6

1. Italian Canadians--Evacuation and relocation, 1940-1945.
2. World War, 1939-1945--Prisoners and prisons, Canadian.
3. World War, 1939-1945--Italian Canadians. 4. World War,
1939-1945--Canada. I. Canton, Licia, 1963- II. Series: Essential
essays series (Toronto, Ont.) ; 61.

D805.C3B49 2012   940.53'1771   C2012-900446-4

Acknowledgements

The Association of Italian Canadian Writers (AICW), in partnership with Guernica Editions and *Accenti Magazine,* and co-publisher Columbus Centre of Toronto wish to thank the Minister of Citizenship and Immigration Canada (Community Historical Recognition Program — CHRP) for making this publication possible. The publication is also financed in part through the generous support of the Villa Charities Family and the Villa Charities Foundation. Heartfelt thanks to the contributors for their co-operation. We are grateful to Marianna Simeone (CBC journalist), Filomena Rotiroti (Quebec MNA) and Salvatore Bancheri (Director, Frank Iacobucci Centre for Italian Canadian Studies, University of Toronto) for writing letters of support. We acknowledge the work of Venera Fazio, Anna Foschi, Agata De Santis, Giulia De Gasperi, Sayeeda Alibhai. For their assistance and excellent advice, we are grateful to Claire Andrews, Laura Clarke, Loe Garavito-Bruhn and Isabel Zucchero. Special thanks go to Program Officer Thérèse Rochefort; and Lucy Di Pietro, Louanne Aspillaga, and the staff of *Italian Canadians as Enemy Aliens: Memories of World War II.* We could not have completed this project without the unconditional support and encouragement of our families, especially Holly and Charlie; Liana, Dario and Decio; Jackie, Medea and GianCarlo.

CONTENTS

Preface
1

JIM ZUCCHERO
Introduction: Confronting the Legacy of Shame
5

LICIA CANTON & JOSEPH PIVATO
Writing the Silence
15

ANTONIO CALCAGNO
Giorgio Agamben, Modern Sovereignty and the Camps:
A Challenge for Canada
31

VENERA FAZIO
Frenzy of Fear: Prelude to the Italian Canadian Internment
41

MICHAEL MIROLLA
Enemy Aliens: How Canada Declared War on Its Own Citizens
69

GIULIA DE GASPERI
The Italians of Cape Breton Island and the Episode of the Internment of Italian-Canadians as Presented in *Down the Coaltown Road*

79

PATRICK MARSH
Oral History in Cape Breton: An Italian Internment History

103

ANGELO PRINCIPE
Italian Canadian Fascist Women and the Government's "Wishy-Washy" Policy

117

JOYCE PILLARELLA
The Italian Internment Experience Seen Through Silence, Spaces and Censored Vision

137

FILIPPO SALVATORE
Guido Nincheri's Fresco Depicting Benito Mussolini in Madonna della Difesa Church in Montreal

157

TRAVIS TOMCHUK
Special Agent 203: The Motivations of Augusto Bersani

163

Frank Giorno & James McCreath
Internee 328, Camp Petawawa, June 1940-June 1941

179

Vittorina Cecchetto
"Don't Speak the Enemy's Language!":
The Impact of the War Years
on Italian Canadian Identity and Culture

225

John Potestio
The Experiences of Italians at the Lakehead
during the Second World War Years

235

Adriana A. Davies
The Black-Shirted Fascisti Are Coming to Alberta

251

Antonella Fanella
The Rebaudengo Family

273

Raymond Culos
Italian Canadian Enemy Aliens Sent to Kananaskis:
Chapter Six of *Injustice Served*

281

Jim Zucchero
Internment and Duliani's *The City Without Women*:
A Case Study for Multiculturalism in Canada

295

Fabiana Fusco
(Translated by Giulia De Gasperi)
From Imprisonment to Writing:
The Case of Mario Duliani's
La ville sans femmes/Città senza donne

337

Venera Fazio
City of a Perilous Legacy

349

Sam Migliore
Painful Memories of a Forgotten Past

355

Preface

In April 2011, the Association of Italian Canadian Writers (AICW), in partnership with Guernica Editions and *Accenti Magazine*, undertook a national literary project to increase public awareness about the internment of Italian Canadians during the Second World War. During this period, about 7,000 Italian Canadians were identified as enemy aliens and obliged to report regularly to the RCMP. Approximately 600, almost all men, were sent to internment camps in Alberta, Ontario, Quebec and New Brunswick. None of the internees was ever charged, yet some were held for more than three years. The internment years not only impacted the families of the interned, it impeded the progress of the entire Italian Canadian community for decades.

Behind Barbed Wire is a collection of short fiction, memoir, poetry, drama and visual art inspired by the internment. *Beyond Barbed Wire*, a co-publication with Columbus Centre of Toronto, is a collection of essays examining the internment from historical, social, literary, and cultural perspectives. The volumes are simultaneously published as print and e-books. A series of articles in *Accenti Magazine* previewed the two companion volumes, launched across Canada in March 2012. The project is funded by the Minister of Citizenship and Immigration Canada (Community Historical Recognition Program — CHRP).

We are extremely proud of our literary project, which was completed in record time. By breaking the silence of past decades, our project bridges the generations and encourages a better understanding of the past so as to avoid repeating the same mistakes.

This endeavour has also given us a unique opportunity to build bridges between individuals and communities across Canada, while emphasizing the work of creative individuals and intellectuals who often work on the periphery of the Italian Canadian community. Let us continue to build bridges. Let us work together on new ventures, not only among writers and artists, but also with other Italian Canadians and organizations at large.

Note: Style choices are those of the individual contributors.

—The Editors

BEYOND BARBED WIRE

Essays on the Internment of Italian Canadians

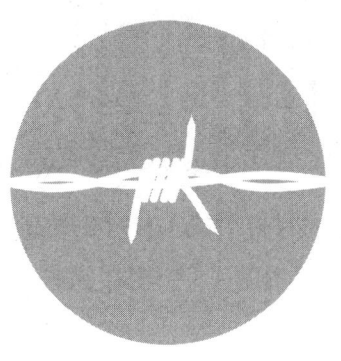

Jim Zucchero

Introduction: Confronting the Legacy of Shame

> *Remembrance shapes our links to the past, and the ways we remember define us in the present ... We know how slippery and unreliable personal memory can be ... But a society's collective memory is no less contingent, no less unstable, its shape by no means permanent. It is always subject to subtle and not so subtle reconstruction.*
> —*Andreas Huyssen*, Twilight Memories

We are honoured and pleased to present this collection of essays about the internment of Italian Canadians — a little known and troubling fact of Canadian history. Producing this volume (in print and e-formats) has been a great responsibility, a wonderful opportunity, and a considerable challenge. The time line for completion of the project seemed impossibly short; the tasks were many and we too few. Now, there is a feeling of excitement in bringing forward the writing presented here; we are pleased at the scope and variety of this collection. It includes compelling first-person accounts of the internment and its effects on the families and communities of those interned.

There are diaries and testimonials as well as commentary and analysis. Some essays offer provocative points to stir debate; others offer thoughtful reflection and posit useful questions. They expose and explore contentious issues and raise important questions about rights and responsibilities, power and privilege, political processes, ethnic identity, collective memory, and many other topics relevant to contemporary Canadian society. They will surely prompt further reflection and promote further analysis. In all, this volume makes a valuable contribution to an important and necessary exercise: the examination of a controversial event in Canadian history, and evaluating some of its long term effects — on Italian Canadians individually and collectively, and on the development of Canadian democracy and multiculturalism.

Some Background Information About the Internment

The story of the internment of Italian Canadians in the 1940s is a paradox. On one hand, it is a little-known episode in Canadian history, even within the Italian Canadian community. On the other hand, it remains a deeply contentious issue that can still elicit strong, polarized responses both within and beyond that ethnic community. Angelo Principe characterized the internment as "a tangled knot." The image accurately conveys the shape and dimensions of the issue; there are many loose ends, pieces that overlap and bear on one another. There are a few incontestable facts: On June 10, 1940 Italy declared war on Britain, France and the Allied countries. Soon after, Canada too was at war.

When Canada declared war on Italy, the government of Prime Minister W.L. Mackenzie King invoked the War Measures Act under the Defence of Canada Regulations. In the weeks and months that followed more than 600 Canadians of Italian descent — including some born in Canada — deemed enemy aliens were arrested and detained in internment camps in Kananaskis, Alberta; Petawawa, Ontario; and Gagetown, New Brunswick. None of the Italian Canadians interned was ever formally charged with committing a crime, yet some were imprisoned for as long as five years. The effects of internment were felt not only by those imprisoned, but also by family members, and in the Italian Canadian communities in which they lived and worked. The extent to which some internees posed a genuine threat to the security of Canadians (through their involvement with fascist organizations) has been an issue of considerable contention. Similarly, the culpability of the government of the day in enacting the War Measures Act has been a matter of heated debate (see *Enemies Within: Italian and Other Internees in Canada and Abroad* (2000)).

In 1990, fifty years after the fact, then-Prime Minister Brian Mulroney offered an apology to Italian Canadians on behalf of the Canadian Government for the events surrounding the internment. In the view of some, his apology was long overdue; to others, he had succumbed to political pressure from those who had developed a simplistic interpretation of the events. Some still maintain that his apology was inadequate because it was not delivered in the House of Commons, so it remains "unofficial." Where are we now in relation to these contentious issues? Has the passage of time — seventy years since the internment, and twenty years since the apology — enabled us to view those events more clearly or provided any new perspectives? The works collected here wrestle with these issues.

This collection of essays is intended for a general readership and not only as a scholarly work for use by academics. Our primary goal has been to produce a volume that provides an accurate overview of the historical events described and critical reflection on the effects of the internment. Editing this collection of essays posed some considerable challenges around technical and logistical points. The obvious issue of repetition was one such challenge; the matter of correctness and accuracy was another. Each of these deserves to be spoken to here.

Repetition of certain facts within these essays was somewhat unavoidable; for example, the invoking of the War Measures Act that enabled the internment is mentioned or discussed in several essays. But the relative emphasis placed on specific details and how they are interpreted is telling and central to this project as a whole. The range of responses — how events are interpreted and examined, demonstrates, in part, why we need to revisit past events and sometimes revise our response to them. Furthermore, this revisioning may cast light on the processes of history. The passage of time may be more likely to affect our intellectual response to troubling events of the past than to bring about changes in our emotional disposition toward them. But the capacity to shift our perception of past events is important if we are to move forward.

Certain themes emerge from the essays here, and there are recurring motifs: silence and bitterness, but also courage and resilience. The distance in time by which we are now removed from those events can provide for a clearer and more nuanced understanding of their meaning and impact. The perspective from which we now reflect on the events of the 1940s enables us to better comprehend their effects and should assist us to move forward constructively with the benefit of new awareness gained.

Every effort has been made to check points of fact to ensure their accuracy. At the same time, some of the issues and events described in these essays are contentious and writers hold different views on some facts. The opinions expressed are those of the authors; they provide useful context and convey various points of view on the topics and issues described.

Some essays rely on memoirs, interviews and the testimony of witnesses, some of whom are family members. Human memory is not mechanical, nor is it perfect; it is prone to slippage, forgetfulness and embellishment. Some of those interviewed were children at the time of the events; now they are elders. How has the passage of so many years shifted their memories and the meaning those memories have come to hold? We have recorded the information received with the understanding that it is prone to all of the vagaries of human memory.

The essays collected here include works by established scholars and by writers who are being published for the first time. The writing of vernacular history and examinations of oral history by some essayists speaks to the broadest objectives of the CHRP project; namely, to give voice to those who have previously not been heard. For some, writing about the internment has been cathartic, a way of exorcising the ghosts of the past. For others, it has provided a means of working toward reconciliation — a much needed opportunity to express the confusion, anger, resentment and emotional pain experienced, directly or indirectly, as a result of those events. Writing about the internments has provided the opportunity to confront the legacy of shame.

But whose shame is it? Where does blame lie? Do subsequent generations of Canadians of Italian heritage still carry the burden of shame from the wartime internments of some in the 1940s, and the requirement imposed on thousands more to report regularly to Canadian authorities? Does the present Government of Canada still bear responsibility for the decisions made by the government in 1940, during a time of war? How is this burden to be managed and disassembled — on both sides? Is a project that aims at commemoration and education a better way to move forward than paying restitution to victims or their families? Is an "official" apology, delivered in the House of Commons still important, and if so, why? How will the Italian Canadian community choose to represent these issues in 2012 — more than 70 years after the fact? These are some of the questions that underlie the essays in this collection.

The essays have been arranged in three sections: the first provides context and scope; the second presents a series of regional studies and offers insight into how the events surrounding internment were experienced in different parts of Canada; the third provides analysis of Mario Duliani's chronicle of internment, *The City Without Women*, the only first-hand account of life as an internee.

Licia Canton and Joseph Pivato's essay "Writing the Silence" provides a brief but comprehensive history of writing about the internment of Italians in Canada and situates that writing within the broader parameters of Italian Canadian writing. They assert that the internment had a profound effect on this ethnic community for generations to follow, as evidenced by the resounding silence and the dearth of writing on this difficult subject. **Antonio Calcagno**'s essay explores fundamental questions about rights, power and the nature of Canadian democracy, from philosophical perspectives. He applies concepts from Giorgio Agamben's work to pose useful questions in determining where we stand today in relation to the troubled history of internment and asks if we are not still prone to the same abuses of power. In her essay "Frenzy of Fear: Prelude to the Italian Canadian Internment," **Venera Fazio** traces the growth of public panic as recorded in several major Canadian daily newspapers as the run-up to the internment. She asserts that the growing frenzy of public fear contributed to the decision of those in power to invoke the War Measures Act. **Michael Mirolla**'s essay "Italian Enemy Aliens: How Canada Declared War On Its Own Citizens" was first published in 1994 and is contemporary with the English translation of Duliani's internment chronicle. It provides a historical overview of the events and expresses a view held by many: that the actions taken were draconian and deeply problematic.

The essays in the middle section provide "snapshots" of events surrounding the internment in various parts of the country, beginning on the east coast and moving west. Some of these essays are also linked in terms of content and method. For example, the essays by **John Potestio**, **Ray Culos** and **Joyce Pillarella** rely heavily on interviews. Others — the essay by **Frank Giorno and James McCreath** on James Franceschini, and the piece by **Antonella Fanella** on the Rebaudengo family — focus closely on a single family and examine how its members were affected by internment. These essays clearly demonstrate that those in positions of privilege were not immune to the force of law or abuse of power.

Giulia De Gasperi's essay examines the events that led to the internment of Italians in Nova Scotia through a critical reading of Sheldon Currie's historical novel *Down the Coaltown Road*, a story set in Cape Breton in 1940. **Patrick Marsh** also uses Cape Breton as a backdrop to examine the evolving view of the internment. His sources are a CBC Radio interview broadcast in 1977 and a second CBC Radio interview recorded in 1991. **Angelo Principe**'s essay presents a different angle on the internment question by considering Italian Canadian fascist women. He asserts that government policy and reaction to the activities of these women was at best uncertain and confused. **Joyce Pillarella** writes about her grandfather who was, by his own admission, an avowed fascist, and who was interned. She intersperses excerpts from interviews with descendants of internees with her personal response to the internment issue.

Filippo Salvatore offers an insightful essay on a fresco by Guido Nincheri of Mussolini on horseback, which adorns the apse vault of the Madonna della Difesa Church in Montreal. His essay conveys both how admired Mussolini was among Italians, and how well respected he was by a broad cross-section of civil society in North America for a time. **Vittorina Cecchetto**'s "Don't Speak the Enemy's Language" demonstrates how Italians in Canada were instantly transformed from integrated members of the community to pariahs, after Italy declared war on Great Britain and France. She notes that this soon led to many Canadians denying their Italian identity. "The Black-Shirted Fasciti Are Coming to Alberta," by **Adriana Davies**, provides useful historical context concerning the nature of fascist organizations in Alberta in the period leading up to the war. Her essay shines a light on the real effects of the internment on the broader Italian Canadian community in Alberta in the post-war years, including the disavowal of "Italianness" by some and the distrust of associating or forming community organizations. She asserts, however, that those who continue to press for reparations are misguided; they collapse crucial distinctions and fall prey to simplistic interpretations of a complex history. **Travis Tomchuk** provides a chilling account of how personal vindictiveness, left unchecked and empowered by the authority of the state, led to great suffering. He examines the case of an RCMP informant, Augusto Bersani, whose reckless conduct led directly to the imprisonment of innocent individuals against whom he sought revenge.

The final section brings together several essays that examine Mario Duliani's internment chronicle *The City Without Women*, a unique and highly influential work. **Fabiana Fusco** highlights some of the ways in which the French and Italian versions of the text differ, and theorizes about the reasons for and effects of these differences. **Jim Zucchero**'s essay examines various aspects of authority in Duliani's text. He focusses on literary dimensions of the text, including the effects of translation, and considers what responses to Duliani's chronicle might suggest about contemporary Italian Canadian culture. **Venera Fazio**'s "City of a Perilous Legacy" intersperses excerpts of *The City Without Women* with excerpts of an interview she conducted with Antonino Mazza, the English translator of Duliani's book. Finally, **Sam Migliore** uses the experience of Italian internees in Cape Breton to illustrate the hardships caused by the internment, and he rebuts the arguments put forth by Iacovetta, Perin and Principe that the Canadian Government's actions in interning Italian Canadians were reasonable under the circumstances.

As a nation, as an ethnic community, and as individuals, how will we remember and manage the impact of injustices perpetrated against individuals and an ethnic group on behalf of the broader community? Can re-examining "the tangled knot" of Italian Canadian internments now help us to become more sensitive to the effects of prejudice, and more astute in developing and implementing more effective laws and policies for the protection of Canadians?

The work of educating people about historic events, social movements, and those who subscribe to different social or cultural norms never stops, but it does become increasingly important. Paradoxically, by raising consciousness about our differences, we become more aware of our similarities and those human qualities that bind us. Revisiting and re-examining difficult episodes from our past allows us to become attuned to the lessons of history that can inform and guide our social policies, laws and practices.

So, what are the lessons of history to be drawn from this episode? That we must be more vigilant about the laws we create to promote security, and about when and how those laws are invoked, especially because the movement of people around the globe has reached unprecedented levels. The capability to move and store information has expanded in ways that were unimaginable just a generation ago, further complicating matters. These two facts heighten the need for greater care and vigilance to prevent abuses of power and the devastating effects of poorly thought out and recklessly administered laws and policies. As many have noted, if we do not heed the lessons of history we are destined to repeat the errors of the past.

It is our hope that this publication can assist in creating positive change; specifically, that those who were victims of state authority can become agents of social change. It is important that the internment of Italian Canadians enter "official" history to be studied further and better understood. Guided by the lessons of the past, we can work toward improving relations across ethnic groups and create more integrated, stronger societies, where mutual respect replaces suspicion, and where caring for others, including those who are different from us, is an expression of our recognition of a common human bond — the true measure of our humanity. Cultivating the growth of such a society will be crucial to the development of Canadian multiculturalism in the twenty-first century. It will require extraordinary generosity, courage, optimism, and imagination: to fight hatred with compassion; to overcome ignorance with awareness; and to extinguish fear with understanding.

Works Cited

Duliani, Mario. *The City Without Women*. Trans. Antonino Mazza. Oakville: Mosaic, 1994.

Huyssen, Andreas. *Twilight Memories: Marking Time in a Culture of Amnesia*. New York: Routledge, 1995.

Iacovetta, Franca, Roberto Perin and Angelo Principe. Eds. *Enemies Within: Italian and Other Internees in Canada and Abroad*. Toronto: UT Press, 2000.

Licia Canton & Joseph Pivato

Writing the Silence

> "Ricordo bene quella sera."
> —*Diario di una emigrante*

Although their body of works is relatively new, Canadians of Italian origin have influenced the evolution of writing and literary criticism in Canada. In 1978, as the editor of the poetry anthology *Roman Candles,* Pier Giorgio Di Cicco brought together previously unheard solitary voices and, by so doing, gave a sense of direction to Italian-Canadian writers. Since then, the appearance of specific collections, anthologies and critical studies — mostly in English but also in French and Italian — has had an important impact on the visibility of our community's literary voices.

Before the 1980s, Italians in Canada wrote in isolation. Their writings did not constitute a conscious body of works. Very early publications include Francesco Giuseppe Bressani's *Breve Relatione* (1653), Antonio Gallenga's *Episodes of My Second Life* (1884), and Francesco Gualtieri's *We Italians: A Study in Italian Immigration in Canada* (1928). Other writers include Anna Moroni and A.A. Nobile as well as Liborio Lattoni who wrote poetry celebrating Mussolini (Pivato 1998).

After the Second World War, it took several decades before Italian-Canadians began writing about the silence, the shame and the secrecy associated with the internment. Thus, Italian immigrants who arrived in Canada in the 1950s and 1960s never heard about the internment of Italians in Canada. Their children did not read about the internment in school. Many in the community wanted to forget about these events where Italian-Canadians had been victims of prejudice and lost their jobs and businesses. Most of those who were directly affected by the internment did not want to talk about it: they were ashamed. "This shameful episode led many Italians to take the extreme measure of denouncing their heritage, even going as far as changing their names to sever any connection to their Italian roots" (Iacobacci 15). As Venera Fazio writes in "City of a Perilous Legacy": "[T]he Italian communities across Canada collapsed ... The communities were rife with confusion, discouragement, and resentment ... The progress of the community, as a whole, was thwarted ..." For the most part, the older generation of Italians in Canada pretended that the internment never happened. Beginning in the 1980s, Italian-Canadian writers and historians began to investigate and write about the internment of Italian-Canadians. But, there has always been a discomfort in addressing this historical event.

The Canadian government's treatment of Japanese Canadian citizens during the Second World War has been well documented and, after many years, their unjust suffering was acknowledged. In 1988, the Canadian government gave a formal apology. Japanese Canadian author Joy Kogawa published the novel *Obasan* in 1981. It became a popular book in high school, college and university courses. Kogawa's *Obasan* presented a critical treatment of the internment of Japanese Canadians in British Columbia and stimulated other ethnic minority groups to re-examine their own buried history. After decades of silence, in the Italian communities of Montreal and Toronto, Mario Duliani's forgotten chronicle *La ville sans femmes* (1945) and the Italian version *Città senza donne* (1946) were rediscovered in the 1980s. This rediscovery was due in part to the work of Italian-Canadian writers and the birth of

Italian-Canadian literature. In 1994 an English version of Duliani's book was published: *The City Without Women* is a translation by Antonino Mazza.

When the Federal Government invoked the War Measures Act in 1970 in Quebec, during the FLQ crisis, some political observers were reminded that the last time the War Measures Act was enacted was during the Second World War. A decade later, writers and academics began to examine the internment of Italians in Canada. Some gave conference papers, others published short articles on the fascist groups and individuals in Canada before the Second World War. Later, a few filmmakers addressed the internment. Today, we have a modest body of works on these historical events.

Elena Maccaferri Randaccio is the first woman of Italian origin to have published in Quebec. Randaccio published *Canada, mia seconda patria* in 1958 under the pen-name Elena Albani, which was reviewed by Mario Duliani in *Il Cittadino Canadese*. Twenty-one years later, in 1979, Randaccio published *Diario di una emigrante* under the name E. MacRan. *Diario di una emigrante* is narrated by Climene, a very strong and determined woman, who describes in detail how her husband Beppe is taken away by two policemen and interned for three years. Climene remembers that night very well. It is the turning point in her immigrant experience. *Diario di una emigrante* is one of the very few fictional works that sets characters within the internment years. In his historical novel *Down the Coaltown Road,* Nova Scotia writer Sheldon Currie describes the struggle of Italians in industrial Cape Breton during the years of the internment. Currie's play *By the Sea — Anna's Story,* based on this novel, was produced by Festival Antigonish in 2001 and by Eastern Front Theatre, Dartmouth, in 2002.

The first Italian in Canada to write about the internment after Duliani was Guglielmo Vangelisti in his 1956 book *Gli Italiani in*

Canada. In two pages he focuses on the suffering of Italian families in Montreal as a result of the arrest of their fathers and bothers (197-198). In his book, *The Italians in Canada* (1969), Antonino Spada devotes only three pages to the internment of Italians in Canada. In his very detailed 387-page book Spada seems to avoid giving many details about these crucial events. On pages 125-127 he gives some historical context for the fascist groups in Canada, one paragraph on the War Measures Act of 1940 and some information on anti-fascist movements. In the rest of his book he only mentions internment in passing. In his profile of Mario Duliani he writes: "After his internment in 1940, he wrote *La ville sans femmes*, which was also translated into Italian" (154). In his brief profile of James Franceschini, Spada notes: "When Italy entered the war JF was interned at Camp Petawawa for a time" (196). Spada was an ardent anti-fascist from the 1930s to the end of his life, so it seems peculiar that he is so circumspect about the arrests and internment of about 600 Italian-Canadians.

In the collection of studies *The Italian Immigrant Woman in North America* (1978), edited by Betty Boyd Caroli, Robert F. Harney and Lydio F. Tomasi, there is one essay titled "La Donna Italiana Durante il Periodo Fascista in Toronto, 1930-1940" written by Luigi Pautasso. The essay concludes with two paragraphs on the internment of 600 men. Pautasso explains that there were also four Italian women jailed in Kingston under the War Measures Act. In her short 55-page book, *All Our Fathers: The North Italian Colony in Industrial Cape Breton* (1983), Esperanza Maria Razzolini devotes three pages to the experiences of Italian miners and their families as men were taken away by the RCMP. She notes that the scars left on these small mining communities, such as Dominion, were evident for decades.

Professor Robert F. Harney was the major scholar of Italian-Canadian historical study. At the University of Toronto he supervised many young academics to pursue this area of research. Unfortunately he died in 1989, at age 50, before he was able to produce his own history of Italian settlement in Canada. The only book we have of his own work is a collection of essays in Italian, *Dalla frontiera alle Little Italies: Gli italiani in Canada 1800-1945* which appeared in 1984. In his final essay "La Little Italy di Toronto 1919-1945," he devotes just three pages to the internment experiences (258-260).

In his 1984 Italian book *Il Canada. L'Italia e il fascismo 1919-1945*, Luigi Bruti-Liberati spends ten pages analysing the internment events in the context of fascist and anti-fascist groups in Canada (190-200). He gives a summary of the reports by Guglielmo Vangelisti, Mario Duliani and researched articles by others. In his sensitively-written book *Canadese: A Portrait of the Italian Canadians* (1989), Kenneth Bagnell devotes chapter four, "Days of Darkness, Days of Despair," to the internment crisis. Bagnell recounts not just the historical facts but also writes brief narratives of individual Italians who were suddenly arrested and later interned; people from all walks of life such as Dr. Luigi Pancaro (a physician in Sudbury), coalminers from Cape Breton, workers from Hamilton and Toronto as well as James Franceschini, the day-labourer turned construction magnate and Canada's first Italian immigrant millionaire.

Issue 53 of *Cape Breton's Magazine* (1990) includes a 20-page interview with Dominic Nardocchio from Sydney, Cape Breton Island. Nardocchio was interned in Petawawa for 21 months. In Stanislao Carbone's *The Streets Were Not Paved With Gold: A Social History of Italians in Winnipeg* (1993), there are six pages on the experiences of the War Measures Act in the Manitoba capital (68-73). Carbone reviews events that occurred in Toronto and Montreal from 1940 to 1941 and contrasts this with the treatment of Italians in Manitoba:

> In Winnipeg, Italians may not have suffered the same degree of hostility as did their counterparts in Toronto or Montreal, but they were subjected to the close scrutiny of the RCMP, to whom they had to report on a monthly basis. Relief payments were suspended and in some cases travel restrictions were imposed. (73)

In their book on the Famèe Furlane, *Rekindling Faded Memories* (1996), Angelo Principe and Olga Zorzi Pugliese make some passing remarks on the internment crisis in the 1940s. In their profile of Dante Colussi-Corte who was president of the Famèe Furlane from 1935 to 1940, they write:

> Colussi's political views were quite unequivocal: he was a strong anti-Fascist. At the outbreak of the Second World War in 1940, he is reported to have burned all the back issues of his anti-Fascist newspaper in his landlord's fireplace. It is likely that he also destroyed the minutes of the Famèe Furlane since the archive now preserves as its earliest document a record book that begins with the meeting of September 15, 1940, and refers to President Colussi's explanation for the suspension of activities during the previous few months and the unavailability of minutes of the previous meeting. (54)

Even though he was a First World War veteran and an anti-fascist journalist, Colussi feared for his life and the Famèe Furlane social club and decided to destroy his papers. He was aware that fellow members Ruggero Bacci and Celeste Cristofoli were interned in July 1940.

Italian Lives, Cape Breton Memories (1999), edited by Sam Migliore and A. Evo DiPierro, contains fieldwork and interviews conducted with members of the Italian communities of industrial Cape Breton (Sydney and Dominion in particular). Section II of the book is dedicated to "The War Years" (87-130) and contains an account of the events by non-Italian miners (100-101) and "Three Women from Dominion" (104-107), thereby giving voice to the recollections of women.

The most scholarly and thorough study of the internment is *Enemies Within: Italian and Other Internees in Canada and Abroad* (2000), edited by Franca Iacovetta, Roberto Perin and Angelo Principe. The volume is a collection of studies by historians who are experts in the field. Principe's authored book on fascism and anti-fascism in Canada, *The Darkest Side of the Fascist Years: The Italian-Canadian Press, 1920-1942*, was published by Guernica in 1999.

Mario Duliani's *La ville sans femmes* is the only eyewitness account of internment and has both the benefits and drawbacks of such a personal chronicle. Susan Iannucci points out that Duliani's text is "a self-vindication, a public act of Canadian patriotism, which is to set him straight forever with the authorities" (211). It is worthy of note that Duliani changed many words and phrases when he produced his Italian version, *Città senza donne,* one year after the original French appeared. (See Fabiana Fusco's essay in this volume.) When Antonino Mazza produced the English version, *The City Without Women,* he used both the French and Italian publications and so produced a third version since he had to decide which words and phrases to translate and which to leave aside.

In her article "City of a Perilous Legacy," Venera Fazio writes about the conversation she had (in 2003) with Antonino Mazza on the internment and his work on Duliani's text. In the exchange, Mazza interprets the emotion and everyday reality that Italians and the Italian-Canadian community lived during the period of the internment. Mazza illustrates the "shame surrounding the subject" that lasted decades, thereby discouraging and silencing any further discussion on the internment

"In the Italian community where I grew up," says Mazza, "people knew about the camps. They would whisper about it, but not talk openly. They tried to keep it a secret ... Imagine, you do not know what you have done wrong or for how long you will be punished ... you live in suspension, in limbo ... you experience a huge torment of being alive and great anxiety."

Filippo Salvatore, in *Fascism and the Italians of Montreal: An Oral History 1922-1945*, interviews thirteen eyewitnesses to the events in Montreal. The interviewees include writer Hugh MacLennan, internees Dieni Gentile and Salvatore Mancuso and anti-fascist journalist Antonino Spada. While he acknowledges the value of the historical research that some academics have done, Salvatore argues that eyewitnesses can share a more human aspect of the internment experience. The author's objective is to show "how the various men and women of different ages reacted to the fact that in a single day they became *enemy aliens*" and to identify "the social, economic and political consequences this subjected them to" (32).

Una Storia Segreta: The Secret History of Italian American Evacuation and Internment During World War II (2001), edited by Lawrence DiStasi, is a volume of essays on the internment of Italians in the United States. As Ken Scambray writes in "Secret Histories": "*Una Storia Segreta* is a major contribution to Italian American studies ... Rather than a footnote that some would rather forget, the revelation of the internment of Italian Americans during the Second World War informs us not only about our status in American society today, but also about our own attitudes towards our past and our identity." DiStasi's book includes memoirs and personal essays as well as academic essays.

In *Veneti in Canada*, a recent volume of essays edited by Gianpaolo Romanato and published in Italy, Angelo Principe has an essay titled "*Il fascismo e gli italo-canadesi 1921-1948.*" There is hardly any knowledge of this historical episode in Italy. Given that Italians in Canada had silenced the episode, they would certainly not speak about it to their Italian relatives. Moreover, many Italian-Canadians still do not know about this historical occurrence.

In *Whoever Gives Us Bread: The Story of Italians in British Columbia* (2011), Lynne Bowen writes about the Italian community in British Columbia from the 1860s to the 1960s. Bowen researched the book by searching newspapers, government records and letters and through interviews. In a recent interview with *The Vancouver Sun*, Bowen says "Many Vancouverites have an Italian neighbour but have no idea how she suffered under the ignorant racism of bureaucrats, politicians or businessmen" (Nov. 5). In Chapter 11, titled "Enemy Aliens," Bowen writes about the internment of Italians in British Columbia. "Whether they wish to talk about him or not, Italians haven't forgotten Mussolini or the war" (256). The same is equally true of the internment experience in Canada. Bowen reiterates the silence and the shame surrounding the subject that every writer and researcher has encountered in writing about the internment.

In his book *Vancouver's Society of Italians*, Raymond Culos addresses the internment of Italians in BC. His most recent book, *Injustice Served* (2012), focuses solely on the internment and how it affected the lives of Italians, and the Italian-Canadian community, in British Columbia. Culos conducted a series of interviews and research over several decades. A foreword by the Honourable Frank Iacobucci and ten chapters are followed by thirteen profiles which give personal accounts of internees or their descendants. The book is in English and in Italian, thereby bridging the language barriers among the generations.

Vittorio Rossi's *Paradise by the River*, a play in three acts, was published by Talon Books in 1998. The same year, the play premiered at the Centaur Theatre in Montreal and was acclaimed by critics. *Paradise by the River* was presented once again at Centaur in 2010, sponsored by Casa D'Italia of Montreal. That same year it was also presented in Vaughan by Toronto's Shadowpath Theatre Company. In the play, Romano is in an internment camp while his pregnant wife Maria deals with the hardship of life without him. The setting alternates between the camp and Ville Émard, where Maria lives. "I decided to tell the story of how this couple who love each other with a child on the way gets ripped apart ..." Vittorio Rossi explains. "You don't have to be Italian to identify with the idea that these struggles really challenged the human condition" (Mirolla 19).

The internment of Italian-Canadians has also been addressed by filmmakers. Paul Tana's *Caffé Italia, Montréal* (1985) caused some controversy by presenting issues such as the internment and the fascist presence in Montreal. Nicola Zavaglia's documentary *Barbed Wire & Mandolins* (1997) gives personal testimony from Italian-Canadians affected by the internment: Domenico Nardocchio of Sydney, Benny Ferri of Hamilton and Bishop Andrea Cimichella of Montreal to name a few. Cimichella was a 19-year-old studying to become a priest when he was confronted by the RCMP and asked to report to authorities every month. "How can you forget ..." says an emotional Cimichella. "Italian means dangerous ... my blood was bad, not the person, not me ..." In the documentary, Antonino Mazza gives statistics: of the 112,000 Italians living in Canada in 1940, 40,000 were born in Canada, 30,000 were asked to report to authorities, eight doctors were removed from the community. "How many doctors could there have been in 1940?" asks Mazza. Compared to other Commonwealth countries "Canada had the most draconian measures during the war against its own people," Mazza concludes. In a recent interview, Nicola Zavaglia recalls his reflections while working on the film: "I just imagined all the anguish and longing of the men imprisoned in what had become once again a wilderness. I was sure, that if I had been alive at that time, I most likely would have ended up in Petawawa. The silence of the land at Petawawa still haunts me" (Canton).

The television mini-series *Il Duce Canadese* (2004), written by Bruno Ramirez and directed by Giles Walker, was aired on CBC TV in English and in French, as *Le Mussolini canadien*, on Radio Canada. *Il Duce Canadese* is set in Montreal during the internment. Three men in the Alvaro family are interned and the lives of their loved ones are disrupted. In an interview with Matteo Sanfilippo, historian Bruno Ramirez reminds us that the fictional account is based on research and interviews with individuals and families who experienced the internment. In writing the script, Ramirez' objective was to ensure that "the viewer is drawn into the story" and "participate in the drama that the characters live." Ramirez says: "It will be up to the viewer, then, to decide ... if those characters deserved the punishment that they suffered" (Our translation).

The silence of past decades will be replaced by a new discourse as a result of recent projects on the internment across Canada. In British Columbia, these include Ray Culos' book *Injustice Served* and Lucia Frangione's play *Fresco*, which recounts the internment through the eyes of a present-day woman. A trilingual documentary film, written by Micol Marotti, is being produced by Media Monkey Productions of Cobourg, Ontario. And the publication of this book, *Beyond Barbed Wire* — and its companion volume of creative works *Behind Barbed Wire* – marks the passage of Italian-Canadians from silent victims to engaged agents of social change. These literary and creative projects revisit a painful period in Canadian history so that we can all move forward.

Works Cited

Albani, Elena. (pseud.) *Canada, mia seconda patria*. Bologna: Edizioni Sirio, 1958.
"A Talk with Dominic Nardocchio." *Cape Breton's Magazine*, Issue 53, 1990, 69-88: http://capebretonsmagazine.com/modules/publisher/item.php?itemid=3421.
"Author sets the record straight on B.C. Italians' contributions - Persecution a forgotten part of their past" in *The Vancouver Sun*. November 5, 2011.
Bagnell, Kenneth. *Canadese: A Portrait of the Italian Canadians*. Toronto: Macmillan of Canada, 1989.
Bowen, Lynne. *Whoever Gives Us Bread: The Story of Italians in British Columbia*. Douglas & McIntyre, 2011.
Boyd Caroli, Betty, Robert F. Harney & Lydio F. Tomasi. eds. *The Italian Immigrant Woman in North America*. Toronto: Multicultural History Society of Ontario, 1978.
Bressani, Francesco Giuseppe. *Breve relatione d'alcune missioni de P.P. della Compagnia di Giesù nella Nuoua Francia*. Macerata: Per gli Heredi d'Agostino Grisei, 1653.
Bruti-Liberati, Luigi. *Il Canada, l'Italia e il fascismo, 1919-1945*. Roma: Bonacci Editore, 1984.
Canton, Licia. "A Conversation with Nicola Zavaglia." Unpublished interview. Montreal, November 21, 2011.
Carbone, Stanislao. *The Streets Were Not Paved With Gold: A Social History of the Italians in Winnipeg*. Winnipeg: Manitoba Italian Heritage Committee, 1993.

Culos, Raymond. *Vancouver's Society of Italians.* Vols. I-III. Madeira Park, B.C.: Harbour Publishing, c.1998-c.2002.
—. *Injustice Served.* Montreal: Cusmano, 2012.
Currie, Sheldon. *By the Sea — Anna's Story.* Unpublished play.
—. *Down the Coaltown Road.* Toronto: Key Porter Books, 2002.
Di Cicco, Pier Giorgio, ed. *Roman Candles: An Anthology of Poems by Seventeen Italo-Canadian Poets.* Toronto: Hounslow Press, 1978.
DiStasi, Lawrence, ed. *Una Storia Segreta: The Secret History of Italian American Evacuation and Internment During World War II.* 2001.
Duliani, Mario. *La ville sans femmes.* Montréal: Société des Éditions Pascal, 1945.
—. *Città senza donne.* Montreal: Gustavo D'Errico, 1946.
—. [translated by Antonino Mazza] *The City Without Women.* Oakville: Mosaic Press, 1994.
Fazio, Venera. "City of a Perilous Legacy". *Accenti Magazine,* Issue 1, March 2003.
Frangione, Lucia. *Fresco.* (forthcoming, 2012)
Gallenga, Antonio Carlo Napoleone. *Episodes of My Second Life.* Vols. II. London: Chapman, 1884.
Gualtieri, Francesco M. *We Italians: A Study in Italian Immigration in Canada.* Toronto: Italian World War Veterans Association, 1928.
Harney, Robert F. *Dalla Frontiera alle Little Italies: Gli italiani in Canada 1800-1945.* Roma: Bonacci Editore, 1984.
Iacobacci, Pasquale L. "Symbol of Resurgence: Montreal's Casa d'Italia." *Accenti Magazine,* Issue 19, 2010: 14-17.
Iacovetta Franca, Roberto Perin, Angelo Principe, eds *Enemies Within: Italian and Other Internees in Canada and Abroad.* Toronto: University of Toronto Press, 2000.

Iannucci, Susan. "Contemporary Italo-Canadian Literature." *Arrangiarsi: The Italian Immigration Experience in Canada.* Roberto Perin & Franc Sturino, eds. Montreal: Guernica, 1989. 209-227.

Jones, Ted. *Both sides of the wire: The Fredericton Internment Camp.* Vol. I. New Ireland Press, 1988.

Kogawa, Joy. *Obasan.* 1981. Harmondsworth, Middlesex: Penguin, 1983.

La Gumina, Salvatore J. *WOP! A Documentary History of Anti-Italian Discrimination.* Toronto: Guernica Editions, 1999.

MacRan, E. (pseud.) *Diario di una emigrante.* Bologna: Arti Grafiche Tamari, 1979.

Marsh, Patrick. *Oral History in Cape Breton. An Italian Internment History.* BA Thesis, Department of History, Sydney, N.S: Cape Breton University, 2008.

Migliore, Sam and A. Evo DiPierro, eds. *Italian Lives, Cape Breton Memories.* Sydney: UCCB, 1999.

Mirolla, Michael. "Vittorio Rossi By the River." *Accenti Magazine*, Issue 19, 2010: 18-19.

Perin, Roberto and Franc Sturino, eds. *Arrangiarsi: The Italian immigration Experience in Canada.* Montréal: Guernica, 1989.

Pivato, Joseph. "Italianistica Versus Italian-Canadian Writing." *Social Pluralism and Literary History.* Ed. Francesco Loriggio. Toronto: Guernica Editions, 1996.

—, ed. The Anthology of Italian-Canadian Writing. Toronto: Guernica Editions, 1998.

Principe, Angelo & Olga Zorzi Pugliese. *Rekindling Faded Memories: The Founding of the Famèe Furlane of Toronto and Its First Years.* Toronto: Famèe Furlane of Toronto, 1996.

Principe, Angelo. *The Darkest Side of the Fascist Years: The Italian-Canadian Press, 1920-1942*. Toronto: Guernica Editions, 1999.

Ramirez, Bruno. *Il Duce Canadese*. Giles Walker (director). Ciné Télé Action, 2004.

—. *The Canadian Duce*. Toronto: Guernica Editions, 2007.

Razzolini, Esperanza Maria. *All Our Fathers: The North Italian Colony in Industrial Cape Breton*. Halifax: Saint Mary's University, 1983.

Romanato, Gianpaolo, ed. *Veneti in Canada*. Ravenna: Longo Editore, 2011.

Rossi, Vittorio. *Paradise by the River*. Talon Books, 1998.

Salvatore, Filippo. *Fascism and the Italians of Montreal: An Oral History 1922-1945*. Toronto: Guernica Editions, 1998.

—. *Le Fascisme et les Italiens à Montréal*. Toronto: Guernica Editions, 1995.

Sanfilippo, Matteo. "Intervista a Bruno Ramirez." Archivio Storico Emigrazione Italiana, November 2006.

Scambray, Ken. "Secret Histories." *Accenti Magazine*, Issue 4, September 2003.

Spada, Antonino V. *The Italians in Canada*. Montreal: Italo-Canadian Ethnic and Historical Research Centre, 1969.

Tana, Paul. *Caffè Italia, Montréal*. Cinema Libre, 1985.

Vangelisti, Guglielmo. *Gli Italiani in Canada*. Chiesa italiana di N.S. della Difesa, 1956.

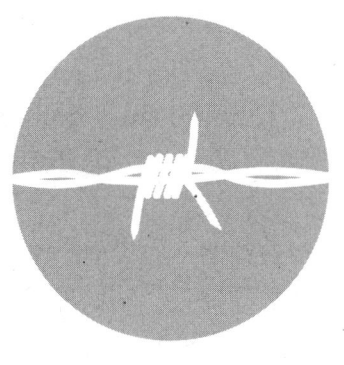

Antonio Calcagno

Giorgio Agamben, Modern Sovereignty and the Camps: A Challenge for Canada

As this volume examines the internment of Italians and Italian Canadians in the 1940s from many perspectives, I wonder whether we can salvage something from the violence and sadness of the camps and learn from their legacy.

My father, Giovanni Calcagno, was a survivor of such a camp, but it was British rather than Canadian. When Italy surrendered during the Second World War, my father was interned in England as a prisoner of war. After the general armistice, he helped transport Italians back to Italy from England and other destinations. Previously, he had served in Mussolini's navy for some thirteen years, was decorated and survived various bombings. After one particularly brutal fight with British ships and aircraft, he was left to die at sea. Fortunately, after three days, he was rescued by a German frigate and taken to Africa to recover.

My father was never interned in Canada, and yet he chose to come to Canada, a former enemy state, to find refuge and build a better life. He returned to Italy occasionally to visit, but he never wanted to live there. I relate these biographical details because I wish to highlight that my father experienced another kind of camp, in addition to the one he was in as a prisoner of war.

As a young navy officer, he was assigned to the temporary internment camps in Athens where, for the first time, he almost lost his life. The Germans had separated women and children from Athenian men in the Piraeus. The women and children were starving.

Allies of the Germans, the Italians were called in to help guard the various campsites. My father despised this duty and he could not bear the suffering of the women and children he was forced to guard. To help alleviate their suffering, he would smuggle food to them. One day, while passing bread to a hungry woman for her children, my father turned to see a German soldier holding a rifle to his head. He was ordered to take back the bread, reprimanded and removed from that particular duty.

My father was a happy man, but he was stoic when it came to pain and suffering. He recounted this story to me only once and, while doing so, he was overcome with horror and fright, on the verge of tears. He was almost shot for a piece of bread. He could not understand why so many people lost their lives for "crazy ideas." Interned at one camp and assigned guard duty at another, he lived the horrible experience of the camps from both sides.

The well-known contemporary Italian philosopher, Giorgio Agamben, takes the camp as one of his central themes. He meditates on the significance of the camp and its consequences, not only for individual lives and peoples, but also for politics or, what he more precisely calls, following German legal theorist Carl Schmitt, the political. He notes that Italians are still creating camps, whether it is for the Roma, who are seen to "plague" Italian cities, or for the Albanian refugees who fled to Puglia, or for the Libyans and other Africans who now seek refuge on the island of Lampedusa.

The camp instantiates itself as a reality in various countries against various peoples, as it did in Canada during the Second World War and at other times in Canadian history, but for Agamben, it bespeaks a deeper reality. The camp is linked to the very notion of contemporary sovereignty, which marks the essence of the modern state, including Canada. If Agamben's claim is correct, then the very political structure of Canada harbours a deep and frightening possibility — a possibility that became a reality with the various internments of the 1940s, and one that may rise again. The camp is not only an act of state in times of war; neither can it be solely explained within the varying frameworks of chauvinism and racism.

Traditionally, three classic forms of sovereignty or autonomy are seen to define any state as a state, making it capable of exercising its essence as a state or polity. First, Aristotle tells us that the polis can carry out its *politeia,* that is, its constitutive essence as a polis, if and only if it establishes what he calls *autarchia,* loosely translated as sovereignty or self-rule. What guarantees this sovereignty is the capacity of the polis to ensure that it does not become the object of attack by foreign powers or that such foreign menace does not prevent it from enacting its constitutive being. Hence, a strong military force is required to ensure freedom from outside attack or threat. Within the state, Aristotle, like Plato, requires that there be guardians and laws to ensure the well-being of citizens dwelling in the polis.

Rome marked the advent of the second form of Western sovereignty. In this form, a state is only a state if it has a strong ruling centre, be it in the form of a leader or a group of ruling officials, and this was the case in Rome, depending upon the various periods of its political history. The strength of the ruler resides in the power to decide who lives and who dies. In employing such power, the ruler can ensure some kind of stability and tranquility of life for and within the state.

Finally, French, British, German and Italian theorists introduced more contemporary forms of sovereignty that do not necessarily depend upon the whims of the sovereign or threat from foreign powers: a sovereignty dependent upon the rule of law. Here, it is the law that is seen as primary and regulative. It would be fair to say that Canada subscribes to this typically modern form of sovereignty.

If one pays close attention to Canadian foreign policy, one often hears about Canada's good intentions of helping her allies establish and maintain both democracy and rule by law. For example, Canada's mission in Afghanistan was intended, in part, to help restore peace and the rule of law. Here at home, the very establishment of the Supreme Court as the ultimate regulative body that can decide on the constitutionality and legality of laws is evidence of Canada's firm belief in sovereign rule established by rule of law.

Agamben rightly tells us that such rule by law is powerful, but he also notes that modern states, including Canada, can — and do — exempt themselves from their own laws, producing what he calls a state of exception. He remarks: "The immediate biopolitical significance of the state of exception as the original structure in which the law includes in itself ... its very suspension emerges clearly in the 'military order' stemming from the President of the United States on November 13, 2001, which authorizes 'indefinite detention' and trials by 'military commissions' (which are not to be confused with military tribunals provided for by the right to war) of non-citizens suspected of participating in terrorist activity.... [T]he term 'state of exception' [is] a technical term that coherently refers to the various juridical phenomena it seeks to define. This term, common to German theories of law (*Ausnahmezustand* and even *Notstand*, the state of necessity) is foreign to Italian and French theories of law, which prefer to speak of decrees of urgency and states of siege (political or fictitious, *état de siège fictif*). In Anglo Saxon legal theory, terms like martial law and emergency powers prevail."[1]

Agamben gives the example of Hitler and the National Socialists. Upon the Nazis' accession to power, they "legally" suspended certain rights and freedoms in the name of state urgency and necessity, aimed at promoting the stability and well-being of the German Reich. Eventually, once the German constitution had been suspended, Hitler and his party ruled absolutely. All modern states to date have possessed this power. They can suspend parliamentary procedures and the rule of law in order to enact a new rule that supersedes the form of due process. For example, Canadian governments of the past have invoked the War Measures Act in order to acquire sweeping powers. Most recently, Pierre Trudeau invoked the War Measures Act in 1970 during the October Crisis.

In a powerful fashion, Agamben argues that in the 20th century — the bloodiest century on record, as Alain Finkielkraut notes — liberal notions of sovereignty, infused with Enlightenment ideals and held so dear for hundreds of years, have never actually materialized. There have always been critical exceptions in which ruling parties or individuals have legitimately and legally taken control of a state in order to carry out what they conceive of as being both necessary and vital for the preservation and well-being of everyone in the state or, frankly, for their own well-being. Usually, as Carl Schmitt notes, the state of exception results in some kind of war, on all kinds of levels, between a formally designated friend and enemy, even between the state and various partisans. Agamben argues that it is the distinction between friend and enemy that results in camps, in which enemy aliens can be interned.

The state of exception, which typifies contemporary Canadian sovereignty, not only draws the distinction between friend and enemy — those favourable to the ruling party and those perceived to be enemies of the party and/or the state, such as our fellow Italians or Italo-Canadians interned here in the 1940s — but also shows what real and absolute power is, and how it functions within the modern state. The state of exception represents the maximum power that a state can legally authorize. Undoubtedly, each time the state of exception is invoked, many rights and freedoms, including *habeas corpus* and the right to a fair trial, are suspended, thus subjecting "enemy" individuals to the desires of the ruling authorities and ultimately creating the need for such things as camps and detention centres.

If Agamben is correct in his political analysis, then the camp is one horrendous expression of sovereignty enacting itself. Following the political thinker Hannah Arendt, who noted that concentration camps first arose not with Hitler, but in the Boer War, Agamben observes that camps breed terror, which ultimately makes totalitarian rule possible. Furthermore, camps dehumanize, stripping individuals of their moral and legal personhood. In her *Origins of Totalitarianism*, Arendt remarked:

> The concentration camps, by making death itself anonymous (making it impossible to find out whether a prisoner is dead or alive), robbed death of its meaning as the end of a fulfilled life. In a sense they took away the individual's own death, proving that henceforth nothing belonged to him and he belonged to no one. His death merely set a seal on the fact that he had never really existed. This attack on the moral person might still have been opposed by man's conscience which tells him that it is better to die a victim than to live as a bureaucrat of murder. Totalitarian terror achieved its most terrible triumph when it succeeded in cutting the moral person off from the individualist escape and in making the decisions of conscience absolutely questionable and equivocal.[2]

My father, Giovanni Calcagno, experienced both sides of the camps produced by modern sovereignty. In the end, both friends and enemies are implied in the camps of modern sovereignty, either as interned or as interning. The Italians and Canadians interned and the Italians and Canadians doing the interning — both of these are products of what Schmitt calls the state of exception. If we really wish to avoid such camps, then we must change the definition of what constitutes our sovereignty here and now.

Agamben offers us a possibility. If anything, the camps reveal our bare life (*la nuda vita*) as human beings — a life stripped of its customs, habits, social and political conventions, a life that simply is. Aristotle, according to Agamben, describes this life as simply being (*haplos*). Rather than sovereignty as the *arché* or organizing and beginning principle of our common life together, why not base political life on the fact that, as human beings, we are bare, fragile life, who, in order to flourish, need one another? Agamben argues that, when we come face to face with bare life in its wretchedness, fragility and utter weakness, we cannot help but stand respectfully before it. We do not wish to destroy it. Rather, we are called to nurture it: for Agamben, this is the beginning of ethics.

The central problem with Agamben's claim is that bare life, at least according to his own description, only manifests itself in dire circumstances such as the camps. Given that we continue to create these camps, to violate and brutally kill others, paying no heed to the call of bare life, which supposedly surges in such acute circumstances, perhaps bare life is not strong enough to curtail the excesses of modern sovereignty. In response to this insufficiency, perhaps we can offer a Canadian solution, but with a twist.

Canadian philosopher John Ralston Saul rightly, I think, notes that Canada is different from other modern states. Unlike its fellow modern states, which were formed by revolutions and nation-state politics that were based on definitions of belonging according to blood, race and ethnic categories, Canada was formed by a federal compromise in which many diverse groups, not only ethnic ones, came together to create a confederate constitutional state.³

Canada was constituted as a weak state, with the flexibility to break down certain problems caused by nation-state politics of blood and race. The traditional categories of race, blood and ethnic belonging were, at least formally, not seen as constitutive grounds for statehood. This is not to say that, practically speaking, questions of race, ethnic belonging and blood did not enter into all kinds of practical political decisions and conflicts that resulted in definite racism, sexism, chauvinism, etc.

If we accept Ralston Saul's political view of Canada's founding as exceptional, why not extend this trajectory? Given that the state of exception is built into the very structure of modern sovereignty, that is to say, given that governments and rulers can exempt themselves from their own laws, could we not eliminate the possibility of the Canadian government becoming an exception to its own laws?

Canada had taken a bold step toward curtailing the broad powers of the War Measures Act. In 1988, Canada passed a new act, called the Emergencies Act, according to which decrees of war and the enactment of certain powers by the cabinet would have to pass through parliament. But the terrorist attacks of 2001 provoked a new act (the Canadian Anti-Terrorism Act) that gave the government sweeping powers. Critics argued that the promise of parliamentary review processes in the 1988 act was never fulfilled. A time limit was set on the powers of the Anti-Terrorism Act, and its powers expired in 2007. However, it is clear that the Emergencies Act could not prevent the government from introducing a new law that overrode the requirements of the Emergencies Act itself. The underbelly of modern sovereignty, namely, the state of exception, remained intact.

I believe that, given the speed and means offered by technologies of all kinds, which allow all members of parliament, both the House of Commons and the Senate, to be readily accessible, we can eliminate the state of exception by inscribing its very negation into the Canadian constitution, immediately after the clause that allows parliament to extend its rule in times of real or "apprehended" war (Part I, section 4, 2). It is supposed that what can, perhaps, prevent the state of exception is the legitimacy of loyal opposition parties that see it as their task to criticize the government in times of duress. But placing in the constitution a clause that explicitly prohibits the suspension of the law by any power, even in times of war and urgent necessity, would give the courts and the people of Canada some form of extended confidence that we have done the maximum possible to avert the real possibility of a state of exception.

To unilaterally give cabinet and the prime minister such sweeping powers as those guaranteed by acts such as the Anti-Terrorism Act in times of grave urgency is to reinforce the view of modern sovereignty. In order to prevent the creation of camps in the future, perhaps we need to suspend such absolute powers and bring urgent matters before all members of parliament and the senate. No one should hold special privileges, especially in times of war: all decisions should come before parliament, thereby guaranteeing to the extent possible, equality for all before the law and no states of exception.

What needs to be rethought are what Locke calls the privileges and prerogatives of the executive branch of government. Perhaps this is one step we can take here in Canada in order to rework modern sovereignty and curtail the possibility of future camps on our own soil. Schmitt notes that it is the nature of the law, especially as it is practised by jurists, to find exceptions. But if we were to inscribe a no-exception clause in the Canadian constitution, we would give maximal force, as best we can here and now, to limiting the possibility of the creation of such camps that is currently inscribed in modern sovereignty itself.

Endnotes

1. Giorgio Agamben, *Stato di eccezione* (Torino: Bollati Boringhieri, 2003), 12–13. Translation mine.
2. In "Totalitarianism," *Part Three of The Origins of Totalitarianism* (New York: Harcourt Brace and Jovanovich, 1951), 150.
3. John Ralston Saul, *Reflections of a Siamese Twin: Canada at the End of the Twentieth Century* (Toronto: Penguin, 1998).

VENERA FAZIO

Frenzy of Fear: Prelude to the Italian Canadian Internment

The internment is the darkest moment in the history of the Italian Canadian community. Few deny the miscarriage of justice. The majority of the men detained in the camps did not pose a threat to national security. "Roughly, it can be said they [the Italians] were suspected not on account of doctrines ... [but] because they obeyed the ambition to show themselves at banquets and in parades organized by the Italian Consulate General, or had the ambition to see their names printed in a local weekly,"[1] writes Mario Duliani in his "documentary novel" chronicling his years behind barbed wire. None of the 619 men and thirteen women detained was ever formally charged with any crime. How and why was this injustice allowed to happen? Without excusing the wrongfulness and to answer these questions, I recreate the prelude to the internment, from May until the middle of June 1940, as documented by three major Canadian newspapers: the *Vancouver Sun*, the Toronto *Globe and Mail* and the *Montreal Daily Herald*.

The newspaper articles, editorials and letters written by citizens reveal a country whose people were more eager than their elected members of parliament to participate in war, and more loyal to their British heritage than to their next door immigrant neighbours. Government and citizens collude to bring about the internment. In hindsight, the will of ordinary Canadians, and the need to contain their terrors of war, prevailed over government restraint. Newspaper content reflects a country devoid of a unifying, positive leadership to the extent that the emotions of fear bordering on hysteria, rage, panic and racial prejudice prevailed.

In May 1940, the eighth month of the war, Canadians are dismayed and alarmed as Germany overtakes France, Luxemburg and the Netherlands. Canadians fear the Motherland may lose the war as Britain seems to be shouldering the brunt of keeping Germany at bay. Up to this point, Canada's participation is minimal. One regiment has been deployed to England and a second one is in training. For Canadians, May is a month of intense emotions and a critical month for the Liberal government. It is a month of citizen unrest and agitation.

The primary source of agitation is fear of fifth columnists. Canadians are bombarded with daily reminders of an internal threat to national security both in the *Globe and Mail* and the *Vancouver Sun*. The *Montreal Daily Herald* begins to include similar news items from May 16 and onwards.

The term "fifth column" widely used in England at the start of the war originated from the Spanish Civil War. Some sources credit General Francisco Franco, while others attribute the phrase to General Emilio Mola Vidal, another Spanish insurgent leader. Whoever used this term first is believed to have said that he had four columns of troops to send against Madrid, while a "fifth column" waited inside the city to stab the defenders in the back at the appropriate moment. The expression took on the wider context to mean "enemies within" (*Montreal Daily Herald* May 25, 1940, 4).

Rather than focusing on the cruelty of Germany's aggression in Europe, some citizens link the "Huns'" conquests to secret sympathizers and/or spies for the Nazis within the conquered countries. One writes: "In the light of what has happened in Europe, Canada is foolish to take chances on Trojan horse stunts. Let us remember Denmark and Norway and nip treachery in the bud" (Toronto).[2] Citizens of Vancouver are also reminded of "Nazi-instigated treason in Norway."[3]

Fifth column activity in Europe gives rise to speculation of sabotage activities within Canada. The *Globe and Mail* describes only one confirmed incidence since the outbreak of war. Several other Ontario episodes are considered suspicious. The Toronto and Vancouver papers also mention a spy ring in the United States that may have spread its tentacles into Canada.

The confirmed Canadian incident "was the attempt by German agents in British Columbia to damage the Consolidated Smelters plant at Trail, one of the nation's most important wartime industries. A letter to the [German] consul [in Seattle] was intercepted and the chief German agent convicted and sentenced to prison for his connection with the plot, details of which have been kept secret."[4]

In this same *Globe and Mail* story referring to the thwarted Trail episode, fire marshal W.J. Scott K.C., in his luncheon speech to the Canadian Manufacturers' Association relays several other violations: In one Ontario factory in which Communists had a strong influence over the Union and personnel, screws were dropped into vital machinery on at least two occasions and electrical transformers were tampered with. Secondly, Scott mentions an attempt to meddle with the cage of a mine hoist in northern Ontario, which if successful would have plunged a number of miners to their deaths. It's not clear from the article whether these events were definite acts of sabotage of the war effort or if the fire marshal is only stating his opinion. Nevertheless, he warns that "the peak" of fifth column activities is yet to come.

In Vancouver, fear of the presence of fifth columnists is expressed when the *Vancouver Sun* admonishes readers to "look well around you, keep your ears open. Britain has 70,000 aliens. How many have we in Canada?"[5] Referring to sabotage in the United States, this same article concludes: "'But they couldn't get into Canada' ... Why not? They got into United States, where the Dies committee dug them up by the shovelful. When it comes to slinking, those German agents can get through knotholes ... This is a war of plain dealing. It is a poor and craven soul who would not deny it even lip service. If such there be, go mark him well."[6]

Convinced of the presence of enemies within, Canadian newspaper editorials attempt to define the extent of the threat and their conclusions are staggering. The *Vancouver Sun*, quoting from the 1941 census, states there may be in excess of 750,000 aliens living in Canada.[7] Not all aliens are enemy aliens, the same article explains. Enemy aliens differ from "friends" by virtue of being citizens of a country with which Canada is at war or former British subjects residing voluntarily in an enemy country. According to this definition, guilt is by virtue of ethnicity rather than legal process. Legally, under the War Measures Act "an enemy alien is subject to seizure, imprisonment and internment. He is not entitled to the benefit of our laws, civil or criminal."[8]

The *Montreal Daily Herald* provides a more accurate estimate of potential saboteurs declaring that in addition to 400 enemy aliens (primarily German Canadians) interned in Petawawa, Ontario and Kananaskis, Alberta, the RCMP registered for observation 14,000 individuals.[9] The *Globe and Mail*, on the following day, quotes a similar number, but without revealing a source, saying there are 16,000 enemy aliens at large.[10] The *Globe* warns the public about these potential spies asking: "How long would 16,000 Canadians retain their freedom in Germany?" This editorial continues: "There is too little watchfulness on the part of the public for fifth-column activities. Something needs to make them realize the possibility of having enemy neighbors and friends, that they may not unwittingly help the foe."[11]

At the beginning of May 1940, the primary suspects of fifth column activities are German Canadians and Communists.

Anti-Italian / fascists sentiments are in the background but not openly expressed in the media until later in the month.

In South Vancouver, where there is a significant German Canadian population, residents are vocal about their mistrust: "English-speaking residents [between Forty-first Avenue and Marine Drive, and Main Street and Victoria Road] suspect that many of the nearly 5,000 Germans living in that marked off area are Hitler sympathizers."[12]

An official of the RCMP counters the opinions of the South Vancouver residents: "We know that there are some Hitler sympathizers in that district. Put it this way — we know their hearts are not with us. But there is no proof of subversive activities."[13] However, English-speaking citizens remain skeptical. A spokesman for the newly formed British-Canadian-Allied Club, an organization whose purpose is to combat nazism and the "unfairness" of Germans monopolizing jobs when many Canadians are unemployed, cites additional incidents of suspicious behaviours by the German community.

Elsewhere in the country, anti-German sentiments are evident from articles such as the one entitled: "Opposes German As New Citizen." Judge R.H. Murray of Halifax delays the application for citizenship of stationary engineer Carl Braun because he (the judge) "was suspicious of Germans and did not favor granting citizen rights to any native of Germany."[14] A citizen had written a letter accusing Braun of being pro-Nazi and anti-British. Braun insists "he held no brief for Hitler or present day Germany"[15] but Judge Murray was not convinced.

Communists are also targets of anger and distrust. One letter from the *Vancouver Sun* reads: "Communism and Nazism are alike as two peas. The fact that they go under different names is all the more reason for alertness. No 'Fifth Column' works under its true colors."[16] Another from the *Globe and Mail* notes:

> Police investigators in Canada believe that thousands of Communists in the Dominion will take active action against this country, instead of confining themselves to peace propaganda when the Soviet leaders consider the time ripe for action. With Communists in this country probably numbering several hundreds of thousands of all ages, the investigators believe the Communist danger is greater in Canada than in Great Britain inasmuch as a large proportion of the Communists here are foreign-born or the children of foreign-born.[17]

The "crime" committed by Communists in Canada and Britain is that they "attacked the present war in pamphlets and in newspapers and have urged an early peace."[18]

In mid-May the newspapers' definition of enemy aliens expands to include fascists and Italian Canadians even though Italy has not yet declared war against Britain and France. A May 15 Toronto *Globe and Mail* article, "Citizens Seek Probe of 5th Column," reveals citizens have been writing letters reporting their distrust to local and federal police:

> Citizens suspicious of their neighbors' actions are asking investigations of small meetings in various homes suspected of housing Communists or Fascist sympathizers ... The letters which have markedly increased during the past week are not from 'crackpots,' but from substantial Canadian citizens who are, to quote one investigator, 'up on their ears' at the latent danger to the country ... (4)

Several days after the *Globe* article, Attorney-General for Ontario, Gordon Conant, in a letter urging Justice Minister Lapointe to place subversive elements in the same category as enemy aliens, subject to internment, includes fascists along with Nazis and Communists.

Underlying the hostility towards enemy aliens is the broader fear of Canada losing her British identity. The period from March 1939 to March 1940 appears to be a peak year for immigration to Canada. Citing immigration statistics of 16,204 immigrants from Europe of which 12,639 were non-British, the *Globe* implores:

> With the Motherland engaged in a life-and-death struggle for existence, heavy immigration from the British Isles is out of the question. But we are not going to build up a British nation in Canada with Germans, Bohemians, Croatians, Hebrews ... [19]

Several editorials debate whether or not it is justifiable to suspend the civil liberties of enemy aliens as allowed by the Defense of Canada Regulations, a subsection of the War Measures Act. The *Globe and Mail* makes a case for temporarily sacrificing democratic principles at home while fighting for democracy abroad: "Can we consistently ask our young men to go to Europe and sacrifice their lives if necessary and refuse to back them up at home in a united spirit? If not, can we allow elements of the community to roam at large discouraging the war effort in any way possible?"[20]

A *Vancouver Sun* editorial answers those who object to the War Measure Act: "If these critics of our British way were compelled to whisper in cellars and cabal in twos and threes, fearful of lifting their voices, they might have some reason to rant about the destruction of civil liberties. But the very fact that they may stand up in a great public park and shout until the trees echo their plaints, is evidence that they are wrong."[21]

Not all Canadians are prejudiced against immigrants or eager to readily condemn suspected enemy aliens. Philip del D. Passy of Port Hope, ON in his letter to the *Globe* (May 17, page 6) objects to the Defense of Canada Regulation that allows a British subject or alien to be detained indefinitely, without trial, provided the Minister of Justice is "satisfied." Del D. Passy also condemns the Attorney General of Ontario proposal to eliminate the right of enemy aliens to access a court of appeal.

Advocating on behalf of immigrants, a columnist for the *Globe and Mail* using the initials L.B. McK. writes: "We show our real character in our treatment of those new Canadians, or so it seems to me. A woman said to me, 'I wouldn't buy a cent's worth from one of them!' 'What,' said I, 'not even if they were naturalized Canadians!' 'No,' she said, 'I wouldn't trust one of them.' How very narrow and unkind is this point of view."[22]

In Vancouver, Lutheran Minister A. Shormann speaks out for his German congregation, deploring the "unchristian agitation / discrimination from the members of the British-Canadian-Allied Club."

But the voices protesting the denial of civil liberties to enemy aliens and Canadian prejudice towards foreigners, whether considered "enemy" or "friendly," are drowned out by the more numerous, strident expressions of anger, suspicion and calls for punishment. Of the three cities represented by the newspapers reviewed here, if frequency of letters to the editor is an indication, Vancouverites are the most vocal, secondly, Torontonians, and thirdly, the citizens of Montreal.

Letters and editorials demanding action against enemy aliens appear in earnest in both the Toronto and Vancouver papers starting on May 15, and May 18 in Montreal. From May 15 until June 21, the *Sun* printed approximately twenty letters and three editorials. A sample of titles, such as "Stop the Fifth Column" (editorial, May 15), "Should Intern Aliens" (letter, May 15), "Clean Out the Fifth Column" (editorial, May 17), "Set Our House in Order Against Fifth Column" (editorial, May 18), "Should Do Something About Aliens," (letter, May 20), "Wants Action on Aliens" (letter, May 23) and "Would Check On Italians " (letter, June 11) reveal the intent of content.

The majority of letters are sent anonymously. Germans and Austrians are most frequently targeted as potential trouble makers. Other letters refer to enemy aliens in general terms and towards the end of May and into June, fascists/Italians become the focus. Internment is the general consensus and some of the writers also favour aliens loosing their jobs and the suppression of alien culture. The tone of the writing is often angry, fearful and/or vindictive. A citizen named "Exactus" in "How to Deal With Aliens" (May 30) provides an example of one of the more punitive letters and is quoted here because he/she brings together the suggestions of other letter writers/editorials:

> Editor, *The Sun*: Sir, I have read your editorials referring to "Fifth Column" activities and elements and I want to congratulate you for the stand you have taken in this connection. I wish to make a few suggestions ... Suspend all citizenship papers. Intern all those who cannot give satisfactory information as to why he or she should retain their citizenship rights now and when the war is over. Intern all others regardless of excuses and pressures ... Aliens should not hold executive positions at any time. Aliens domiciled here of aggressor nationality should be immediately discharged from employment ... All foreign language schools should be declared illegal ... Foreign Clubs come under the same category. Aliens should

> not be allowed to settle in communities at present ... British people should be brought here in large numbers over a period of years ... (4)

The *Globe and Mail* prints nearly three-quarters the number of letters as the *Vancouver Sun,* but gives indication the numbers printed are far fewer than those received. On May 25, on the editorial page (6), under the heading "Tardy War Effort Arouses The Canadian People; More Vigorous Measures Vehemently Demanded," the editor explains that only five letters are selected for publication among the "avalanche" received. The *Globe* letters and editorials take a broader view point than that of the *Sun* by calling for greater participation in the war effort and by being critical of the secrecy and passivity of the federal government:

> It is undeniable that there is a deep dissatisfaction from one end of the country to the other among people concerned about the war effort. While grave fear has arisen lest the Allies prove unequal to the huge tasks facing them, it is coupled with the feeling that Canada remains little more than a complacent partner in the struggle ... Part of this may be due to the inexplicable silence since the election ... The Prime Minister may have reasons for keeping the public in the dark. If he has, they are not good enough ...[23]

Later in May, the *Globe* denigrates parliament, referring to it as "the Ottawa Steam Roller" when the Liberal majority shouts down the Hon. Herbert A. Bruce as he asks the Justice Minister to take a more realistic view of the war and order immediate restrictions of subversive activities and the internment of enemy sympathizers.

The mail chosen for publication supports the *Globe*'s anti-government stance. For example, in one of the five letters published on May 25 titled "Feeble Effort Thus Far," the author describes the war efforts of the government using the same words as indicated by the title. Two days later, the *Globe and Mail* includes an additional five letters under the heading "Readers of The Globe and Mail Voice Dissatisfaction Concerning Complacency at the Capital — Consensus Is That Cabinet Has Been Derelict," including one correspondence asking for the Prime Minister's resignation.

One letter differs from others included by the *Globe* and exposes a chilling dimension to the attitude towards enemy aliens: "H.R." encourages citizens to "snoop" on their foreign neighbours for the purpose of reporting suspicious behaviours to the authorities. ("Two Nazis Interned," letter, May 31).

The *Montreal Daily Herald* reports on anti-fifth column sentiments across the county but devotes less space, in general, than the other two newspapers to publishing editorials and letters written by citizens. Regarding enemy aliens, it does include one editorial and three letters. The editorial (May 31) titled "The Fifth Column" condemns Nazis and fascists. To control the threat of enemy aliens, one citizen proposes a Home Guard while a second suggests an organization similar to the French Foreign Legion. The third person, Mrs. G.F.M., echoes sentiments similar to those expressed by the *Vancouver Sun*'s Exactus. Despite the few editorials and correspondence, several *Daily Herald* articles indicate that the attitudes of a significant number of Montrealers towards enemy aliens mirrors those of the majority from the other two large centres. (It is noteworthy that fascists in Montreal were the first to be arrested in the country even before Italy formally declared war.)

On May 22, a *Daily Herald* news item reporting on a speech by Captain Reverend Norman Rawson to the Montreal branch of

Political cartoon from the *Globe and Mail*, May 30, 1940.

Purchasing Agents regarding the dangers of Nazi fifth columnists ends with the following report: "It was understood that yesterday, a delegation of Westmount citizens, apparently not satisfied with present methods of RCMP and Ottawa in connection with Fifth Column activities, called at RCMP headquarters and asked for details on the work being done by the police at the present time."[24]

On May 28, 10,000 Montrealers from all nationalities convene at Atwater Market to hear the dangers of the fifth column. (Toronto hosts a similar mass rally on May 22 when a crowd of 20,000 gathers at Maple Leaf Stadium.)

The letters and editorials of all three newspapers expose a Canadian population ensnared in a frenzy of fear and paranoid in its estimation of the numbers of fifth columnists at large. Mob hysteria pervades. Lacking confidence in the leadership of authorities, citizen groups meet with the intention of either taking action of their own or exerting pressure on elected officials. The call to strike forcefully against enemy aliens begins in Vancouver and then sweeps across the country. The catalyst for action is Britain's arrest of 3,000 enemy aliens along her east and south-eastern shores on May 13.

On the eve of May 13, a group of Vancouver ex-servicemen declare themselves the "sixth column." Their three objectives are to broaden the scope of the War Measures Act by enacting a national scheme of registering every person of alien origin, suspending all applications for naturalization by foreign residents and establishing tribunals throughout Canada with full powers to issue warrants for the arrests of "any such person deemed necessary for the protection of the State."[25]

The demands of the "sixth column" are similar to the British-Canadian-Allied Club that had been meeting since the beginning of May. In its petitions to the Federal and Provincial governments, this Club includes the additional request that Canadian employers give preference to British and allied citizens.

On May 14, the Lower Mainland executives of the Canadian Legion pass a resolution to be sent to the Prime Minister Mackenzie King demanding internment of every alien enemy and "that all naturalized Canadians who were formerly alien enemies be put under police supervision."[26] One of the Legion delegates, Walter Stone, emphasizes: "We have thousands of enemy aliens and sympathizers in our midst. Today it is the Germans. Tomorrow it may be the Italians. Within the month it may be the Japanese. Something must be done."[27]

Two days later, several groups of Vancouver veterans meet, including the 31st Battalion Association with its proposal to form a vigilante organization. On May 17, the *Sun* prints a strong editorial endorsing the plans of both Mayor Hume of New Westminster and Mayor Telford of Vancouver to register all males over sixteen in order to determine who is a fifth columnist. The editorial also approves of Britain's leadership regarding internment and the formation of an armed citizen Home Guard to protect the country from spies within and from external enemies. "The time to clean up the Fifth Column is now,"[28] the editorial proclaims.

Legion chapters and/or groups of ex-service men meet across the country making similar demands as their Vancouver counterparts. In Edmonton, 1,000 service men gather insisting on a national plan of defense and to organize a mass meeting to help set up a defensive force. Zone Eight of the Canadian Legion of Hamilton, ON meets to demand a corps of vigilantes. Other interest groups join forces with the Legion and veterans. On May 21, The Quebec Legion Branch petitions the Prime Minister to include a sweeping investigation by the RCMP of subversive activities by Nazis, fascists and Communists. Other terms of this urgent petition involve:

declaring illegal organizations of any national group, other than those of nationalists of the Allied countries and the firing of all enemy aliens, Nazis, fascists, Communists and their sympathizers from any employment which would enable them to help the enemy.

Other interest groups and prominent individuals echo the pleas of the Legion branches and veterans. In Saskatoon, the Junior Board of Trade urges formation of a youth guard of young men contemplating enlistment, who could also form the nucleus for a home defense organization. The Vancouver Police Commission sends an urgent telegram on May 18 to the Prime Minister advising him of the "strong feelings against enemy aliens"[29] and asking "whether 'adequate' care has been taken to control any possible subversive activities." It ends with the plea that the board be taken into the government's confidence on "what steps have been taken."[30]

In Toronto, Mayor Ralph Day takes the initiative in contacting the Government to install a Home Guard and register all males. The Police Association of Ontario, on May 24, passes a resolution that all subversive organizations be declared illegal.

On May 20, the Federal Government responds to the mounting pressure and sets up a special committee of Parliament to consider the broad question of fifth columnists. The next day, Mackenzie King makes a pivotal speech to the House of Commons attempting to reassure Canadians the Government is on top of the war effort. In regard to enemy aliens, he pleads:

> The Government has taken all possible steps to prevent sabotage and subversive activity ... Our efficient Royal Canadian Mounted Police and other branches of the Government are fully aware of the situation and have taken action whenever warranted. I wish however, in this connection to make two appeals. I appeal to all citizens of foreign extraction to

remember that they are living in a land which is fighting to maintain the freedom which they now enjoy ... I appeal also to all members of the public to refrain from persecution and panic action against harmless and law-abiding people who share our life and in most instances our common citizenship.[31]

The Prime Minister's even-tempered speech is met with criticism, increased pressure and demands for his resignation. In the Senate, the Right Hon. Arthur Meighen, in a scathing denouncement, demands immediate action for Canadian participation in the war. The Senator appeals for a reorganization of Government that would bring about the united support of Canadians. The call for reorganization of Government is taken up by the *Winnipeg Free Press*, recognized by other newspapers "as the most powerful and consistent supporter of the Government in Western Canada."[32] The *Montreal Daily Herald* on May 31 reports the Parliament sat for ten days "under intermittent demands from Conservative benches for the Prime Minister's resignation."[33]

Citizens continue to demand action as their letters discussed here previously indicate. Additional "advocacy" groups such as The League for Patriotic Action organize in Toronto and across the country. The League's charter asks for full mobilization of the war effort including defense against enemy aliens. In late May, the Scarborough, ON Charter Veterans' Council votes on nine resolutions pertaining to the prosecution and investigation of enemy aliens, including a request to the Provincial Government to ensure school boards scrutinize teachers regarding their loyalty.

Within days of Mackenzie King's speech, there is evidence the will of citizen and partisan groups will prevail. On May 23, the Minister of Justice, Ernest Lapointe, speaking in the House of Commons, predicts a forthcoming more intensive round up of enemy aliens.

A week later, even though fascist organizations have not yet been declared illegal, the RCMP strike at the heart of the Canadian fascist party, known as National Unity Party, with warrants issued to eight members of the party leadership. "Similar arrests were made in other cities."[34]

On June 5, Parliament strikes a vigorous blow at enemy aliens. Sixteen organizations are declared illegal including the communist party and fascist groups. All commissioned officers of the RCMP are made Justice of the Peace for the purpose of issuing search warrants.

On June 10, Italy declares war on England and France.

On June 12, of the three newspapers, The *Globe and Mail* provides the most comprehensive coverage of the round up of Italian Canadians in Ontario and Montreal. Mysteriously the *Vancouver Sun* does not report any local arrests but on June 21 provides details on the internment of eleven fascists, all members of the National Unity Party. The *Globe and Mail* on June 12 includes in their articles:

> Police have been preparing for the last three weeks to swoop down on members of the Fascist Party and other Italian organizations the moment war was declared. The word came yesterday, prepared instructions were taken out of the headquarter vaults and wired to the different cities. There are now more Italians in custody than there are Germans ...[35]

In a separate column, the *Globe* states:

> A gigantic roundup of Italian residents was launched by Federal and city police simultaneously with Italy's declaration of war, and the swift, smoothly executed raids in the forty-eight hour period netted hundreds of aliens ... In Toronto,

> Windsor and Hamilton, centers of large Italian populations the civic authorities cooperated with Royal Canadian Mounted Police in rounding up Italians ... Italian clubs and restaurants were raided and searched from top to bottom ... the prisoners were given no warning of their impeding arrests. The police closed in on them in a lightning move and men were taken from their homes in a daze.[36]

The police are equally thorough in Montreal where the roundup brought scores of persons into custody within thirty-six hours. Under the supervision of Federal officers, Provincial Police took command on bridges leading from the island. The Community Centre, Casa D'Italia, was cordoned off and customs and immigration officers watched exits by train and boat. There were additional raids on downtown buildings, among them the Italian Chamber of Commerce.

On June 14, The *Montreal Daily Herald* provides insight into a community in crisis when two thousand Italian citizens report for registration as required by order of the RCMP: "Hundreds of them, mostly women thronged headquarters ... seeking advice and information concerning husbands, sons or other relatives who have fallen into the police dragnet."[37]

The *Globe and Mail* realizes Canadians have been unjust to the Italian community. Responding to the demonstrations in which eleven Italians shops were damaged in the aftermath of June 10, an editor writes:

> The *Globe and Mail* abhors the thought of witch-hunting. There is no necessity for an army of amateur sleuths to spy upon and persecute persons of foreign origin ... We suggest that the Minister of Justice call into conference at once the

Attorneys-Generals of the nine provinces for the purpose of establishing a protective force that will forestall enemies within our midst in a judicial manner free from hysteria.[38]

Conferences of the nature recommended by the *Globe and Mail* are never organized. Abandoned, Italian Canadians are left to cope, scapegoats of war-induced terrors, to face their own fears, including the uncertainty and the isolation felt by the men imprisoned behind barbed wire, and the anxieties experienced by their families and Italians in general, across the country, as they struggle to survive in a primarily hostile environment. Internment of some Italian Canadians, likely members of the fascist organizations, was inevitable, a reality of war-time procedures. However, if it had not been for the thirst of fellow citizens for punitive action, the RCMP and local police would not have cast such a wide and indiscriminate net. Society has a right to protect itself from its enemies, but in a just nation, the force deployed for the purpose of protection would not exceed the threat posed.

Endnotes

1. Mario Duliani, *The City Without Women*, trans. Antonino Mazza, (Oakville: Mosaic Press, 1994) 123.
2. "Let Us Forestall Treachery," editorial, *Globe and Mail* 6 May 1940: 6.
3. "750, 000 Aliens Enjoy Full Canadian Rights," *Vancouver Sun* 14 May 1940: 13.
4. "Says Sabotage Already Tried Near Toronto," *Globe and Mail* 2 May 1940: 4.
5. "It Can't Happen Here," editorial, *Vancouver Sun* 4 May 1940: 1.

6. "It Can't Happen Here," editorial, *Vancouver Sun* 4 May 1940: 1.
7. "750, 000 Aliens Enjoy Full Canadian Rights," *Vancouver Sun* 14 May 1940: 13.
8. "750, 000 Aliens Enjoy Full Canadian Rights," *Vancouver Sun* 14 May 1940: 13.
9. "Legion Demands Suppression Of Subversives In Country," *Montreal Daily Herald* 16 May 1940: 9.
10. "A Dependable Home Guard," editorial, *Globe and Mail* 17 May 17 1940: 6.
11. "A Dependable Home Guard," editorial, *Globe and Mail* 17 May 1940: 6.
12. "Displaying of Swastika Charged in S. Vancouver," *Vancouver Sun* 8 May 1940: 21.
13. "Displaying of Swastika Charged in S. Vancouver," *Vancouver Sun* 8 May 1940: 21.
14. "Opposes German As New Citizen," *Globe and Mail* 1 May 1940: 1.
15. "Opposes German As New Citizen," *Globe and Mail* 1 May 1940: 1.
16. "Out Go the Communists," editorial, *Vancouver Sun* 7 May 1940: 4.
17. "Citizens Seek Police Probe of 5th Column," *Globe and Mail* 15 May 1940: 4.
18. "Citizens Seek Police Probe of 5th Column," *Globe and Mail* 15 May 1940: 4.
19. "Keeping Canada British," editorial, *Globe and Mail* 9 May 1940: 6.
20. "Safety National In Scope," editorial, *Globe and Mail* 18 May 1940: 6.
21. "Personal Liberty," editorial, *Vancouver Sun* 2 May 1940: 4.

22. L.B. Mck., "This and That," *Globe and Mail* 1 June 1940: 1.
23. "An Anxious Country Waits," editorial, *Globe and Mail* 15 May 1940: 6.
24. "Warns That Enemy Is Organized Here," *Montreal Daily Herald* 22 May 1940: 5.
25. "'Sixth Column' Formed by Ex-Servicemen to Combat '5th' Column: Registration Proposed For All of Alien Birth," *Vancouver Sun* 13 May 1940: 13.
26. "Internment of All Enemy Aliens Proposed After Investigation of S. Vancouver Situation," *Vancouver Sun* 14 May 1940: 13.
27. O. Pip, "Internment of All Enemy Aliens Proposed After Investigation of S. Vancouver Situation," *Vancouver Sun* 14 May 1940: 13.
28. "Clean Out the Fifth Column," editorial, *Vancouver Sun* 17 May 1940: 10.
29. "Police Board Asks Ottawa for Information on Security Steps," *Vancouver Sun* 18 May 1940: 19.
30. "Police Board Asks Ottawa for Information on Security Steps," *Vancouver Sun* 18 May 1940: 19.
31. "Address Of Premier King Delivered Before Parliament," *Montreal Daily Herald* 21 May 1940: 6.
32. "Much More Must Be Done," editorial, *Globe and Mail* 28 May 1940: 6.
33. "Grit Unity Stands Off Tory Attack," *Montreal Daily Herald* 31 May 1940: 13.
34. "Police Say Unity Party Is Smashed," *Montreal Daily Herald* 31 May 1940: 1.
35. R.A. Farquharson. "Suspects Are Placed in Receiving Stations Preparatory to Camps," *Globe and Mail*, 12 June 1940: 4.

36. "Raids in Ontario Net Guns and Black Shirt Uniforms," *Globe and Mail* 12 June 1940: 4.
37. "Montreal Italians Rush to Register," *Montreal Daily Herald* 14 June 1940: 3.
38. "An Appeal to Mr. Lapointe," editorial, *Globe and Mail* 12 June 1940: 6.

Works Cited

Duliani, Mario. *The City Without Women.* Trans. Antonino Mazza. Oakville: Mosaic Press, 1994.

Globe and Mail:

A Canadian. "What of the Cost?" Letter. 27 May 1940: 6.
"Action Asked By Meighen." 22 May 1940:1+.
"A Dependable Home Guard." Editorial. 17 May 1940: 6.
A Liberal. "Senator's Hardy's Letter Resented As Attempt To Throttle Press." Letter. 23 May 1940: 6.
"Ask Full Mobilization Of Canada's Resources To Meet German Peril." 31 May 1940: 4.
"A Mockery and a Disgrace." Letter. 25 May 1940: 6.
"An Appeal to Mr. Lapointe." Editorial. 12 June 1940: 6.
"An Anxious County Waits." Editorial. 15 May 1940: 6.
Anxious Veteran. Letter (untitled). 25 May 1940: 6.
Beamish, Royd. "Red-Tinged Bodies Banned Along With 'Cultural' Societies." 6 June 1940: 1+.
Belfour, D.A. "Outlawing Communists." Letter. 24 May 1940: 6.
Beston, B. James. "Britain Rounds Up 3,000 In Enemy Alien Sweep." 13 May 1940: 1.
Canadian Born and British-Bred. "Help Urgently Wanted." Letter. 27 May 1940: 6.

"Citizens Seek Police Probe of 5th Column." 15 May 1940: 4.
Coates, L. Ernest. "Time To Speak Out." Letter. 25 May 1940: 6.
"Corps To Fight Fifth Column Here." 18 May 1940: 13.
D.S. Letter (untitled). 27 May 1940: 6.
Farquharson, R.A. "Do Anything To Aid Unity." 22 May 1940: 1.
Farquharson, R.A. "Suspects Are Placed in Receiving Stations Preparatory to Camps." 12 June 1940: 4.
"Fault Not With the People." Letter. 27 May 1940: 6.
"Feeble Effort Thus Far." Letter. 25 May 1940: 6.
"Intern First Probe Later, Veterans Urge." 27 May 1940: 4.
"Keeping Canada British." Editorial. 9 May 1940: 6.
"Let Us Forestall Treachery." Editorial. 6 May 1940: 6.
"Many Citizens Proffer Help In War Effort." 24 May 1940: 4.
Mck., L.B. "This and That." 1 June 1940: 1.
"Much More Must Be Done." Editorial. 28 May 1940: 6.
"Opposes German As New Citizen." 1 May 1940: 11.
Passy, del D., Philip. "British Principles in Danger." Letter. 17 May 1940: 6.
Patriot. "Wants New Leader." Letter. 27 May 1940: 6.
"Police Await Orders On 16 Banned Groups." 7 June 1940: 4.
"Police Body Endorses Anti-Subversive Action." 24 May 1940: 4.
R.H. "Two Nazis Interned." Letter. 31 May 1940: 6.
"Raids in Ontario Net Guns and Black Shirt Uniforms." 12 June 1940: 4.
"Safety National In Scope." Editorial. 18 May 1940: 6.
"Says Sabotage Already Tried Near Toronto." 2 May 1940: 4."Sees Move Helpful but Ineffective if Courts to Be Used." 6 June 1940: 1+.
"Subjects Are Placed in Receiving Stations Preparatory to Camps." 12 June 1940: 4.
"The Ottawa Steam Roller." Editorial. 27 May 1940: 6.

"Toronto Mass Meeting To Ask Disloyalty Curb And Greater War Effort." 21 May 1940: 4.

Taylor, J. "Hangs Head in Shame." Letter. 25 May 1940: 6.

Wellington, A. "War Effort Drags Down." 27 May 1940: 6.

Montreal Daily Herald:

"Address Of Premier King Delivered Before Parliament." 21 May 1940: 6.

"Ammunition, Guns and Black Shirts Taken in Ontario Round Up of Italians." 12 June 1940: 2.

"Ask Elimination Of Fifth Column Here." 27 May 1940: 3.

"Curb on National Groups, Guard on buildings, Full RCMP Probe Are Declared Urgent." 21 May 1940: 3.

"Donnell, Jim. "Suggests Auxiliary Legion." Letter. 31 May 1940: 4.

"Eight Held Following Two Raids." 30 May 1940: 3+.

"Four Provinces Assist Anti-Fifth Column Move." 23 May 1940: 8.

G.F.M., Mrs. "Canada For Canadians." Letter. 11 June 1940: 4.

"Grit Unity Stands Off Tory Attack." 31 May 1940: 13.

Hunter, Louis V. "Move Gains For Home Guard To Check 'Fifth Columnists.'" 18 May 1940: 2.

"Legion Demands Suppression Of Subversives In Country." 16 May 1940: 9.

"Legion To Offer Services Against 'Fifth Columnists' Here." 23 May 1940: 3.

"Montreal Italians Rush to Register." 14 June 1940: 3.

Munro, Ross. "M.P.'s Press Government For Even More Action On War." 25 May 1940: 6.

"Origin Of The Term 'Fifth Column.'" 25 May 1940: 4.

"Police Say Unity Party Is Smashed." 31 May 1940: 3.

R., C. "A Home Guard." Letter. 18 May 1940: 4.
"Revamping Sought On Citizen Act." 25 May 1940: 3.
"See Laxity With Aliens In Canada." 28 May 1940: 3+.
"The 'Fifth Column.'" Editorial. 31 May 1940: 4.
"Warns That Enemy Is Organized Here." 22 May 1940: 5.
"5th Column Activities." 30 May 1940: 5.

Vancouver Sun:
A Canadian. "Should Intern Aliens." Letter. 15 May 1940: 6.
"Adrian Arcand and Others in Custody in East." 30 May 1940: 12.
Alberni. "Should Do Something About Aliens." Letter. 20 May 1940: 4.
An Old Veteran. "Would Check on Italians." Letter. 11 June 1940: 4.
"Ask Gov't to Suspend All Naturalization." 7 May 1940: 13.
Another Canadian. "Points to Real Enemy." Letter. 22 May 1940: 6.
"Be Prepared. Recalls Huns of 1914-18." Letter. 21 May 1940: 4.
British-Canadian Allies Club, Member. "Ban German Language." Letter. 24 May 1940: 10.
Campbell, Edith. "Urges Canada to Wake Up." Letter. 21 June 1940: 10.
Canada First. "Deport Nazi Stooges." Letter. 7 June 1940: 10.
Canadian. "Questions on Aliens." Letter. 15 May 1940: 6.
Canadian Logger. "What to do with Aliens." Letter. 8 June 1940: 4.
"Clean Out the Fifth Column." Editorial. 17 May 1940: 10.
Davison, Jas. "Aliens in Government." Letter. 21 May 1940: 4.
D.C.M. No. 1637L. "Fifth Column Is Here!" Letter. 15 May 1940: 6.
"Displaying of Swastika Charged in S. Vancouver." 8 May 1940: 21.

Exactus. "How to Deal with Aliens." Letter. 30 May 1940: 4.

"'Fifth Column' Watched, State Ottawa Ministers." 17 May 1940: 1+.

French, C. "Sees Need for Home Guard." Letter. 17 May 1940: 10.

"Gov't Bans Dozen Organizations: Communists, fascists, Labor Defense League." 5 June 1940: 1+.

"Insist on Action to Curb 'Fifth Column.'" 16 May 1940: 17.

"It Can't Happen Here." Editorial. 4 May 1940: 1.

"Parliament to Probe 'Fifth Column': Gov't Announces Drive On Subversive Elements." 20 May 1940: 1+.

"Ottawa Plans Alien Roundup." 23 May 1940: 13.

"Out Go the Communists." Editorial. 7 May 1940: 4.

"Parliament to Probe 'Fifth Column': Gov't Announces Drive On Subversive Elements." 20 May 1940: 1+.

"Personal Liberty." Editorial. 2 May 1940: 4.

Pilcher, Capt. J.W. "We Ought To Prepare." 4 June 1940: 4.

Pip, O. "Internment of All Enemy Aliens Proposed After Investigation of S. Vancouver Situation." 14 May 1940: 13.

"Police Board Asks Ottawa for Information on Security Steps." 18 May 1940: 19.

R., "Supports Mayor's Stand." Letter 22 May 1940: 6.

Schormann, A. (Rev.). "Lutheran Pastor Answers". Letter. 18 May 1940: 4.

"Set Our House in Order Against Fifth Column." 18 May 1940: 17.

"'Sixth Column' Formed by Ex-Servicemen to Combat '5th' Column: Registration Proposed for all of Alien Birth." 16 May 1940: 1+.

"'Sixth Column' Opens City Office: S. Vancouver Church Target for Vandalism." 20 May 1940: 13.

Stimson, J.N. "Wants Action on Aliens." Letter. 23 May 1940: 4.

"Stop the Fifth Column." Editorial. 15 May 1940: 6.

"Sudden Drive Made Against Unity Party." 24 May 1940: 2.

Unemployed. "Enemies in Our Midst." Letter. 17 May 1940: 10.

Yours for Canada. "Behind Barbed Wire." Letter. 27 May 1940: 4.

"Vancouver and Valley Veterans Begin Organizing 'Flying Columns.'" 17 May 1940: 21.

"Wells Gray Warns of 'Fifth Column': "People Here Who Are Not Our Friends." 18 May 1940: 19.

"300 War Veterans Join 'Flying Column': Old Soldiers Will Combat Subversion." 21 May 1940: 13.

"750,000 Aliens Enjoy Full Canadian Rights." 14 May 1940: 13.

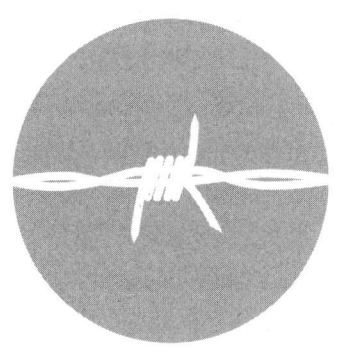

Michael Mirolla

Enemy Aliens: How Canada Declared War on Its Own Citizens

(Note: This article was written in 1994 and appeared originally in *The Eyetalian Magazine* and in *Accenti* Fall 2011)

Sending civilians to internment camp without trial simply because of ethnic origin was not then, is not now and never will be accepted in a civilized nation that purports to respect the rule of law. On behalf of the government and people of Canada, I offer a full and unqualified apology for the wrongs done to our fellow Canadians of Italian origin during World War II.
— *Then-Prime Minister of Canada Brian Mulroney. Statement made outside the House of Commons, Nov. 2, 1990*

To my mind, the application of the time-honoured principle of British justice, that a man is innocent until proven guilty, makes it impossible to curtail the activities of these slimy, subversive elements that are at work in not only this province but throughout the country.
— *Gordon Conant, Ontario Attorney General, May 7, 1940*

When Il Duce marched to war Monday, he threw the switch setting in motion machinery which carried out the largest, most thorough and smoothest roundup of enemy aliens and suspects in the history of Montreal.
— *Excerpt from* The Montreal Gazette, *June 12, 1940*

> "Down with the Jackals" — Toronto Residents Cry, As Windows of Italians' Stores Are Smashed
> — *Headline in* The Globe and Mail, *June 11, 1940*

So, who were these "slimy, subversive elements," these "enemy aliens and suspects," these "jackals"? Well, there was Antonio Capobianco, an accountant at the National Harbors Board in Montreal. The fact he'd been born in Canada and had a brother in the Canadian army didn't prevent his being hauled away in handcuffs. And Joseph Costantini of Ottawa, owner of the Prescott Hotel. And Dr. Vittorio Sabetta, the only Italian medical man in Sault-Ste-Marie. And Dr. Luigi Pancaro of Sudbury. And James Franceschini, the man whose company had built many of the roads in Ontario. And Luigi Scattalon, a coal miner in Dominion, NS. And shoe repairer Francesco Zaffiro of Hamilton. And Luisa Guagnelli from Niagara Falls, arrested while her son was in the bath and not even allowed time to dress him.

The exact number of those arrested between June 10 and the end of October, 1940, isn't known, but the figure could be as high as 6,000, with another 17,000 fingerprinted and photographed for police records. These RCMP records still exist today, despite the efforts of internees and there descendants to have the slate wiped clean.

In Montreal, in what was dubbed "the largest, most thorough and smoothest roundup of enemy aliens and suspects in the history" of the city (*The Montreal Gazette*, June 12, 1940), over 2,200 were nabbed in one day. In Toronto, 3,000 were detained in the month of June alone. The majority were released after detention lasting up to a month. The rest were sent to one of four camps: Camp Petawawa in Ontario; St. Helen's Island in Québec; and two camps in Fredericton, New Brunswick.

According to official statistics, 597 Italian Canadian men were taken to Camp Petawawa. Eyewitness reports put the figures at closer to 700. Of these, more than 85 per cent were Canadian citizens, people who'd sworn allegiance to the King and who considered Canada their country.

Also arrested and interned were 13 women, some of whom, like Luisa Guagnelli, were taken to the Women's Penitentiary in Kingston.

The men were jailed for periods that extended to three years and more, with an average stay of 16 months. Guagnelli was released from prison in the fall of 1943, after Mussolini resigned and Italy surrendered to the Allies.

And of what crime exactly had these men and women been accused? What acts of treason had they committed? Why had they suddenly been branded as "slimy, subversive elements," "enemy aliens and suspects," "jackals"? The arrests were carried out under the 1939 Defence of Canada Regulations (informally known as "The Enemy Aliens Act"), made possible thanks to the War Measures Act of 1914. (Yes, the very same one used in 1970 by Pierre Trudeau during the FLQ crisis.) Section 21 of the Defence of Canada Regulations gave the Minister of Justice the right to hold without trial anyone whom the Minister felt could possibly act "in any manner prejudicial to the public safety of the state."

The then-Minister of Justice Ernest Lapointe took this in the broadest way possible and was quick to take measures to make sure "enemy aliens" wouldn't subvert Canada's fabric. On June 13, 1940, he said in the House of Commons: "The very minute that news was received that Italy had declared war on Great Britain and France, I signed an order for the internment of many hundreds of men whose names were on the list of the RCMP as suspects."

In the propaganda press of the day, this was hailed as an incisive and well-planned operation that nipped subversion in the bud. *The Montreal Gazette* of June 12, 1940, reports:

> Armaments ranging from powerful rifles, shotguns, revolvers and automatic pistols to sawed-off baseball bats and home-made blackjacks were seized by the police ... Transfer of the enemy aliens suspected of possible 'fifth column' or sabotage activities was begun yesterday when a group of those held were moved in buses to an undisclosed destination ... Customs, excise and immigration officers watched exits by train and by boat. Businessmen previously sworn in as RCMP special constables dropped their work and went to assigned spots as soon as they heard the zero hour had come.

So one would expect, of course, that such a thorough rounding up of such a large number of suspected saboteurs would eventually yield substantial criminal charges. Perhaps, there might be revelations of an underground network of fascist sympathizers working to undermine the Canadian war effort. Or even actual proof of sabotage against the security of the Dominion — such as people sending off signals to waiting Italian submarines, or plans for blowing up public buildings.

As a matter of fact, not one Italian Canadian arrested and detained under the Defence of Canada Regulations was ever charged with — let alone convicted of — any act of sabotage or disloyalty during the war. Not one! Their only crime was to have an Italian name or to belong to one of three clubs: the Sons of Italy, the Dopolavoro and the Fascio. Granted, some of them, through misguided loyalty to their homeland or simple nostalgia, did sign up for as many Italian groups and associations as possible, including the Fascio, which had connections with the fascist party in Italy.

But, of those interned at Camp Petawawa, less than 100 had actually been members of the Fascio.

That, however, didn't prevent the RCMP from rounding up everyone they could get their hands on: from millionaires to lawyers; from doctors to bricklayers; from bandleaders to university professors.

Some were taken out in the middle of the night; others in front of their families; still others on their way to or from work and not even permitted to inform their families. Their papers, invoices, receipts and private letters were confiscated. Doctors and lawyers had their confidential records taken away as evidence, and for names that might lead to further arrests.

In Montreal, the men were herded into military barracks where they had to sleep on the floor. Some were led through the streets while hostile crowds insulted them. In Toronto, they were taken first to the Don Jail, then to the CNE Automotive Building and finally to the Stanley Barracks. From there, they were taken by train to their final destination — Camp Petawawa.

Suddenly, decent, law-abiding men found themselves in an isolated camp, 160 kilometres northwest of Ottawa, in the middle of dense bush and surrounded by a pair of barbed-wire fences that were constantly patrolled by armed guards with orders to shoot anyone caught trying to escape.

The conditions may not have been of concentration camp severity — families could send gifts; the food was edible; they were allowed one 24-line letter per week; and no one was beaten or physically tortured. But it wasn't quite the paradise that Ernest Maag, a Red Cross delegate from Montreal, reports in an October 3, 1940 letter:

> The Camp ... is beautifully located in the forest. The climatic conditions must be called ideal ... The accommodations for

the prisoners are absolutely first class ... Sports and walks, recreational activities, classes, etc., are very well taken care of and organized.

Almost sounds like a retirement home, doesn't it? In truth, the men were separated from their families, forced to wear oversized shirts with red bulls-eyes on their backs (easier targets in case of attempted escapes) and made to perform tasks such as building roads and clearing land for the princely sum of 20 cents a day.

Having been accused of no crime, they couldn't understand what they were doing there, why they were being treated like convicts. And their sentences were open-ended, adding to the stress: some were released after a few months; others remained in the camp until the war was over. Many were depressed and worried sick about their families back home.

As Antonio Capobianco says in a June 13, 1992, article in *The Montreal Gazette*:

> Our families were not allowed to visit or write for the first year of our internment. Hundreds of Italian families were left to fend for themselves; often they were poor and hungry ... Many of the internees' families feared for their lives, thanks to the MacKenzie King government's false accusation branding them as enemy aliens, saboteurs and fifth columnists.

This inability to interact with their families proved to be the hardest thing for the internees to take. Most had been brought up to be the providers. Many had come to Canada on their own at first to lay the groundwork for the rest of their families. To be once more separated for months and sometimes years was a devastating blow.

And it didn't help to hear the news from outside the camp: angry mobs in the heart of the Italian district in Toronto smashing store windows and calling for revenge; the boycotting of Italian stores by housewives who considered it a patriotic duty; violence in Nova Scotia where coal miners refused to work alongside Italians; the freezing of bank accounts so that not even the wives of the internees could make use of their savings; the confiscation and even selling off of their property, property which in many cases wasn't returned.

But, for many, being imprisoned, losing their jobs, and being taken away from their families were all things they could eventually learn to live with. What they couldn't stand was the idea that they might be branded as traitors — while at the same time their brothers and sons were fighting for the Allies.

Says Ralph Esposito, a member of the officer training corps in Montreal when the "Enemy Aliens Act" was passed:

> Pretty ironic, isn't it? ... My father was taken away with no right under the law to have a lawyer ... He was six months in Petawawa without a trial while I was in officer training for the army! ... When he came home, he was a walking phantom. (*The Montreal Gazette*, Nov. 11, 1990).

Some managed to adapt to the camp conditions better than others. Dr. Pancaro, for one, became chief medical officer at Camp Petawawa and tried his best to maintain a cheery outlook on life. Band leader Frank Ferri from Hamilton organized a camp orchestra. He played for the internees and, on occasion, even the guards, with a memorable Christmas Eve concert solely for his jailers.

Others were completely broken by the experience. James Franceschini not only lost most of his businesses but also developed throat cancer. When he was released for medical reasons, he discovered that the government was intent on taking away his few remaining businesses.

For some, the worst was yet to come. A month after he was released from Camp Petawawa, Antonio Capobianco was told by his boss at the National Harbors Board that he needn't bother return. Joseph Costantini died in 1951, never really recovering from the fact he'd been separated so long from his family. Luisa Guagnelli would return home to find her husband and son waiting for her. But, at the same time, she faced suspicion and mistrust from people with whom she'd worked for years.

There followed several decades where many Italians were embarrassed to admit their origins. Some waited years before telling anyone about their ordeal; others even went so far as to change their names and to invent new backgrounds for themselves. This hurt not only those who were interned but also their children and even grandchildren. The missed opportunities were felt not only in stalled careers but also in a loss of culture and self-worth.

One of the questions most often asked is: How is it that this internment has been so little publicized? Why is it that even after then-PM Brian Mulroney issued an apology (albeit an unofficial one outside parliament), some still raise their eyebrows in disbelief when the subject is brought up?

Part of the answer may lie in the fact people find it hard to believe that a country with an elected parliament would arrest and intern its own citizens, without laying any charges whatsoever. And without ever finding a single one guilty of anything.

Another reason may be the attitude of the internees themselves, personified by the writings of Mario Duliani, a respected journalist, prize-winning playwright and man of letters who, in 1936, had been invited to Montreal by none other than Eugène Berthiaume, editor of *La Presse*.

Duliani was arrested in Montreal and held for forty months at Camp Petawawa and at a camp outside Fredericton, N.B. In 1945, he published a fictionalized account of his internment titled *La ville sans femmes*; in 1946, it was published in Italian as *Città senza donne*. In his book, not once does he question why he's being arrested. Nor does he rail against the political system that has effectively taken him away from a successful career: by 1937, he'd already made a name for himself by founding the French-language section of the Montreal Repertory Theatre.

Rather, he advocates that the internees put the ordeal behind them and go on with their lives, saying that the internment "seemed wholly justified by the political and military situation of the moment." And this was the attitude held by most of the internees — a type of fatalism, coupled with a sense of nostalgia and longing to be once again amid family. It was almost as if, in some sense, the men felt guilty despite not having committed any crimes — that internment was an expiation for some guilt they had brought on themselves for some reason or other.

On his arrival at Camp Petawawa, after the train journey from Montreal, Duliani writes:

> At last, here we are, in barracks, in the depths of a forest, in the middle of the night, with this atrocious feeling of being imprisoned, who knows for how much longer, not knowing what our loved ones might be going through, aware that they will not learn for several days that we are no longer near them, that we will not see them again for some time to come.

That Duliani's journal represented the only book-length first-hand account of life in Canada's internment camps didn't prevent its rapid descent into obscurity. And, in keeping with some unwritten code of silence about the period, it was only in 1994 that an English version of this valuable document appeared titled *The City Without Women*, translated by Antonino Mazza.

But that's only par for the course. After all, didn't it take 50 years for the government of Canada to recognize that a great wrong had been done to some of its most ardent citizens — and to issue, if not a formal apology, at least a form of *mea culpa?*

One can't help but feel it is this lack of questioning that has kept a dark period in Canadian history hidden for such an intolerably long time. And has left a black mark hanging over an entire community. As one internee says:

> The deprivation of my freedom, being torn from my family, being robbed of time, the loss of my money, all this I might still learn to live with without complaint! ... But what I cannot come to terms with is the idea that my wife, a Canadian, and my Canadian-born children, may suspect I have betrayed *our* country!

Still, it may not be too late. There's definitely a lesson to be learned here, one that is needed just as much today as it was in 1940. Perhaps, with the charged political climate and the tendency to place the blame for the country's problems on its newest arrivals, it is needed today more than ever.

That lesson is: Never again must answering "yes" to "Are you Italian (or Somali or Pakistani or Iraqi)?" lead to the summary denial of the rights of citizenship in this country. The price to pay for capturing a few potential subversives is just too great.

Giulia De Gasperi

The Italians of Cape Breton Island and the Episode of the Internment of Italian-Canadians as Presented in *Down the Coaltown Road*

During my PhD program at Ca' Foscari University, Venice, our department organized a round table discussion on the topic of memory, censorship and writing[1] to give us as students the possibility to showcase our field of research and interests. I presented a paper on Mario Duliani's *The City Without Women* on the topic of the internment of Italian-Canadians in Canada during World War Two.[2] It became quickly evident, while researching my paper, that there was not much literature available on the topic; and, when I began conducting my fieldwork[3] with Italian-Canadians in Cape Breton Island, Nova Scotia, I realized that it was and still is a difficult subject to discuss.

When I arrived at Saint Francis Xavier University to conduct research towards the completion of my doctoral thesis, I did not know that I would be embarking on a new research project even before finishing my PhD. It was through students in my Italian class that I first learned about the presence of Italians in Cape Breton Island. I then read *Italian Lives, Cape Breton Memories*[4] and learned about the Italians of Sydney (whose ancestors came mostly from the central regions of Marche, Abruzzo and Molise) and those of Dominion (from the north of Italy, in particular from the province of Treviso), the former working in the steel plant, the latter in the coal mines.

The need to learn more about these communities, with a particular emphasis on the Dominion one because of our shared communal background (I am originally from the province of Treviso), prompted me to search the printed and archival material available and to explore the history of the community by conducting fieldwork. I learned that, outside Cape Breton, little was known about these communities and about the internment of some of their members during World War Two.[5]

Cape Breton writer, Sheldon Currie, took it upon himself to fill the void by telling the story of the Italians of Cape Breton and the episode of the internment. He felt the need to do so because that void was also his void. Born and raised in Reserve Mines, a small mining town just outside Sydney, he grew up during the 1940s and does not remember the war years. But even after the war ended, he does not recall hearing anything about the way Italian-Canadians were treated during the conflict. He discovered the episode of the internment while reading an article in *Cape Breton's Magazine*. This was an interview with Dominic Nardocchio, a well-known and respected shoemaker from Sydney who was interned in Petawawa for 21 months.[6] Currie wrote *Down the Coaltown Road*, in an attempt to tell a story very few knew and very few seemed willing to discuss.[7] In a climate of general discomfort and whispers, literature can play a crucial role, giving voice to, and becoming a vehicle of expression for, the Italians of Cape Breton and the difficulties they faced. An historical novel, it also provides a picture of these Italian communities, describing their role and position within the larger community.

The novel[8] is set in fictitious Coaltown, a small mining town in industrial Cape Breton Island that mirrors life in the numerous mining towns that dotted the coast along the Atlantic Ocean. The Prologue and Epilogue are set in 1965, whereas the rest of the story takes place in 1940. The opening and closing chapters tell the story of Sister Helen Perenowsky and her quest for understanding, forgiveness and acceptance. But these chapters also offer the reader a detailed and precise description of life in Cape Breton after the end of War World Two. A blanket of decay and peacefulness has fallen over the landscape and the buildings (namely the church, the glebe house and the convent, representing the Catholic faith, a recurring theme in the novel and a distinctive feature of Currie's writing) that overlook the Atlantic Ocean. The drastic change is expressed by the words of a woman who is picking wild strawberries on a cliff: "It's hard to imagine the goings-on here twenty-five years ago when the war was on."[9] Indeed the Prologue ends with an imaginary peacefulness and stillness surrounded by things long gone and forgotten:

> The sun-drenched day is calm. The ocean around the coast from Sydney Harbour to Indian Bay is flat. [...] On this day there is no hint of menace on the surface or in the depths of the sea. On land every reminder of former menace is gone or going: the artillery batteries, the searchlights, the signal stations, the fortress observation posts, anti-aircraft guns. The bunkers now nothing but deteriorating, windowless, [...] And around the bunkers nothing but the grass and the ash-covered chunks of rotting and rusting gear and equipment of long-ago soldiers, junk treasurers for the archeologists of war.[10]

The desolation and sense of stillness presented in the Prologue are in contrast with the planning and plotting of Anna Pellegrina, whose last name is self-explanatory of a character struggling to find her place in the world. One of the main characters in the novel, she relates the events of her life in the first person (her accounts are in italics). It is 1940 and Anna is a young girl who lives in La Prudenza, an Italian town by the sea. Life for Anna is described as typical for a girl who is expected to learn how to become a good housewife. Feeling constraint and with no hope for her future, she decides to emigrate to Canada. Anna knows that "it was the men who went to Canada. The women went with them, or sometimes after them. And I [Anna] knew they wanted coal miners in Canada."[11] It is uncle Pietro, already in Canada, who informs Anna about life in the country. During my fieldwork in Cape Breton I collected many oral narratives about emigration from Italy to the island. In general it was the men who first came to work and save money, and often their coming to Canada was not intended to be a definite migration. If with time they decided to stay, they would then go back to Italy to get married or would send for their families. And it was through correspondence or through agents sent by the coalmining companies to recruit workers that news of jobs spread.

Because it was uncommon for a single woman to come to Cape Breton, Anna marries Tommasio (by way of mastering to perfection all the tricks of female seduction) and together they immigrate to Canada. They arrive in Coaltown where "most of the Italians in Cape Breton live [...]. Most of them work in the pit."[12] This description reflects the equation wherein coalmines attracted northern Italians and steel plants meant work for southern Italians. Anna and Tomassio settle down and he finds work in the pit.

The plot line alternates between the voice of Anna and the omniscient voice that tells the story of Father Rod MacDonald, a young veteran who has lost an eye trying to save the life of Franco, Anna's cousin, while at war in Europe. Father Pat Mancini, Father Rod's good friend and companion during the assignment to save Franco, is now also a veteran, having lost an arm during the rescue mission. Once all three are discharged from service and arrive in Cape Breton as war heroes, Father Rod is sent to Coaltown:

> [I]t looked like it was about to be a trouble spot now, certainly, and perhaps until the war ended. The yahoos were already persecuting Canadians with German names and now the Italians would be in for it. At least in Coaltown there were lots of Italians so it should be manageable.[13]

It is through the eyes and thoughts of Father Rod walking around Coaltown that the historical, cultural, social and economic complexity of Cape Breton Island is presented and described to the reader:

> [T]here are two Cape Breton islands, two cultural islands separated from the mainland by the Strait of Canso. When he heard the other students talking about home in Cape Breton, he knew it wasn't his home they were talking about. He went to the library to look at the map. The island as a whole is divided into two land masses that look on the map like two upflung arms of an exasperated Nova Scotia reaching out into the North Atlantic. The dual arms are separated by the salty inland sea, Bras d'Or Lake. North and west of Bras d'Or Lake lay Inverness and Victoria counties, referred to as "the country" by the migrants, among them Father Rod's parents, who came from their Celtic and Acadian farms and villages, the men to work in the mines, the single women to work as domestics or clerks, or attend nursing schools in Glace Bay. To the migrants of the coal towns who came from Italy, Germany, France, Poland, the Ukraine, Africa, and China, "the country" was a green expanse on the map as undifferentiated as the

white expanse of the Northwest Territories. To the south and west of Bras d'Or Lake is Richmond County, also "the country". And finally, to the south and east, Cape Breton County, industrial Cape Breton, containing Sydney, the only city on the island, built around the steel plant, and Glace Bay, the largest town in Canada, the commercial centre of the half-dozen or so smaller towns built around coal mines. [...] Two islands on an island. One an island of farms and music and Gaelic, and the other an island of steel and coal.[14,15]

In this industrial scenario of steel and coal, where "[f]ew families could afford a car or truck, and since the war began all vehicles, as well as many foods and some articles of clothing, were rationed," the Italian community of Coaltown stands out:

> Looking out over the rows of company houses, he could identify most of the Italian dwellings by the gardens in their back yards. About two hundred families lived in Coaltown. [...] Most of them came from northern Italy after World War One, [...] the Italians were now a rural people living in an industry town. [...] [They] created their new-world farms in "miniature", in their backyards. They loved good wine, good food, and good music, and they provided it for themselves and for each other and for anyone else gracious enough to lean over their fences and share a bit of gossip.[16]

This description reflects the oral narratives I have collected during my years of fieldwork from the Italian-Canadians of Dominion. Adjectives like "hard-working" and "self-sufficient" and statements that underline the efforts made to become part of the larger community while maintaining Old World traditions are paralleled in many recollections. This brief description also provides important actual facts about the Italians of Cape Breton that worked in the coalmines. The majority of them, as noted earlier, came from Northern Italy after the end of War World One. Most of them were farmers, living in towns such as Castelfranco Veneto, Riese Pio X, Possagno, Crocetta and Giavera del Montello, and having a difficult time providing for their families. The opportunity to come to Canada was met with optimism although working in the mines was challenging. Italians have always been described by Cape Bretoners[17] as hard-working people, and not averse to long shifts or difficult physical labour. At home, either company houses or residences they built themselves, they turned their backyards into vegetable gardens, built small barns to house poultry, cows, pigs. They eventually opened several stores. Their generosity was well known. As was their ability to make home-made wine and meat products derived from hogs, following traditions brought from Italy.

In this setting of integration, adjustment and continuity, with the war raging on, everyone looked at Italy, at Mussolini and at what he would say and do next. Because of their great number, particular and close attention was paid to the Italians of Cape Breton and for this reason Father Rod was sent there, to be of help to and provide support for the parishioners, if the need arose.

Tomassio, Anna's husband, is not much liked. He is arrogant, boasting and walks down the street as if he owned the entire town. He epitomizes the macho hot-tempered Mediterranean. Angelo, their son, known as Gelo, is in love with Sadie, but her father doesn't approve: "He hates you 'cause you're Italian. Not bad enough you're a Catholic. At least you can stop being a Catholic. Not much you can do about being an Italian."[18] This hatred is also verbally expressed by her father: "If you think you're gonna bring a goddam grandchild of Mussolini into this house, little miss, you got another think [sic] coming"[19] and by the use of terms such as "dago" and "wop" throughout the novel: "He [Gelo] was called wop, Dago, and bohunk more often now, and not so often in jest, but he brushed it off."[20] Episodes like this were common during the war years when intolerance and ignorance put a stop to many friendships, although we must not forget, as is emphasized in this novel by the strong bond between Anna and Ceit, that some people helped and were of great support to the families in need.[21]

In the novel the wariness of the situation is underlined also by the decision made by the bishop to postpone Confirmation in Coaltown:

> "He [the bishop] is a bit leery to come to Coaltown because of the Italian Thing."
> "The Italian Thing?"
> "Yeah. The Italian Thing. It's only a matter of time until Mussolini brings Italy into the war. The day it happens will be an interesting day in Coaltown and everywhere else in the country. The newspapers are already filling up with hostility. You remember what happened to people with German names last year."[22]

Anna is also worried about the "Italian Thing". She is especially worried about her husband, Tomassio:

> But I knew too that Tomassio was strutting around like Mussolini himself, he even walked down Coal Road to the Italian Hall wearing a Mussolini shirt until I burned it in the kitchen stove. [...] Even the Italians at the Italian Hall were embarrassed with him not to mention nervous he might get them all arrested and the hall closed.[23]

The Italian Hall is *la Sala Italiana*, in Dominion, built, financially and physically, by the members of the Dominion Italian Community Club in 1936-37 as a place for the members and their families to meet and socialize.[24] The minutes recorded since 1936 show that, around the beginning of 1938, there had been troubles and slandering about the Hall and its members. Discussion led to the passing of a motion that prevented members from discussing politics during the meetings. In the books the minutes are then suspended between January 1940 and May 1948 with a short entry on October 1947.[25] Oral accounts say that the Royal Canadian Legion tried to take the building over, but was eventually prevented to do so.

Currie paints, with precise and direct strokes, the scene, laying the foundation for the important events that are to follow. Through a general presentation and description of Cape Breton's dual realities, followed by a picture of every day life in Coaltown as it moves closer to the war, the author prepares us for the climax reached with the arrest of Tomassio by the RCMP soon after Italy declared war on June 10, 1940. On that day Anna is at home with her friend Ceit. Although "in most Italian families, the men made the wine,"[26] in Anna's as well as in her family at home in La Prudenza, the women are the custodians of the secrets of making good home-made wine.[27] In the midst of the process, Gelo comes home and for a few minutes there follows an everyday discussion between mother and son on the importance of healthy eating, a plate of spaghetti waiting for him in the pantry. This familial atmosphere is suddenly interrupted by the bursting open of the front and back doors. Two RCMP officers are looking for Tomassio. The room freezes, with only Anna's thought suspended in mid air: "She'd heard rumours the Mounties would 'round up the Italians' after Mussolini got into the war with Hitler. Was this it?"[28] Gelo is able to flee the house with an excuse and fetch Father Rod, seen in the whole community as not only the priest but also a mentor and counselor. Although there are no formal charges pressed against Tomassio because he did "nothing as we know about yet,"[29] the "explanation" given to all of those who had a husband, father, brother taken away, he is suspected of spying. At the same time, Tomassio is at his work place, ready to cash his cheque, only to find out he has been fired. Tomassio walks home, and is surrounded by RCMP officers when he enters. Father Rod's presence helps calm things down, but Tomassio is nonetheless taken away and put into the county jail. Anna, like many other mothers and wives, is now desperate: "What will I do if they take him? I got no money of my own."[30]

It is in this extremely tense situation, where there seem to be no more certainties, that a new concept is introduced. Italians are now "enemy aliens": "Alien. Is that what they're calling us?" asks Anna. Her friend Ceit tries to explain the absurdity of it all:

> It's our own people saying it, not just the Mounties, [...] [t]hat is the worst of it. It's people's own neighbours. If you can imagine that. They're bothering the kids at school. They're bothering the ones that own the stores and they're bothering the miners in the pit.[31]

Anna's sense of worthlessness and helplessness epitomizes the way other women that were directly affected by this event felt: "I was never so cross at myself in my life, just sitting there almost speechless and totally useless."[32] A plausible explanation for this absurd situation was not easily found. Orders were sent from Ottawa to "round up" residents of Italian origins who might be suspicious. There was a list with names and anonymous calls reporting more people. Tomassio and others were locked up in the County

Jail waiting to be sent to internment camps, leaving wives and mothers at home trying to make sense of what was happening and trying to find a way to support their families. Father Rod, the spokesperson for the Italians in Coaltown, pays a visit to Sergeant Archimbault and asks why Tomassio has been arrested. Sergeant Archimbault explains that he has received orders from Ottawa to "round up" people:

> "Round up who?"
> "It's supposed to be fascists, but I can't find any fascists."
> "So what's the point?"
> "We have our theories. They've got fascist organizations in Montreal and Toronto. The leaders are well known. I suppose if they're going to intern people from Ontario and Quebec, they figure they have to treat the rest of the country equally."
> "You believe that?"
> "Who knows? Probably a bit of envy in there too."
> "Envy?"
> "All the real action is on the coast, submarines sinking ships in the Gulf, convoys shipping out from Sydney, coal production, steel production in the news everyday, they want to get in on it. And I suppose they figure if there are Italians in Cape Breton, there must be fascists there too, just like in Toronto, Montreal, and Ottawa. Sometimes the farther away from a situation the more clearly you think you can see into it."[33]

In the town of Dominion, two individuals were sent to the internment camp in Petawawa, where they were held for two years.[34] Eventually family members were able to communicate through letters, but the tone of the oral narratives collected stressed an extremely difficult time. In the novel, the episode of Tomassio and the other Italians that wait in the county jail and are verbally assaulted by a group of individuals echoes the narrative provided by Nardocchio in *Cape Breton's Magazine*.[35]

In the novel the situation worsens when the other miners refuse to work in the pit together with the Italians. Tomassio's best friend and partner in the pit speaks up during the riot:

> Who are we talking about here? These Italians are the same people that stood with us in the strike in '25.[36] They arrested Tomassio. Yes. What for? Who knows? Tommy was my buddy in the pit for years. I'd trust my life with him. These people are friends. We work with them, we play ball with them, hockey, most of you go to church with them. They're neighbours. They're buddies in the pit. Our buddies. [...] How's your memory? Do you remember the strike in '24? Do you remember '25? Do you remember hunger? Do you remember how many Italians brought around food from their gardens? I'd bet there's not a man standing in front of me whose family didn't get at least one armload of vegetables. And what about the winter of '25? Pickles, preserves, dried fruit, salt meat, fish. What about you, big mouth? Did you eat Italian vegetables in '24? Or did you eat enemy alien vegetables?[37]

Italian miners were shut out for nine months during which the other miners refused to work in the pit with them. Their guns were also confiscated. The situation gets even worse. Lucia Gato and Maria Goretti visit Father Rod:

> "We're losing our homes."
> "What do you mean?"

> "The Mounties took our men. They said if we don't have men in the pit, we can't live in the company houses.
> [...]
> Some men came around. Said we got a week to get out. Where we gonna go? And they're gonna cut off relief. We'll have no money to pay rent. Or buy food. We got kids. We can't go for work. Even if there was work."[38]

Father Rod offers help and support. He represents all of those who provided assistance to those in need during these hard times. Italians were also resourceful, they helped and were helped and soon the "round-up" was over.

> "[...] why is the round-up over?" Father Rod asked.
> "I guess they realized it was a stupid idea in the first place. We told them that. We're still watching a few people on their list but I think it's pretty well done."
> "What about the men they took to Minto and Petawawa already? Everybody knows they're not spies or whatever it was they were put away for."
> "I don't know. I guess they'll let them go sooner or later."[39]

This brief dialogue sums up the absurdity of the situation, and shows how things went back to "normal" and people had to accept explanations such as: "They handed us the list along with our orders. We obeyed. It's war. With the war on, people feel they can justify anything."[40]

It would be misleading to state that life went back to normal. There were a lot of scars. Even though the "round up" was over, some of the men interned did not come home right away and, once families were reunited, some decided to move away and re-settled in places such as Guelph, Ontario. The way Italian-Canadians were treated might not appear as harsh as the way in which Japanese-Canadians were dealt with in terms of the numbers involved and the measures taken against them. But was internment really necessary or was it a "stupid idea in the first place"? Were Italian-Canadians really enemies? Did they really represent a threat to the country they had chosen as their new homeland? Even the way in which the Canadian Government dealt with the two communities after the end of the War was different: the Japanese-Canadians received formal apologies and compensation, whereas Italian-Canadians are still waiting for an official redress. What has happened that made their situation different?[41]

Down the Coaltown Road gives voice to this chapter in the lives of Cape Breton's Italians and to the episode of the internment of some of the members of their community. It does this without pointing fingers or naming names, by piecing together history, oral accounts and the "truths" of those who lived through it, thus releasing the sense of discomfort and unease that have always filled the room when trying to discuss this difficult topic in Canadian and Italian histories.

Endnotes

1. *Giornata di Studio "Memoria, censura, scrittura"*, 25 March 2004, Ca' Foscari University, Venice, Italy.
2. My article is "Mario Duliani e *The City Without Women*. Lo strano caso degli internati italo-canadesi durante la Seconda Guerra Mondiale," in *Memoria Scrittura Censura. Quaderni del Dottorato in Studi Iberici, Anglo-americani e dell'Europa Orientale*, Università Ca' Foscari, Venezia, 2005, pp. 265-76.

3. Preliminary fieldwork in Dominion was conducted in the winter of 2009. Extensive fieldwork was carried out during the summers of 2009 and 2010, thanks to two subsequent Helen Creighton Folklore Society Grants-in-Aid. In this article I will refer to material collected during my fieldwork on those occasions.
4. Edited by Sam Migliore and A. Evo DiPierro and published by UCCB Press in 1999, *Italian Lives, Cape Breton Memories* is an invaluable source of first hand accounts of life before and after emigration from Italy.
5. For detailed information about the Italian presence in Cape Breton, see Sam Migliore, "Introduction," pp. 11-13 about the history of emigration and settlement; and Esperanza Maria Razzolini Crook, "All Our Fathers: The North Italian Colony in Industrial Cape Breton," pp. 16-23 about the Northern Italians, in *Italian Lives, Cape Breton Memories*. Articles on the Italian community of Dominion are "'The Hall was Us': Roles and Functions of the Italian Hall, *La Sala Italiana*, in the Italian-Canadian community of Dominion, Cape Breton Island, Canada," in *Folk Life* by the author and "La Comunità Italo-canadese di Dominion, Isola del Capo Bretone, Nuova Scozia," in *Veneti in Canada*, co-authored with Frank Canova.

    For information about the war years and the episode of the internment of Italian-Canadians in Cape Breton Island see Section II — "The War Years" of *Italian Lives*, pp. 87-122; "War Wounds: Painful Memories of a Forgotten Past," by Sam Migliore in *Racial Profiling and Borders: International, Interdisciplinary Perspectives*, pp. 175-201; and Patrick Marsh's BA thesis *Oral History in Cape Breton. An Italian Internment History*.

Literary works based on the episode of the internments of Italian-Canadians of Cape Breton are, to my knowledge, *Down the Coaltown Road* by Sheldon Currie, the novel which is the topic of this article, and *By the Sea — Anna's Story*, a play based on the novel and produced by Festival Antigonish in 2001 and by Eastern Front Theatre, Dartmouth, in 2002.

Barbed Wire and Mandolins, a 47-minute long documentary about the episode of the internment, features, among the interviewees, Dominic Nardocchio from Sydney, Cape Breton.

6. "A Talk with Dominic Nardocchio," *Cape Breton's Magazine*, Issue 53, pp. 69-88, published on 1 January 1990.
7. Interview with Sheldon Currie, 9 August 2009.
8. The novel is a mix of friendship, love, sex, faith, betrayals, mysteries, murders and murderers but not all the events told in the book will be discussed here. However, to be thorough I will provide a brief synopsis of the storyline. The novel opens and closes in 1965 in Coaltown. The main character of the initial and ending chapters is Helen Perenowsky, a very tall and blond girl who doesn't fit in with the rest of her classmates. Her mother dies young and Helen is left with her father, a loner, and a brother who leaves to go to War. One day, at the end of Mass, she is approached by a handsome young man and the two spend some time together, travelling around the coastline, first in her brother's motorcycle and then in his boat. This handsome man, very mysterious, takes her to the prom. They have a wonderful time and end up spending the night together. In the morning he is gone, taking with him the

letter her brother had left her with instructions of his whereabouts. The man was a German spy who gets in touch with her years later (in 1965) to apologize. In the meantime, however, Helen had become a nun, having given up the daughter that was born from their only night together. The daughter writes her a letter inviting her to her wedding.

Anna is another, if not the most, important, character in the story. In Italy she marries Tomassio, the two immigrate to Canada and settle in Coaltown. Tomassio finds a job working in the mines. They have a son, Angelo. Tomassio is a difficult man, arrogant and boastful who has an affair with Cathy's husband, Wilfred, known as Ump because of his position in baseball games. Cathy is the mother of Sadie, Angelo's girlfriend. Because of Tomassio and because he is Italian, Ump disapproves of their relationship. Anna knows about Tomassio's affairs. After Tomassio is taken to the County Jail, he escapes and hides in Cathy's attic. In the meantime Anna, during one of her usual long walks, gets almost raped by Ump whom she pushes away making him fall down the cliff. Tomassio, on the run, is now suspected of the murder of Ump. When he tries to escape into the woods from Cathy's house, he is caught again and jailed once more. He succeeds in escaping one more time only to be beaten to death. His body is found by Helen.

Father Rod MacDonald, recently arrived in Coaltown to keep an eye on the Italians, is the peacemaker, the counselor, the mentor, the person everyone goes to in time of need. He is, however, an enigmatic figure who still dreams of the nurse who took care of him while in the hospital in Europe and who has sex with Anna, now his housekeeper, who tries to protect herself from the risk of Father Rod telling, other than the police and without mentioning her name, that she is the one who killed Ump.

The novel ends with the funeral of Tomassio and the confirmation of the children of Coaltown.

9. P. 14.
10. P. 15.
11. P. 19.
12. P. 45.
13. P. 47.
14. Pp. 53-4.
15. Not the specific topic of this paper, but worth mentioning here is the idea presented in this passage of the two islands on an island, two separate realities that live side by side. Other solitudes to add to the ones of the French and the English presented by Hugh MacLennan in his novel *Two Solitudes*. MacLennan was well aware of the many solitudes present in Canada, his own ancestors coming from Scotland, and he wrote about this aspect of Canadian society in many of his essays.
16. Pp. 56-7.
17. One such Cape Bretoner is Lennie Stephenson, former postmaster of Dominion, who became a very good friend of the community and helped many Italians with paperwork and documentation. When I interviewed him during the summer of 2009, he spoke several times about what hard-working people these Italians were (Dominion, 27 July 2009).
18. P. 71.
19. P. 72.
20. P. 110.

21. Racism and discrimination were not directed exclusively at Italians, although after 10 June 1940 Italians were especially targeted. In the novel there is an interesting exchange of words between Father Rod and Theresa Papadopoulus, an old lady who is sick with T.B. and who is at the hospital. Father Rod goes to visit her:

"Cute, aren't they [two nursing students who would check on her]," Theresa said. "And innocent as daylight. They come every half-hour, to check on me. They seem happy enough to see that I'm still alive. But the first time they came, my eyes were closed and they came up close to make sure I was still breathing. 'She's okay,' I heard one of them say as they walked away. Then the other one said, 'We're sure getting a lot of them these days, pretty soon there won't be any beds for white people.'"
"White people?" Father Rod repeated.
"Yeah. Can you believe it? Of course, they think I'm an Italian because my name isn't Murphy or MacNeil. They don't realize what they're saying, they're so young, but you can see what's in the air." (206)

See also Migliore's Introduction in *War Wounds*, pp. 175-76.
   Also interesting to note from the perspective of the Italian-Canadians in Dominion is their use of the term "English" as encompassing everyone who was not Italian. The term does not seem to have a negative connotation.
22. P. 82. The conversation is taking place between Father Rod and Sister Mary.
23. P. 143.
24. For more information about the Italian Hall see the author's article "The Hall was Us" in *Folk Life* and pp.

263-68 in *Italian Lives*.
25. Permission to examine the records of the minutes was given to the author by Frank Canova, current President of the Dominion Italian Community Club.
26. P. 110.
27. The episode of the wine reminds me of an account I collected about the RCMP bursting into the house and disposing of barrels of wine that was recently made by the family. A gesture that was not necessary, especially in those circumstances and in the view of the fact that wine was also a source of income, but that stays with the individual who witnessed it for the rest of his life.
28. P. 113.
29. P. 114.
30. P. 118.
31. P. 118.
32. P. 104.
33. Pp. 120-21.
34. See also *Italian Lives, Cape Breton Memories*, pp. 102-7.
35. "A Talk with Nardoccio," pp. 77-8.
36. For more information on the agitations of the early 1920s, see Robert J. Morgan, *Rise Again! The Story of Cape Breton Island from 1900 to Today*, book 2, pp. 57-65.
37. Pp. 179-80.
38. P. 197.
39. Pp. 253-4.
40. P. 255.
41. These issues are presented and discussed from different perspectives and points of views in two seminal works: *On Guard for Thee: War, Ethnicity and the Canadian State, 1939-1945* and the more recent *Enemies Within: Italian and Other Internees in Canada and Abroad*.

Works Cited

Books

Currie, Sheldon. *Down the Coaltown Road*. Toronto: Key Porter Books Limited, 2002.

Duliani, Mario. *The City Without Women*. Translated by Antonino Mazza. Oakville: Mosaic Press, 1994.

Enemies Within: Italian and Other Internees in Canada and Abroad. Edited by Franca Iacovetta, Roberto Perin and Angelo Principe. Toronto: University of Toronto Press Incorporated, 200.

Italian Lives, Cape Breton Memories. Ed. by Sam Migliore and A. Evo DiPierro. Sydney: UCCB, 1990.

MacLennan, Hugh. *Two Solitudes*. Toronto: Macmillan Company of Canada, 1951.

Morgan, Robert J. *Rise Again! The Story of Cape Breton Island from 1900 to today*. Book 2. Sydney: Breton Books, 2009.

On guard for thee: war, ethnicity and the Canadian state, 1939-1945: a report on the proceedings of the conference held 25-27 September, 1986, at the Donald Gordon Centre, Queen's University. Edited by Normal Hillmer, Bohdan S. Kordan, Lubomyr Y. Luciuk. Canadian Committee for the History of the Second World War, 1988.

Articles

"A Talk with Dominic Nardocchio," *Cape Breton's Magazine*, Issue 53, 1 January 1990, 69-88. Available on line at: http://capebretonsmagazine.com/modules/ publisher/item.php?itemid=3421&keywords=Nardocchio

De Gasperi, Giulia. "Mario Duliani e *The City Without Women*. Lo strano caso degli internati italo-canadesi durante la Seconda Guerra Mondiale." *Memoria Scrittura Censura*.

Quaderni del Dottorato in Studi Iberici, Anglo-americani e dell'Europa Orientale, Università Ca' Foscari, Venezia, 2005, pp. 265-76.

— "'The Hall was Us': Roles and Functions of the Italian Hall, *La Sala Italiana*, in the Italian-Canadian community of Dominion, Cape Breton Island, Canada," in *Folk Life: Journal of Ethnological Studies*, Vol. 49, No. 2, 2011, pp. 142-53.

— and Frank Canova. "La Comunità Italo-canadese di Dominion, Isola del Capo Bretone, Nuova Scozia," in *Veneti in Canada*. Ravenna: Angelo Longo Editore, pp. 229-242.

Migliore, Sam. "War Wounds: Painful Memories of a Forgotten Past," in *Racial Profiling and Borders: International, Interdisciplinary Perspectives*. Jeff Shantz, ed., 1. Lake Mary, Florida: Vandeplas Publishing, 2010, pp. 175-20.

Unpublished material:

Currie, Sheldon. *By the Sea — Anna's Story*. (a play)

Marsh, Patrick. *Oral History in Cape Breton. An Italian Internment History*. BA Thesis, Department of History, Sydney, N.S: Cape Breton University, 2008.

Minutes of the Dominion Italian Community Club, 1936 to present time.

Interviews:

Currie, Sheldon. With the author. 9 August 2009.

Stephenson, Lennie. With the author. 27 July 2009.

Fieldwork:

De Gasperi, Giulia. With several members of the Italian-Canadian Community of Dominion, Cape Breton Island, 2009, 2010.

Documentaries:

Zavaglia, Nicola. *Barbed Wire and Mandolins*. National Film Board of Canada, Canada, 1997

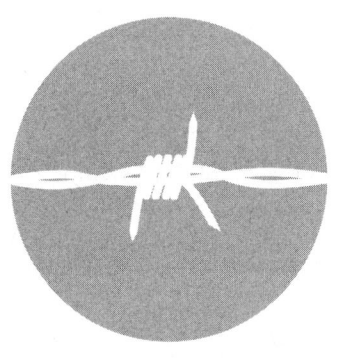

Patrick Marsh

Oral History in Cape Breton: An Italian Internment History

The subject of the internment of Italians in Canada evokes a variety of emotions and assessments among scholars. It is undeniable that the internment of Italian-Canadians in various cities across the country had a profound effect on each community. At the same time, it is important to understand the federal government's position on detaining potential threats to national security. Generally speaking, the scholarship surrounding Italian-Canadian internment was seen from one of two perspectives. One typically viewed internment as a negative event in Canadian history and perceived the Canadian government's actions as unjust. The other perspective, while acknowledging the questionable nature of internment, sought to defend the government's actions by explaining the connection between Italians and the rise of fascism across the globe during the 1930s and 1940s. The two perspectives have had a polarizing effect on the scholarship, creating a need for new ground to be broken.

This essay seeks to briefly explore the two perspectives of Italian internment scholarship as well as suggest a new direction for research through oral history. With oral history, scholars can probe with the same questions posed in both scholastic perspectives, but also break ground by exploring the concepts of collective memory as well as attach a more personal, human element to the history of the internment of Italians in Canada.

The internment of Italian Canadians was presented to the general public as a negative event in Canadian history in the 1997 documentary *Barbed Wire and Mandolins*. Some surviving internees, including Dominic Nardocchio of Cape Breton Island, relived the events of their arrest more than fifty years later.[1] The documentary noted some of the undisputed aspects of internment, such as the invoking of the War Measures Act at the beginning of the Second World War, the mobilization of the RCMP on 10 June 1940 to seize "enemy aliens," the transportation of internees to camps, and the general description of the camp in Petawawa, Ontario.[2] Despite this level of detail, the film's focus was on the effect the process of internment had on the internees, their families, and their communities.[3]

Of the interviewed internees, Nardocchio's testimony is particularly interesting. He vividly describes the events that happened to him on the day he was picked up by the RCMP.[4] Nardocchio, a working class citizen in Cape Breton, insists he does not understand why he was taken away. He was aware that Italian-Canadians were taken away because they were believed to be "fifth columnists" and traitors to Canada, but he maintains his innocence.[5] Whether or not Nardocchio and the other internees who were interviewed were truly supporters of Mussolini's fascist regime in Italy appears to be a question left for another documentary; there was mention of possible connections within the communities to the fascist regime through church groups and social clubs such as the Sons of Italy, but no concrete accusations were made.[6] Some of the internees explained that there was a sense of Italian pride within the community during the earlier years of Mussolini's regime to the middle of the 1930s, when Italy invaded Ethiopia.[7]

Sam Migliore's *Italian Lives, Cape Breton Memories* is another source that views internment as a negative event in Canadian history. Migliore focuses on collected stories and interviews of Italian Canadians impacted by internment. Migliore and sociologist John deRoche's interviews included the Nemis family, whose members were miners who emigrated from Italy to Dominion, Nova Scotia. They also interviewed non-Italian miners who worked with Italian Canadians who provided an account of the time leading to internment.[8] Catherine MacDonald-Nemis's account described attitudes towards Italian Canadians during the Second World War. In her brief interview she explains that during the war years, local miners did not want to work with Italians.[9] Once the wartime fear had dissolved, however, relationships returned to normal and the dislike of Italian workers in the mines waned.[10] Another interviewee, an activist, blames the government for propagating the xenophobia seen in the mining towns; he also blames the government for the Italian workers losing their jobs.[11]

Italian Lives also argues that the government took a considerable amount of time to acknowledge the internment and offer restitution. In an address by then Prime Minister Brian Mulroney to the NCIC and the CIBPA[12] on 4 November 1990, a formal apology was made.[13] Mulroney stated that "what happened to many Italian Canadians is deeply offensive to the simple notion of respect for human dignity and the presumption of innocence."[14] He admitted that many arrests were based on membership of Italian Canadian organizations.[15] Migliore explains that these arrests happened across the country to men like Michele (Mike) LaPenna who belonged to groups like Dopolavoro (After Work) and suffered because of this affiliation.[16]

Published nearly a decade before Migliore's work, *On Guard for Thee: War, Ethnicity and the Canadian State, 1939-1945*, is another text that views internment as a negative event in Canadian history. A discussion of the government's actions during the war when dealing with ethnic minorities and refugees is prominent in the text.[17] A number of authors in the book were "critical of the suspension of civil liberties, the cruel impact of a fearful and xenophobic public opinion, and the overzealousness and even immorality of the government's actions."[18]

On Guard for Thee specifically intended to ridicule government mistakes and policies during difficult war years. According to the book, those who were rounded up by the RCMP were immediately taken to local headquarters to be fingerprinted and photographed.[19] Over the entire course of the war, the book claims, no Italian Canadian committed an act of sabotage, and the concept of a "fifth columnist" to the Italians was confusing and nonsensical.[20] To Italians, fascism was not as much a political ideal as it was a revitalization of Italian pride. It was possible to see their positive opinion of Mussolini's regime in its early years as a proud moment easily confused by the Canadian government with being a danger to their country.

In opposition to the view that internment was a negative event in Canadian history is some recent scholarship that challenges both internees and the government for wrongdoing during the Second World War. The book *Enemies Within: Italian and Other Internees in Canada and Abroad* features an introduction by Franca Iacovetta and Roberto Perin that discusses the key issues of internment, the first of which was that of achieving a balance between the civil liberties of minorities and the needs of majorities.[21] Another issue is the activity of the government during the war years. This includes the invoking of the War Measures Act, the RCMP's speedy mobilization, and spying on people suspected of belonging to a "fifth column".[22] The third major issue was the reaction of the public and the government to the act of internment.[23]

Iacovetta dismisses the central thesis of *On Guard for Thee* that internment was a "war against ethnicity" and that the government did little except cave to the wartime hysteria and xenophobia that was building across the country.²⁴ This caving was reinforced by the government's supposed arbitrary incarceration of people based on incomplete and vague information scraped together just in time for Italy's declaration of war.²⁵

The spread of fascism in Canada is a recurring theme of *Enemies Within*. In an introduction to a chapter dedicated to the question, Iacovetta illustrates that fascism began to take hold in Canada's Italian communities very early on.²⁶ Mussolini's regime encouraged the spread of fascism in Canada's urban "Little Italies."²⁷ However, there was a distinction between those who were emotionally supportive of Mussolini's rise to power and those who were actually committed to the fascist regime; Iacovetta labels them "black sheep" and "black shirts" respectively.²⁸ Fellow *Enemies Within* scholar Angelo Principe notes that the basis for arrests does appear arbitrary.²⁹ Innocents were jailed, while men who were well-known leaders in the fascist community, like A.D. Sebastiani and A.S. Biffi, were not interned.³⁰ In addition, about twenty men labelled "Mafiosi", who had nothing to do with fascism, were arrested too.³¹ Principe explains that men with questionable and uncertain links to fascism were arrested.³²

Luigi Bruti-Liberati, another author featured in *Enemies Within*, focuses on the RCMP and the nature of its mobilization. A committee devoted to monitoring fascist activity in Canada was established by March 1936, likely a response to Mussolini's invasion of Ethiopia the previous December.³³ A document had been produced by the government as early as 1926 titled "Fascism (Italian) in Canada." By 1931, concrete evidence was compiled that supported the notion that there was a fascist enclave in Canada.³⁴ Once Mussolini invaded Ethiopia, the project took a more formal shape and the monitoring of major urban areas where large numbers of Italians resided, like Montreal and Toronto, was underway.³⁵

Bruti-Liberati also asserts that despite previous information, the RCMP may not have been aware of the documentation of the fascist activity.[36] The information collected may not have been accurate due to the sources often being paid police informants. This could also explain why some Mafiosi were arrested with no affiliation to fascism.[37]

Italian internment continues to be a controversial debate fuelled by the concept of state responsibility and the impact on Italian communities. Oral history in particular has been valuable to uncovering the impact of the Second World War on ethnicities in Canada. *Enemies Within* states that interviews, private letters and memoirs are the kinds of sources that have been used to shed light on aspects of internment not easily revealed by government documents, security files of the RCMP, and archival records.[38] Oral history is important to both sides of the argument. It also offers the possibility of re-framing the important issues of internment. Collective memory and the circulation of stories and memories is a fresh perspective on the subject. In conducting oral interviews, the debate can move away from traditional schools of thought which polarizes the scholarship.

As it becomes increasingly difficult to obtain sources for interviews, scholars must rely on accounts already collected. For the purposes of this essay, two CBC broadcasts were used to supplement oral testimonies. The first is a broadcast that took place on 27 September 1977 on CBC radio.[39] This interview included two interviewers — a man and a woman, and three male subjects. One of the men was called Besso or Basso (likely the former since it is a common surname in Cape Breton); another went by the name of Johnny. The third man's name was unintelligible. The atmosphere of the interview itself was light-hearted, with jokes and laughter at various intervals.

The second broadcast is a CBC report from 1991, around the time that there was immense political pressure on the Mulroney government to make amends to Italians for the "mistakes" made during the Second World War.[40] The reporter, Joan Melanson, went into the field and interviewed a number of families about the subject of internment, asking questions that often sparked tension. She interviewed Dominic Nardocchio (later to be included in the documentary by Zavaglia cited above), an internee at the camp in Petawawa; Carmella Scattalon, her husband Luigi, and nephew Londo; Ralph Gatto; Leno and Theresa Polegato; and a non-Italian friend of the Italian community, Nelson Beaton. All of these subjects were at one point residents of Cape Breton and, with the exception of Beaton, were part of Cape Breton's Italian community. It is important to note that only Nardocchio experienced the internment firsthand, while the Scattalons had one member of the family interned who was not present for the interview. The rest were part of the peripheral fallout of internment.

Any notion that the community has one consistent opinion to the question of internment is dashed by these two interviews. In the case of the first oral testimonies, the topic is slowly introduced by the interviewers. They begin with talk of Italian identity on the island, a reunion organized by a friend, M. Serrato, followed by the emigration of Italians to the island after the Second World War.[41] Several minutes into the interview, the subject of internment is introduced as the result of a question asked by one of the interviewers about Dominic Nardocchio.[42] The topic is then discussed for about fifteen minutes by all interviewees.[43] From this brief mention of internment in an interview that discusses Italian life in Cape Breton, it can be gleaned that the men in the interview do not discuss the subject with a great deal of animosity.[44] Both Besso and Johnny come to the conclusion that the wartime paranoia was either propagated by a few people within the workplace in Cape Breton or it was a way for the government to cripple Italian pride.[45] Still, Besso discusses the subject in a matter-of-fact-tone and explains that, since that time, people have matured and Italians are no longer looked at as being from "outer space".[46] It also appears that the interviewees have a desire to put the ordeal behind them, and move on to more important issues in the community, such as preserving their Italian heritage.[47]

The second oral testimony is a fourteen minute report dedicated solely to the subject of internment. Contrary to the relaxed atmosphere of the 1977 interview, the 1991 piece unfolds with a great deal of tension due to the interviewer's methods and the topic now appearing to be more sensitive. In this report, which was recorded six years before *Barbed Wire and Mandolins*, Dominic Nardocchio mirrors that lack of understanding.[48] Nardocchio's frustration is shared by the rest of the Italians interviewed by the CBC reporter. The Scattalons, for example, erupt into an argument after reporter Joan Melanson begins to ask about names of possible fascists or "fifth columnists" within the community.[49] The response as to how to deal with internment as a subject over fifty years later is met with different responses. Leno Polegato believed that the history should remain in the past.[50] Carmella Scattalon also wants the history to remain behind them.[51] Ralph Gatto and Londo Scattalon believe it was a product of the war.[52] Nelson Beaton, the Italian sympathizer, believes that Cape Bretoners should offer a mass apology to the Italians.[53]

Despite the diversity of response within the community, there are some key themes that are mentioned in both interviews. Family remains a critical point of interest within the community. The 1977 CBC broadcast deals with the subject of the Italian community from its beginnings to the current day. Over time, the interviewees variously mention events in terms of family memories.[54] For the two more vocal participants, Besso and Johnny, when discussing their arrival in Cape Breton near the beginning of the 20th century, both recall leaving family members behind or that there were ties with Italians who had already immigrated to Canada.[55] Compared to Italy, they believe that family relationships are closer within the community.[56] This sentiment is best demonstrated in their discussion of the reunion sparked by M. Serrato around the same time of the interviews.[57] Additionally, when they recall the migration of many Italians to Ontario or the move to the Mira region in Cape Breton, they do so by remembering the names of the families who moved.[58] Finally, when discussing the future of the Italian community in Cape Breton, Besso and Johnny both mention the lack of interest in using the language and continuing the customs by the next generation, although they do not put the blame solely on the most recent generation for this.[59]

The second interview also includes the importance of family in the Italian community. It is mentioned in passing that Dominic Nardocchio did not have enough time to say goodbye to his wife before he was taken away to Petawawa.[60] Carmella Scattalon recalls the event mostly through her role as both sister-in-law to one of the internees and as a mother.[61] She explains to the reporter that she turned out her home's lights in order to make the angry citizens leave their home alone.[62] As she sat with her children in the dark, she sent her husband Luigi Scattalon to check on his sister-in-law at their family store.[63] Luigi recalls a skirmish with police and his decision to go into hiding to protect his family.[64] Ralph Gatto recalls his wife's relaxed, calm approach to dealing with the wartime paranoia.[65] Near the end of the interview, the Scattalons erupt into an argument over the names of people within the community.[66]

The second topic that arose in both interviews was the politics of internment. In the case of the first interview, the informants subscribe to the belief that "those were the times" and now all is forgiven.⁶⁷ Italians were put on the spot by accusations of being part of Mussolini's "fifth column," a group of citizens who were determined to bring down the government of an opposing nation through guerrilla tactics. The interviewees do not specifically mention this sentiment, but they recognize that the government took action against a possible threat to national security through internment.⁶⁸ Local politics, specifically in Cape Breton, were mentioned in the conversation. Johnny warns the interviewers that they do not want to "get started on Dominion," but Besso states that Dominion was home to "a few big mouths" at the time of the war and they were part of the problem in the community.⁶⁹ He points out that there were only a few within the mining community who made working with Italians a problem.⁷⁰

The second broadcast places internment in a national and global context by the juxtaposition of sound clips of Italian leader Benito Mussolini and wartime Prime Minister Mackenzie King.⁷¹ Interestingly, the concept of fascism is only brought up twice in both interviews. The 1977 interview mentions one event where a man the community knew was a fascist visited to recruit.⁷² Besso explains to the interviewers that in 1936 or 1937, a man came from Montreal looking to recruit fascists within the Italian community.⁷³ As Besso states: "He was a real fascist." He also says that the man held meetings before disappearing shortly afterward.⁷⁴

In conclusion, these two interviews reveal several key points. First, the lack of homogeneity amongst the Italian community; there is no encompassing perspective among the community. From reading and listening to first-hand accounts, there is the sense that something virtually unforgivable had happened. According to Dominic Nardocchio, near the conclusion of the 1991 interview, if someone is innocent and has not done wrong, they cannot be paid back for wrongful treatment, no matter how much money is offered.[75] Adversely, many in the community, such as Besso and Johnny from the 1977 interview, and the Scattalons, and Ralph Gatto from the 1991 interview, the subject should be buried and allowed to fade away from memory. Many appear to want to let time heal the wounds of the community and to focus on the future of the community. These diverging opinions aside, there is a common template for the Italian responses: the importance of family, the local politics of the war, and the silence regarding fascism. That said, every Italian Canadian citizen recognizes that their experience was difficult and traumatic. The window is rapidly closing for the opportunity to document first-hand accounts of internment or arrests that took place during 1940, but the new direction the scholarship can take does not necessarily have to rely on only personal experience. Family and community experiences have the potential to answer many questions surrounding internment as well as open the door to new ones, including how to move on from what is perceived as one of Canada's more negative events in its history.

Endnotes

1. Nicola Zavaglia, *Barbed Wire and Mandolins*, National Film Board of Canada, Canada, 1997
2. Ibid.
3. Ibid.
4. Ibid.
5. Ibid.
6. Ibid.
7. Ibid.
8. Sam Migliore, *Italian Lives, Cape Breton Memories*, (Sydney: University College of Cape Breton Press, 1999), p. 98

9. Ibid., p. 98
10. Ibid., p. 98
11. Ibid., p. 101
12. National Congress of Italian Canadians and the Canadian Italian Business Professional Association respectively.
13. Sam Migliore, *Italian Lives, Cape Breton Memories*, (Sydney: University College of Cape Breton Press, 1999), p. 121
14. Ibid., p. 121
15. Ibid., p. 121
16. Ibid., p. 121
17. Norman Hiller, "The Second World War as an (Un) National Experience," *On Guard for Thee: War, Ethnicity and the Canadian State, 1939-1945*, (Ottawa: Canadian Publishing Centre, 1988)., p. xvii
18. Ibid., p. xvii
19. Bruno Ramirez, "Ethnicity on Trial: The Italians of Montreal and the Second World War," *On Guard for Thee: War, Ethnicity and the Canadian State, 1939-1945*, (Ottawa: Canadian Publishing Centre, 1988), p. 72
20. Ibid., p. 73
21. Franca Iacovetta and Roberto Perin, "Italians and Wartime Internment: Comparative Perspectives on Public Policy, Historical Memory, and Daily Life," *Enemies Within: Italian and Other Internees in Canada and Abroad*, (Toronto: University of Toronto Press, 2000), p. 3
22. Ibid., p. 3
23. Ibid., p. 3
24. Ibid., p. 5
25. Ibid., p. 6
26. Ibid., p. 24

27. Ibid., p. 24
28. Ibid., p. 24
29. Angelo Principe, "A Tangled Knot: Prelude to 10 June 1940," *Enemies Within: Italian and Other Internees in Canada and Abroad*, (Toronto: University of Toronto Press, 2000), p. 28
30. Ibid., p. 28
31. Ibid., p. 28
32. Ibid., p. 28
33. Luigi Bruti Liberati, "The Internment of Italian Canadians," *Enemies Within: Italian and Other Internees in Canada and Abroad*, (Toronto: University of Toronto Press, 2000), p. 77
34. Ibid., p. 77
35. Ibid., p. 78-79
36. Ibid., p. 81
37. Ibid., p. 81
38. Franca Iacovetta and Roberto Perin, "Italians and Wartime Internment: Comparative Perspectives on Public Policy, Historical Memory, and Daily Life," *Enemies Within: Italian and Other Internees in Canada and Abroad*, (Toronto: University of Toronto Press, 2000), p. 14
39. The Beaton Institute, "The Italian Community in Dominion." *CBC Radio Interview* on 27 September 1977, unknown interviewer, T-941on CD.
40. The Beaton Institute, "Italian Internment in World War II." *CBC Radio Report* on 23 February 1990, Joan Melanson reporting, T-2387 on CD.
41. "The Italian Community in Dominion," T-941
42. Ibid.
43. Ibid.
44. Ibid.

45. Ibid.
46. Ibid.
47. Ibid.
48. "Italian Internment in World War II," T-2387
49. Ibid.
50. Ibid.
51. Ibid.
52. Ibid.
53. Ibid.
54. "The Italian Community in Dominion," T-941
55. Ibid.
56. Ibid.
57. Ibid.
58. Ibid.
59. Ibid.
60. "Italian Internment in World War II," T-2387
61. Ibid.
62. Ibid.
63. Ibid.
64. Ibid.
65. Ibid.
66. Ibid.
67. "The Italian Community in Dominion," T-941
68. Ibid.
69. Ibid.
70. Ibid.
71. "Italian Internment in World War II," T-2387
72. Ibid.
73. Ibid.
74. Ibid.
75. Ibid.

Angelo Principe

Italian Canadian Fascist Women and the Government's "Wishy-Washy" Policy

The fascist State and the Catholic Church argued, each for different reasons, that a woman's main role in society was in the home. As child bearers, women were targeted by the fascist Regime with the aim of increasing the Italian population, since "number," in the fascist military view, "was power." To this end, the Regime rewarded women who gave birth to a large number of children. The Catholic Church, on the other hand, with an eye to morality, preached that women should stay home, have children, nurse them and look after their families. Hence, both Church and State had a common view of women's role in the family and in the society: the relegation of women to humanitarian and nursing functions.[1]

Often in the conflicting discourses over what constituted the most appropriate form of "womanhood" and "motherhood," significant differences characterized the political understanding between the Church and the State both in Italy and within the Italian communities abroad. Overall, Italian Canadian fascist women like Italian women in general, though often relegated to a subordinate position, did not always fit into such a passive role. In fact, when Italian men — fathers, brothers and husbands — were interned, women were able to adequately take care of their families and look after community associations such as the Order Sons of Italy (OSI).

I.

To align Italians abroad to the new policy of fascist Italy regarding women, in the Thirties, just after the 1929 Conciliation Pact between the State and the Catholic Church, the Consuls brought into the community those institutions which fascism had create at home in order that women and children might serve the regime's expansionist aims. The *Opera Nazionale Balilla* (ONB), which in 1937 became *Gioventù Italiana del Littorio Estero* [GILE], was imported into the Italian Canadian communities. The ONB first and the GILE after enrolled boys and girls in four age groups: *Figlie della Lupa*, age 6-8; *Piccole Italiane*, age 8-14; *Giovani Italiane*, 14-18; *Giovani Fasciste*, 18-21. And the local Italian Catholic churches gave the Consuls a hand. In Toronto, for example, the Italian Feminine Fascio before the establishment of Casa d'Italia on Beverly St. met every last Sunday of the month in the basement of St. Agnese Catholic Church, at Grace and Dundas Streets.

To stimulate the interest of Italian Canadian women youth in joining fascist organizations, Donna Giovanna Brigidi, the wife of the Italian Consul in Montreal, spoke regularly to their mothers organized in the *Opera Maternità e Infanzia* (OMI), illustrating for them the "Fascist Woman's Mission" in the new Italy. She argued that the fascist "female organizations have the useful function of educating the young woman in body and mind in order that she may completely carry out her mission within the limit of the family." This function, both physical and spiritual, brings out a new and harmonious awareness in the Italian woman, she concluded.[2]

Women were the key to induce Italian Canadian female youth to join fascist clubs and athletic associations, to march in parades dressed in fascist uniform, black skirt and white blouse, sing fascist songs, and attend classes teaching the Italian language. The youth, girls and boys, garbed in fascist uniform, participated in the many rallies and public displays that fascists organized throughout the year wherever there was a sizeable Italian community. The young fascists who distinguished themselves in the gym and in studying the Italian language were rewarded with a medal. In Montreal, in 1935, nine girls received a gold medal, eight silver and thirty-three bronze.[3]

At the end of the school year, for the girls and boys attending fascist schools, there was a display of gymnastics attended by the parents of the youth involved and fascist authorities. At the 1935 gymnastic display, dignitaries such as Italian Consul Brigidi and the Mayor of Montreal, Camillien Houde, attended. Addressing those assembled, Mayor Houde said: "It might not be too far away the day in which even in Canada necessity urges us to follow the example of the Italian nation and fight victoriously the evils affecting society."[4]

Further, the most disciplined and distinguished athletes of the Canadian fascist youth, generally daughters and sons of local fascist leaders, were from 1932 on rewarded with a dream vacation either to a beautiful beach resort or to a healthy mountain camp in Italy. There they were housed with similar minded youth from around the world and completed the indoctrination they received back home by being plunged into Italian life and fascist ideology. The Italian trip was a successful experience of indoctrination with young women, like Ersilia Sauro and a Miss Fiorentini. Both young women were members of the GILE and both enjoyed their Italian vacations.

In Rome, Fiorentini happened to witness the Guglielmo Marconi fascist State funeral: "The entire population in the *Urbe* paid homage to the memory of such an immortal scientist," she wrote.[5]

She was, probably, not aware that Marconi was honoured mainly because he was a fascist. In fact, regarding science itself, a year later, Mussolini's government closed the prestigious Roman school of physics and dispersed its equipment because the scientists were either Jews or not fascists. Three of them, the Nobel Prize winner Enrico Fermi, Benedetto Rossi, and Emilio Segré moved to the USA and helped America to build the world's first atomic bomb.

In a long letter to the fascist weekly *L'Italia Nuova*, Ersilia Sauro described her dream-like experience first in Naples and than in Rome. But she was overwhelmed on being there for Il Duce's speech:

> ... Among all the memories, the one that remains most vivid in my mind is the day that we saw *Il Duce* for the first time. I confess that standing before that Great Man, who has done so much good for Italy and who is adored by the entire nation, my eyes were filled with tears and my heart with emotions. The Duce [...] who looked at us was [...] a tender and affectionate father [...] Oh, if all Italians living abroad could see that smile!
>
> I tell you frankly that if I had seen nothing else, the Duce's smile and the words he spoke at the final gymnast display on September 10 would have been enough to make that trip a happy experience.[6]

She went on quoting Mussolini's words to the world-wide youth gathered in Rome before their departure: "As you leave Italy remember that the *Tricolore* [the Italian flag] of the *Patria* is always your companion." She closes her letter expressing the desire to return to Italy and cry out once again: *Duce! Duce!*

When the Montreal fascist weekly *L'Italia Nuova* published this letter, the winds of war were in the air and the RCMP had had for some time even fascist women and their organizations under observation. In October 1937, S.T. Wood, assistant commissioner of the RCMP, issued a memorandum requesting information about the various Italian women's fascist organizations. Wood was concerned about the strength of the *Fascio Femminile*, whose members promoted fascism among the young and collected funds to support Italy's invasion of Ethiopia. In Montreal, which was the site of the largest Italian Canadian community, there were six branches of the feminine Fascio, the same number as the men's organization. There were also women's branches in Toronto, Hamilton, North Bay and Vancouver. In addition women could join feminine lodges of the OSI and the Dopolavoro groups. Toronto's feminine section of the Dopolavoro organization was 200 members strong.[7]

II.

When Italy entered the war on 10 June 1940, most Italian men who occupied executive positions in the Fascio across Canada or in one of the associations under fascist control (the "Order of the Sons Italy," the "Italian World War Veterans Association," the *Opera Nazionale Dopo Lavoro*, and the *Patronato Scolastico Italiano*) were interned to camp Petawawa. Save for four, Italian fascist women, who occupied leading positions in the fascist clubs and affiliated organizations, were not troubled except for an initial questioning by the RCMP.

In fact only on 4 October 1940, four months after the rounding up of most of the men, did N.A. Robertson, chairman of the I-D C (Inter-Department Committee) which was in charge of internment, write Attorney General, Ernest Lapointe. In the letter, he requested the Minister's consent to "detain, interrogate, warn and release on the same date" ten Italian women who were the top and most active leaders of Italian feminine fascism in Canada. Six of them resided in Montreal: Dr. Laura D'Anna, Giuseppina

Di Ioia, Carmela Frascarelli, Fosca Giubilei, Antonietta Mancuso, and Rosa Spinelli. Three of them were in Toronto: Etelvira Frediani, Filomena Riccio, and Maria Spaziani. Francesca Olivieri lived in Hamilton, ON.

In the letter Robertson also informed the Minister that all ten women were naturalized Canadian citizens. He further stated that: "The files of the RCM Police disclose that these persons have been active members of the feminine Fascio, which organization is considered a menace to the welfare of the State, and it is considered that they should be examined by Department Consul and warned that internment will result from any further participation in matters pertaining to the Fascio."[8]

The list was headed by Dr. Laura D'Anna. The RCMP had abundant documentation about this lady's extensive fascist activities. In 1934 she organized Montreal's Feminine Fascio and became its director, a position which she held continuously to the day Italy entered the war. She was the fiduciary of four of the six sections of the Montreal feminine Fascio: namely Ville Emard, Mile End, Montcalm and Lachine. The RCMP's report went on to describe her as a "stunning beauty" and listed all the other important positions she occupied in Quebec's Italian fascist galaxy: "President of the *Maria Pia di Piemonte* club and held the same office in the Lodge *Maria Pia di Savoia* as well."

Undoubtedly she was very active and well connected with fascists who counted. She was a close associate and collaborator of Consul Brigidi's wife Giovanna. For example, the fascist weekly *Italia*, 20 April 1935, reported that in Mile End district, the Feminine fascist group met on Sunday, 14 April 1935. The purpose of the meeting was dual: to organize the distribution of some clothing to needy Italian children and to wish a happy Italian vacation to Donna Brigidi, wife of Consul. Presiding the meeting, Laura

D'Anna spoke about "the feminine Fascio's work among Italian mothers and their children." Present at the meeting were some fascist leaders with their wives and a "group of *Giovani Italiane*."

Furthermore, Dr. D'Anna had been very active in the Dopolavoro and the Sons of Italy, and she put particular effort into raising funds for the *Befana Fascista* and the fascist Summer camps. Because of her influence throughout the community, she was chosen as Godmother of the *Unione Abruzzese Gabriele D'Annunzio*: Abruzzo was the Region of Italy where she hailed from. She was also a member of the "Italian Moral Front". The RCMP considered Dr. D'Anna the most active and dangerous fascist woman in Canada and asked the I-D C for her "internment".

A second report, however, written eight months later by the same Police agency and signed by Chief S.T. Wood, gives a completely different view of Dr. D'Anna. She had, in the mean time, collaborated with the RCMP: at least two men who had been released from internment, were once again interned. They were Vincenzo Poggi and Domenico Scalera. With respect to Poggi, Dr. D'Anna stated as follows: "Poggi was a member of the OVRA sent to Canada to conduct propaganda and I know that he was paid by Rome and that the International Press Service operated by him under the direction of the Italian Consul Brigidi together with [Camillo] Vetere, was paid for by Rome." Even Rev. Scalera (a protestant minister who had taken Bersani's place at the Italian Protestant Church of the Redeemer in Montreal) was re-interned on Dr. D'Anna's declaration.

Regarding Laura D'Anna the RCMP reported that being a confidant of the Italian Vice Consul, she "has recently provided this Police Force, with a statement which definitely established Scalera's membership in the Fascio and his activities in the OVRA." The report further states: "During the past six months, this lady has provided the Force with information of inestimable value, the genuineness of which has been authenticated." In closing, it stated: "No inducement was extended and she imparted the information with sincerity above question."

Because of her collaboration, Commissioner Wood asked that her husband, Dr. Antonio D'Anna, be released from internment camp and sent home:

> Since both he and his wife are intelligent and cultured people, they moved in the higher circle of society in the Italian colony and were thus thrown into constant association with the Italian Consular Officials who, we know wield absolute control over the colony and could make or break the career of any compatriot whose ideology did not conform in with that prescribed by Rome (see Appendix).

In the category described by Commissioner Wood were those Italian merchant internees who did some import-export dealings with fascist Italy and whose business depended entirely on the Consul's will. But none of those were released.

The charges against the other nine Italian women were in general similar to the one we have described above involving Dr. Laura D'Anna, but in much lesser proportion. They were accused of having had a leading role in the feminine Fascio of their city or area in which they resided and also of being leaders in one or two of the associations affiliated with fascism like the Order Sons of Italy, the GILE, in the Dopolavoro etc. They all had, like Dr. D'Anna, their men interned and most of them were the sole bread winners of the family. Carmela Galardo-Frascarelli symbolizes these women's commitment as well as their ideological confusion. She was a remarkable woman: though bright and dynamic, she did not see through the profound contradictions in which she lived. A 1940 report of the RCMP called Frascarelli "a fanatic fascist".[9]

The RCMP had much material proving its charges against the women in question. Agents fluent in the Italian language went through the collection of the two main fascist weeklies. The first was *L'Italia* which in 1937 was sold to Giulio Romano and became *L'Italia Nuova*. Published in Montreal, this weekly also served the Italians living in Nova Scotia, New Brunswick and the mining Italian colony of Cape Breton. The second was the Toronto *Bollettino Italo-Canadese*, owned by Perilli and edited by Tommaso Mari, which served Italians living in Ontario and Manitoba. The examination of these two newspapers gave the RCMP the necessary documentation to make up the political profile and extended involvement of each of the women in question with fascism and its affiliated organizations. Not one of them was interned. The Italians living in British Columbia and the prairies read *L'Eco d'Italia*, published in Vancouver from 1936 on. Its files were used for the internment of men. However, in those two provinces no Italian women were interned or, as far as we know, taken in for questioning as had happened in Quebec and Ontario.

III.

Except for Michelle McBride, historians have ignored the Canadian women internees. The reason for this neglect is probably due to the tiny number of women involved, 21 in total across Canada. They had been charged under section 21 of the Defense of Canada Regulations which gave the state power to arrest and intern anyone suspected of being able to act against the safety of Canadians and/or the security of the State. Those 21 women were interned in a special section of Kingston Penitentiary reserved for female inmates. Four of those 21 women were Italian Canadians, all from Ontario. They were Maria Pressello of Windsor, Venera Lo Bosco of Welland, Luisa Guageneli of Niagara Falls, and Maria Fontanella of Toronto.

Of the other seventeen (17) inmates twelve were German, three were Belgian, one was Austrian, and one, Gladys McDonald, was Anglo-Canadian. She was the only communist woman to be interned. As organizer and secretary of the provincial branch of Saskatchewan Communist Party, MacDonald "was caught mimeographing an outlawed newspaper, *Factory and Furrow*, and was incarcerated for a year."[10] At the end of her prison term, she was interned. According to Warden Allan, she was such a model inmate that he "recommended her release" because she was eager "to aid Canada in its war effort." In asking for her release, Warden Allan probably took into consideration that, after Hitler's attack on the USSR, communists all over the world switched their view of the war from a confrontation between "two capitalist blocks" to a "democratic war against Nazi-fascism."

Strangely enough Maria Pressello, neither a fascist nor involved with any other political party, was the first Italian woman to be retained and interned as early as June 14, 1940 and taken to Kingston Penitentiary three (3) days later, long before the I-D C showed any interest in the Italian fascist women. She was the only one of the twenty-one women internees to be "isolated" from the other inmates, Italians included. The reason for her arrest and internment probably was, we assume, not police investigation and factual proofs but anonymous letters and hear-say reports. This stresses the idea that at the core of the Canadian State at that tremendous hour rather than strength and rationality fear and confusion reigned.

The other three Italian women taken to Kingston Penitentiary had, like nine of the ten Italian women discussed above, been active in the Fascio and in some of the other fascist affiliated associations. They were, however, neither particularly active nor more dangerous than the nine who were left undisturbed at home. This points once again to the reigning confusion which led authorities to be influenced by the demands of the mob.

Among the leading fascist women of Toronto, only the 55-year-old Egilda Fontanella was singled out for internment. Throughout the 1930s, four *Fiduciarie* (women leaders) followed each other to head the feminine section of the Toronto *Fascio Principe di Piemonte*. The first one was Elisa Rebbecca Palange whom Rome ordered Vice-Consul Giorgio Tiberi to replace because she was Jewish. Etelvina Sartini Frediani succeeded her in 1935 and held that position for twenty-four months. Because of her fascist activity, she was fired from her job and she decided to resign as fiduciary of the Fascio. Her position was taken by the financially well off Egilda Fontanella in 1937. Two years later, in 1939, Filomena Riccio succeeded Fontanella.

Egilda Fontanella applied for Canadian Citizenship in 1939 and it was not granted for her fascist involvement. She was the only fascist woman of Toronto to be interned and she resented it. In a defiant letter to the Minister of Justice, she wrote: "Although I am not a naturalized Canadian I beg to inform you that I have been a law abiding citizen of Canada and object very much to being interned."[11] The reason for her internment was, we believe, dual: she was not married and therefore without family responsibility; and because her brother, Dr. Pasquale Fontanella, the most important Italian fascist in Ontario, was able to evade internment. As soon as he heard on the radio that Italy had declared war on France and England, he took a train for the United States. Dr. Fontanella was one of the *"Triumviro"* (three men) who in 1926 founded the *Fascio Principe di Piemonte* in Toronto. The other two founders were the painter Vittorio dell'Angela and Francesco Gattuso. The Trio had the collaboration of Camillo Vetere of Montreal who, at the time, was the appointed "Fascist Trustee" for Canada.[12]

Further, during the financial campaign for Toronto's *Casa d'Italia* in 1934, Dr. Fontanella together with Pasquale Molinaro collected $95, the largest sum after the Consul Tiberi who headed the list of collectors with $358.[13] Moreover Fontanella often represented the vice Consul in community events when the diplomat could not attend. One of these instances was the annual ball of the *Italo-Canadese* Society. Representing the Consul, Fontanella met two officials of the newly founded Independent (anti-fascist) Italian Veterans Association, G. Ferrari and R. Laudadio. In meeting them Fontanella addressed them with threatening words: "If you persist in this action against the [fascist] National Veterans Association, your families and relatives in Italy could suffer unpleasant consequences."[14] This provoked a strong reaction from the anti-fascist Toronto bimonthly, *L'Emigrato*.[15] The main reason for interning Egilda Fontanella might have been fear that her brother could, through her, impart secret orders to local fascists.

The twenty-nine-year-old Venera Lo Bosco was arrested on September 9, 1940. According to the RCMP, she "has for several years been the teacher of Italian school which was organized by the Cristophoro [sic] Colombo Club" in Welland, ON. The just mentioned club came to be through the initiative of two fascists, Giuseppe Rettura and Dr. Ignazio Scozzafave. Scozzafave was interned when Italy entered the war; Rettura like Dr. Fontanella "avoided internment by fleeing to the United States at the inception of hostilities between Italy and the British Empire."[16]

To document its case against Lo Bosco, the RCMP used the files of the fascist weekly *Bollettino italo-canadese* (*Bollettino* here after). In fact that paper often reported her fascist activities in the

Welland and south Ontario area. For example, on September 27, 1935, the *Bollettino* wrote that Venera Lo Bosco attended the inauguration of the *Cristopharo Colombo* Society; in the September 13 issue of the following year, 1936, it reported that she was appointed Secretary of the said society. Further, on February 21, 1936, the *Bollettino* reported that Lo Bosco had been a teacher at the fascist school and referred to her as attending a theatrical performance given by her students. The following year, 1937, Dr. Scozzafave praised Lo Bosco for her activities as a teacher at the Italian school. Even Vice Consul Colonna praised Lo Bosco for her activities in the fascist school [May 18, 1939].

She was also actively involved in the *Italo Balbo* Lodge of the Order Sons of Italy. The Lodge was named after a leading Italian fascist, and she spoke to its members on September 24, 1937. Furthermore, as Fiduciary of the Welland Fascio, she escorted a group of GILE teenage members to the fascist camp in Italy in 1938. [*Il Bollettino*, August 25, 1938]. Even the New York *Progresso Italo-Americano*, in the January 9, 1940 issue, reported that Lo Bosco had been the Grand delegate of the *Italo Balbo* Lodge to the annual convention of the North America Order Sons of Italy.[17]

The other Italian internee was Luisa Guagneli. Before being taken to Kingston Penitentiary, she spent six weeks in the Toronto Don jail working in the kitchen. At Kingston the Warden was alarmed because, through hearsay, he learned that Guagneli was able without authorization to communicate with people outside the jail. To uncover the root of this communication, he set up an investigation, as he was particularly anxious to learn if correspondence had been arranged at the prison without his authorization.

Using an interpreter, Warden Allan questioned Guagneli. She admitted that before being interned she had taught "fascist subjects" [sic] under the direction of the Rev. Joseph Monahan.

According to the Warden, the mentioned Rev. might have been a "Father Giuseppe". She, however, "denied any effort on her part to maintain correspondence with any person, and most emphatically denied knowing a woman named 'Rita Mazza'." Although satisfied on this point, Warden Allan was, nevertheless, suspicious of this woman. He was on guard since she did not collaborate during the interrogation and, therefore, he still gave her case his special attention. He instructed Matron Vera Cherry that letters and any other form of communication to or from Guagneli should be very carefully examined.

Since his investigation bore no fruit, he was on guard to prevent Guagneli from resuming the activities which, the Warden suspected, she has practiced during her incarceration in Toronto. Regarding this point, Warden Allan wrote: "It would now appear that Guagneli did not conduct the correspondence in question from this institution, but there is the possibility that the letter was sent out during her stay at the jail in Toronto." Following this line of thinking, he wrote a letter, dated December 18, 1940, to the Governor of the Toronto Jail asking him if a woman named Rita Mazza worked there and if she might have come in contact with Guagneli:

> In connection with investigation we have conducted [...], it has been intimated that she [Guagneli] might have been employed in the Kitchen there, where she could have contacted one "Rita Mazza," and, through this person, have been in communication with friends on the outside.

The letter continued by asking to "confirm or deny" that Guagneli had, during her stay at the jail, been employed in the kitchen and if a worker, named Rita Mazza, was there at the same time: "It would be appreciated if you could inform the undersigned of the location of employment if any, of the Guagneli woman during the incarceration at the jail. It would also be of assistance if we could be advised whether or not a person by the name 'Rita Mazza' was there at the same time."[18]

Due to a growing number of women incarcerated for criminal acts, the Penitentiary needed space. The authorities made room by sending the political internees home. The first of the four Italians to leave was Maria Gilda Fontanella. She had arrived on September 14, 1940 and left it on February 18, 1941. A week later, on February 24, 1941, even Luisa Guagneli was set free. Maria Pressello and Venera Lo Bosco were released on July 8, 1941. Regarding them, Warden Allan, in a letter to the C.I.O. Department of the Secretary of State, wrote: "Under direction of your office Venera Lo Bosco and Maria Pressello have been released from the Internment Section of the Prison for women." They took the CNR 5:52 evening train heading for their respective homes.

IV. Conclusion

As we have seen the Canadian Government policy regarding fascism in general and Italian fascist women in particular has three stages: first curiosity, then acceptance and then a wishy-washy position. In fact, it was only after three months following Italy's entry into the conflict that the government remembered there were Italian Canadian fascist women and decided that the most active among them should be warned only and sent home. The policy guiding the government regarding Italian fascist women was at best confused and chaotic.

The government and the RCMP's way of dealing with Quebec's fascist women, Italians as well as French Canadians, peculiarly stands out. In that province, the fascist female movement was well organized and the strongest of the country, but the Catholic Church and the strong contingent of MPs from that province made sure that fascist women were not disturbed.

In Toronto, only Fontanella was singled out while the other three feminine fascist leaders were left undisturbed. The other two fascist internees, Venera Lo Bosco and Luisa Guagneli, coming from small Italian communities in peripheral cities, were in no position to create any disturbance to the Canadian war effort or lend any help to the enemy. Completely meaningless was the long internment of Maria Pressello. It seems that, regarding female internment, the country lacked a vision and sound leadership. Instead, political short sightedness, mob feeling and confusion reigned supreme.

V. Appendix

This memo from T.S. Wood, Commissioner, RCMP, to the Minister of Justice, dated May 28, 1941, suggests how Dr. Laura D'Anna avoided internment and got her interned husband released:

> SECRET MEMORANDUM TO THE RIGHT
> HONORABLE THE MINISTER OF JUSTICE
> Re: DR. ANTONIO D'ANNA.
> Montreal P.Q.
>
> It is desired to bring to your attention certain circumstances concerning Dr. Antonio D'Anna, Montreal, an Italian physician, who was detained for interrogation on June 10, 1940, and subsequently interned pursuant to the provisions of Regulation 21 of the Defense of Canada Regulations, which

I feel warrants his release from internment on compassionate ground.

2. The subject arrived in Canada from Italy during February, 1930, accompanied by his wife, Dr. Laura D'Anna. He acquired Citizenship through naturalization on June 7, 1937. This couple have two children, aged seven and four years, who were born in Montreal. The family returned to Italy for three-months visit during 1938.

3. Investigation performed by this Force into the ideology and activities of the subject disclosed that he was an active participant in the Fascio of Montreal and its auxiliaries. In the course of examination performed by Mr. Gerard Fautex, K.C., Department Council, the subject admitted past membership in the Fascio but stated he had neither paid dues nor attended meetings of the Fascio following 1938.

4. Since both he and his wife are intelligent and cultured persons, they moved in the higher circles of society in the Italian colony and were thus thrown into contact association with the Italian Consular officials who, we know, wielded absolute control over the colony and could make or break the career of any compatriot whose ideology did not conform with that prescribed by Rome. Since the subject was the official physician of five Italian societies, there is reason to believe that his ostentatious display of fascism may have been adopted to further the interest of his medical career.

5. The subject's wife, Dr. Laura D'Anna, was the Directress of the Feminine Fascio of Montreal and collaborated extensively with the Italian Consular Authorities in administrating the affairs of the Fascio. During the past six months the lady has provided this Force with information of inestimable value,

the genuinity [sic] of which has been authenticated. No inducement and she imparted the information with a sincerity above question.

6. With respect to her husband, Dr. Laura D'Anna quite frankly states that he was a member of the Fascio but she points out that he did not propagandize that ideology and his affiliation was largely the result of the existing circumstances, in that his practice would have suffered had he acted otherwise. Furthermore, he wished to visit Italy to acquaint his parents with his Canadian-born children and did not wish to invite difficulties with the State Authorities of Italy. Following their return from Italy, her husband gradually severed his Fascist connection. Dr. Laura D'Anna assures us that, despite her husband's previous deportment, [he] will give no cause for concern.

7. In the circumstances, it is felt that the liberty of the subject does not constitute the danger that was originally anticipated and I recommend that he be released from internment.

Yours Faithfully
[signed] S.T. Wood

APPROVED [signed Ernest Lapointe]
Minister of Justice

Endnotes

1. See Patrizia Dogliani, *L'Italia fascista, 1922-1940,* Milano: Sansoni, 1999: pp. 88-150.
2. See Luigi Pautasso, "Donne Italiane Internate," *Quaderni Canadesi,* anno 1, n. 1, 1977.
3. The following are the names of the gold medalists: Camilli

Iolanda, Sarsano Emma, Martellini Giuseppina, Bartolini Bianca, Procopio Caterina, Piperni Olivia, Manucci Ada, Guardo Ada and Ialente Assunta.

4. See *L'Italia* (Montreal), May 18, 1935. His pro-fascist stand led Houde to the internment camp at Petawawa.
5. *L'Italia Nuova*, September 25, 1937. Further in the same issue, the fascist weekly initiated a petition "to give a main artery of Montreal the glorious name of Marconi."
6. *L'Italia Nuova*, October 15, 1938.
7. CSIS, Vol. 7, Re: Fascism — Italian — in Canada. Aug. 1938.
8. RG 18, vol. 3563, File: part of file # 11-19-2-3, vol. 5, Minister's Order — Italian: letter dated, Ottawa, October 4, 1940.
9. NAC, Memorandum to the Inter-Department Committee, Ottawa, 23 September 1940; 40 D269-1-D-754; MWJ/LIJ; Re: Mrs. Carmela Frascarelli (female). Montreal, PQ.
10. See Michelle McBride, "The Curious Case of Female Internees," in *Enemies Within* (Edited by Franca Iacovetta, Roberto Perin, and Angelo Principe), Toronto: University of Toronto Press, 2000, p. 164.
11. NAC, RG 73, vol. 74 (inv. 63), file #23-1-12.
12. See Angelo Principe, *The Darkest Side of the Fascist Years*, Toronto: Guernica, 1999, p. 42.
13. See, "La seconda ondata per la Casa d'Italia," *Il Bollettino Italo-Canadese*, December 4, 1936.
14. See the bimonthly *L'Emigrato* (Toronto), N. 5, March 30, 1932.
15. Idem.
16. NAC, RG 30, E-163, vol. 14, File 161, memorandum to The Inter-Department Committee, Re: Antonio Amendola, Welland, ON, dated 21-1-1941.
17. NAC, The RCMP report, dated, Ottawa, 27-8-40. 40 D 269-1-E-1164.
18. NAC, RG 73, Acc, 80-81-253, box 63, file 23-1 pt. 1.

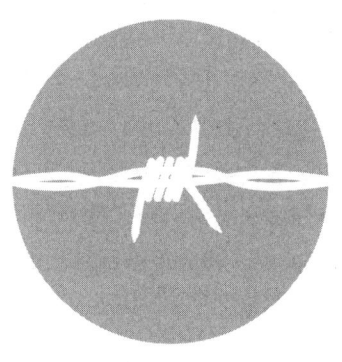

Joyce Pillarella

The Italian Internment Experience Seen Through Silence, Spaces and Censored Vision

This essay examines the silence surrounding the internment experience, linking my archival research with a visit to the former camp in Petawawa and the life-history interviews I conducted in Montreal. These will be part of an archive being compiled and housed at the Columbus Centre in Toronto.

My grandfather was a fascist. I'm an oral historian. Unfortunately, I began to practice my craft after everyone who was interned, died. I first learned about the "concentration camps" at home — this is the label that is used by many families in Montreal to refer to the camps. My grandfather, Nicola Germano, was interned for a total of three years and eight months at the Petawawa and Fredericton internment camps.

Born in 1887 in Ururi, Campobasso, Nicola served as a sergeant in the Great War. A fiercely proud Italian, he never hesitated to scribble in his books: *"Chi per la Patria muore, ha vissuto assai."* Knowing he had served in the trenches, I knew this was not simply a slogan to him. Nicola immigrated to Montreal in 1920. He went to work as a labourer at Canadian Tube and Steel in Ville Emard, an industrial working-class district in Montreal. He was a board member of the Italian Veterans' Association and the Fiduciario of the Fascio in Ville Emard. I was told that he gave the Roman salute, as he was escorted away by RCMP officers on June 10, 1940.

Growing up, I remember hearing about the practical jokes Nicola used to play at the internment camp and about his adventures with

Montreal mayor Camillien Houde. Upon release, his former employer refused to rehire a "criminal," so he had to find work at another steel mill in Lachine.[1] This anecdote served the purpose of communicating the injustice rather than the actual status of "second-class prisoner of war." The stories were weaved loosely together into a distorted narrative of camp life that skipped huge gaps of time and experiences. The lack of balance in the stories wasn't due to a faulty memory; it was simply an absence of memories.

Eventually, I found documents and war medals "filed" in the *cantina* (wine cellar). My mother had recycled her father's black shirt into a skirt lining. Apparently it was an excellent quality of silk. Clearly, my family did not attach any nostalgia to these items, judging from the way they were misplaced. This ambiguous message was saying: it was worth preserving, but who's listening?

The first turning point came after I started reading essays by Roberto Perin, a leading historian on the topic of internment in Canada. His concern, which is shared by other leading scholars in this field such as Gabriele Scardellato and Franca Iacovetta, is that too often we are presented with a simplified version based on "selective evidence," which inevitably removes agency from the internees.[2] This notion was challenging the family narratives I was accustomed to hearing. My grandfather never denied his beliefs, but the "innocent" motif was present. After two days of heated debates on the phone with Perin, I came to the conclusion that I needed to contextualize my "family story" with the historical evidence available.

This led me to the National Archives in Ottawa. The evidence informed me how the Italian consular services duplicated the fascist groups that existed in Italy and regrouped organizations such as The Sons of Italy under their control.[3] The power the *fascisti* had over the colony extended into social life, relief efforts, politics, commercial ventures, education, culture and individuals. I'm not implying that an Italian "had" to be a fascist in Montreal; in fact, most were not. However, if someone had to do business with Italy for professional or personal reasons, it would have been in their interest, at the very least, to appear to be a fascist sympathizer if they wanted to get things done with an Italian institution.[4]

No one can argue that during wartime, a country has to protect its citizens from any potential acts of sabotage from enemies within. During peace time, a citizen has to commit an unlawful act for the authorities to take action. During war time, the Minister of Justice gave himself the authority to take measures to *prevent* an act from being committed that would be prejudicial to the state. The conflict and the gaps between the documents and the oral history lie here. It was up to the agents' discretion to identify "potential saboteurs," in other words, men who should be interned based on *what they might have done*. On the other hand, the family members I interviewed recalled "their" reality — what their fathers could not have done. The oral testimonies make me question the validity and context of the evidence collected by the agents.[5] Meanwhile, the families I spoke to stated that they were never properly informed as to why the man was being interned. This silence is at the root of much of the misinformation.

Fragmented primary evidence left me in a challenging position to interpret the decisions. Files were incomplete or destroyed, evidence was missing, arrest reports from the Montreal police and jail records have vanished, and the local Italian newspapers from the 1930s have frittered away. For instance, recommendations to intern individuals were generally based on one of the following: affiliation to the Italian Consul and fascist authorities; evidence gleaned from pro-fascist newspapers which reported activities and events in the colony; seized records that confirmed associations to clubs and testimonies from dubious paid and unpaid informants.[6] Exhibits which sustain the accusations are not included in personal files that report the circumstances for individual arrests. The documents provide a semi-proof, because the evidence isn't always complete. For instance, what does "spreading anti-British propaganda" mean exactly? Where is the evidence that was seized from the fascist clubs? Why were some protagonists in the fascist clubs not arrested? How were the informants' lists evaluated? Further research may uncover some of these answers. What is certain is that the written sources I have consulted so far establish how the Italian colony and fascist organizations were perceived by the authorities and reconstruct the experience from the point of view of the Canadian authorities.

In 2004, I was contacted by the producers of a television show called *Past Lives* to be the subject of an episode.[7] They asked me if there was anything I'd like to investigate about my past. The first thing that came to mind was my grandfather and the internment. With the help of the producer, I was able to visit the former site of Camp 33 in Petawawa. Going to a historical site associated with suffering can be considered borderline "dark tourism." However, I didn't see myself as a tourist or voyeur. My grandfather had been there and somehow I felt I had a right to walk on his turf.

My expectations of this visit to the past were unrealistic. There was practically nothing there. This affected me and made me realize that this chapter in Canadian history had been cast aside. I needed a marker to tell me something happened here. But realistically a commemoration would go unnoticed because this area is strictly off limits to the public. Thinking about the physical landscape today, I see how it reflects the emotional landscape in the life stories. They both share a sense of abandonment.

I conducted life-history interviews in Montreal in 2011 with the families of men who had been interned. I was excited about the possibility of uncovering new evidence and possibly filling in the gaps. The stories I collected immersed me into their world and into that time period. They are personal impressions of the times. Sometimes statements contradict archival documents, but this doesn't invalidate them. Rather, they add interpretation and meaning.

Alessandro Portelli, who has changed the paradigm of how we approach oral sources, reminds us that "memory is not a passive depository of facts, but an active process of creation of meanings."[8] In other words the narrators are shifting between their point of view today as older people to their childhood memories in order to "make sense of the past" while putting "their narrative in historical context."[9] Nevertheless, the life histories are grounded in the everyday experience which adds context and helps us see the event from a private viewpoint. While the narrators were able to offer counterpoints to the archival evidence, they came to the interview with more questions than answers about the internment.

What these experiences have in common is silence, emptiness and gaps. Each approach reveals a part of the grand narrative that still remains fragmented. As an oral historian, I'm fascinated with silence. What does it mean? What's not there? Is there a pattern? What can we learn from it? As I search for the answers, now begins my journey to Petawawa.

The production crew and I were driving up from Ottawa on the night of October 28, 2004. There was a full moon, and there had been a solar eclipse the night before. We were heading north on Highway 17. The railroad tracks run parallel to this road, surrounded by forest and silence. When I think back to that silence, I realize it was foreshadowing things to come.

The only light on the road to the town that night was the moon and occasional headlights. I couldn't help thinking how appropriate the number of this highway was. Seventeen is considered a bad-luck number for Italians, and this was the "road to the unknown" for the internees who travelled it back in June 1940. Like them, I felt nervous anticipation in my gut, not knowing what to expect or how I'd react. Unlike them, I knew exactly where I was going, why I was going and when I would leave. I didn't have fear. They did. They had no idea what to expect and no release date to look forward to. While the men were being displaced to what was to them an unknown destination, the families back home were about to deal with the consequences of those actions. French philosopher Michel Foucault explains the spectacle of public punishment as a drama that serves as a judicial ritual.[10] The spectacle of the arrests on June 10, 1940 — that is, the two RCMP officers who rounded up the men — one on each side of the accused — reverberated with fear within the Italian colony, and left a symbolic "chalk trace" around the family. Once "the body" was removed, the families too had to face displacements in their lives.

Sandra Corbo was four years old when her grandfather Achille and uncle Nicola Corbo were interned. Achille, a ladies' wear designer and tailor, was also vice-president of the founders of the Saint Joseph Orphanage that was on Saint André Street. Achille's son, Nicola, was a prominent notary. At the time of the internment, Sandra's grandmother was very ill and consequently Sandra's parents had to work to cover the medical expenses and support the family. They decided to place Sandra at Saint Joseph Orphanage, assuming that she would be well looked after, considering her grandfather was one of the founders. Sandra lived there from the age of four to the age of six, and she still feels the pain of that displacement.

> Sandra Corbo: I still have to deal with it. I was put into an orphanage. I was in hell for two years. The nuns were terrible. There was a big gate and you couldn't see out. I was interned.

My grandfather (Achille Corbo) was 57 years old when he was interned. He had lived in Canada for 40 years. That was his question — why? He was more Canadian than Italian. He loved this country and had no interest in visiting Italy. I wanted to know what happened. I didn't ask questions because I wasn't encouraged. I'm 73 years old and it still hurts like hell. I still don't have any answers.

Question: Why do you think you felt discouraged from asking questions?

Sandra: It was the shame brought on the family. We were criminals. The feeling of not being worthy ... of being considered a traitor, an enemy alien.

Question: But if your grandfather knew he did nothing wrong, how was it shameful?

Sandra: It's the public perception reflected back on you.

Question: How would you describe your grandfather after the internment?

Question: My grandfather was not the person he used to be. He was silent, sad, he always had a far-away look in his eyes. There was no real communication. A lot of anger and pain. They were never given a chance to get it out in the open.[11]

The themes in Sandra's story parallel her grandfather's: the loss of freedom, being removed from family and society without an option, and the pain of living with an injustice. Despite the roles the Corbo men played in the Italian colony, Sandra interpreted their loyalty to Canada by the roots they had planted in this country. A sense of justice was never established for her family, which she reveals — as many other families have — through their unanswered questions. Sandra explains the consequence of the internment and how it marked the families in a public way. The notion of "who you are" versus "how others see you" was a double punishment that attacked their sense of self and their public persona.

Back in 1940, approximately 256 Montrealers travelled this road to the internment camp. There are two train stations close to the army base — one at Chalk River and one at Petawawa. The prisoners of war were met at the train station, where they were transferred to small tarpaulin-covered trucks for the remainder of the journey. Driving along the dirt road, I heard nothing but the sounds of the rocks hitting the vehicle and felt every bump on the road. I couldn't help imagine what it must have been like for those men; the tension and the anxiety must have amplified with each sound. We'll never know what any of them were thinking.

Giuseppe and Antoinetta Visocchi had seven children. They lived on Mozart Street, with their backyard to what was then called the Shamrock Market. While Giuseppe was interned, his bank account was frozen, his wife Antoinetta had no relief, and neighbours and family were afraid to help for fear of having contact with an internee's family. The oldest daughter Tommassina recalls how in those days women couldn't sign the lease, and when her mother turned to Father Evangelista at Madonna della Difesa Church to sign the lease on her behalf, he dismissed their situation in a mocking way and added: "They haven't thrown you out yet?"[12] The family experienced severe trauma during this period. Tommassina and her sisters, Elisa, Rosetta and Josie, have never felt closure with this experience. Josie explains how her father was after two years of internment:

> Maybe he was depressed. He was always sitting in the parlour alone. Maybe he was scared of what they would do to him again. My father was very depressed. He was crying for us. He would always listen to *La Traviata*. Over and over again. I don't know. He never spoke to us about the internment. Why didn't we ask? He must have suffered a lot. They did something to him. What did they do to him? We have no one to tell us.[13]

The sense of solitude Josie describes was felt by many families. Spoken with sadness, it inevitably puts the past self into question with the present. The precious answers that lie in what wasn't told or what wasn't asked, leave the story unfinished and leaves the family member to imagine what they could have done and what they should have known. Neither feeling settles well.

The next morning our television crew arrived at the entrance of the military base, where we had to go through a check point to register ourselves and our vehicle. We were introduced to Sean, the ranger who was going to be our guide. He gave us a security briefing: "Do not touch anything; do not wander off; let me lead; there are still things left underground that can explode."
   The internees were given more than a briefing upon their arrival; they were given a new identity. Relieved of their possessions, which were basically what they were wearing at the time of arrest, they were now outfitted in prisoner uniforms with a red target on the back of their shirts and jackets and a red stripe sewn on their right pant leg. This made them easy targets, should they attempt

an escape. Furthermore, the uniform signalled their new status. Their former identity had been stripped — men became prisoners of war, names became numbers, honour was replaced with humiliation. Whether their internment was an instrument used by the Canadian authorities to convey power or was the result of misinformation, from the beginning the men knew that their internment was an act of injustice. Regardless, they had to adjust to their new status. Deeper reflections about this experience don't seem to have been discussed within the families.

Historian Luisa Passerini has done extensive oral history research with working-class Italians who lived through the fascist years in Torino, Italy. She has examined self-representations in the memories. Passerini's analysis helps us understand how mentalities, the interpretation of personal history and personal survival techniques, are reconstructed in narratives.[14] Because the men passed on so few recollections to their family, we have to examine beyond what's there. We need to consider why certain stories were selected and look for links. This takes on meaning because so few things were discussed. For example, almost all the families from Montreal will recall a personal anecdote of Montreal mayor Camillien Houde, who was interned. This component of "self-representation," to use Passerini's words, adds a sense of respectability. I think this was a way for the men to validate to their families that they were not criminals, and it was their way of exemplifying that the internments were unjust. It allowed them to shift their image from a common prisoner to a respectful internee.

The former Petawawa internment camp is located on Centre Lake. It takes about 25 minutes to reach it from the entrance to the military base. The camp was set up in a wide open space in the middle of the woods. There are deer tracks everywhere. Centre Lake acts as a boundary to the camp on one side and the forest surrounds everything else. At one end of the camp, trees were replanted, which gives an accurate idea of the width of the camp. Using a blueprint of the camp and the topography, I was able to envision the space. A compass doesn't work well because of the interference from the metal left underground. Similar to the compass that couldn't orient me that day, there were no "instruments" in place to orient families through the internment. They too had to rely on a mix of sources with varying degrees of accuracy.

Originally, there were two barbed wire fences that closed off the camp. The only markers left are four cement posts with some iron bracing still attached. The map suggests that these may have been the main entrance to the camp. The space between the posts is approximately ten feet wide, which seems narrow. However, Sean (the ranger) explained that in those days trucks were smaller than they are today. There was another entrance labelled as the "Japanese Gates." These posts are the only trace of the camp. I interpret these detached pillars as a metaphor for the men who were the pillars of their families and the detachment the families lived during the internment and the internees after their release. Embedded in these recollections is silence.

Antoinette Palmeri was twelve years old when her father Vito was interned. Her perspective illustrates how news travelled in her private and public spheres and, more importantly, how she was informed and uninformed of what was happening.

> Antoinette: We had no news, no news at all. It was said they were in Bordeaux Jail. So my mother went (to Bordeaux) and they said: "[The prisoners] had just left. They're not here anymore."
>
> Question: Did they tell you they sent him to Petawawa?

Antoinette: We found out when we got one of those letters. It said prisoner of war 465. There was no explanation, then from one person to another we found out he was prisoner of war ...

Question: Did you know other girls who had their fathers arrested? In school? Did you talk about it with other girls?

Antoinette: No. No. We didn't want to talk about it. First of all, we didn't know where they were. And secondly, we were kids! Talk about what? We didn't understand why they were arrested ... we didn't understand fascism. We were too young, we didn't know the sense of it.

Question: Did the nuns in school talk?

Antoinette: No, no, no, no ... Not at all. Not a word. The class was mixed. There were French, Italian. So it was better ... 'cause it would have been a big story ... A monsignor came once to talk to all these families who were interned. And I got a dress. I didn't need a dress. We needed food. A dress? My mother used to sew. We kissed his ring and that was it, good-bye.[15]

News came to the families in random, informal ways. Nor was information being disseminated through official means or through the daily newspapers. One only has to scan the microfilm of the dailies to see that the news ended shortly after the arrests. We also have to consider that the interviewees were young at the time. Antoinette showed me a letter written by her father from the camp which doesn't make much sense to her: "It's written in code. My mother must have understood what he was really saying." We analyzed it together and clearly there were nicknames and other meanings intended in the text. The private correspondence may have been trying to bridge gaps of silence.

As I stood in the empty space of the former camp in the middle of the forest, I couldn't help feeling that nothing ever happened here. I had mixed feelings of anger and sadness. It was as if those men were never there — like waking up from a bad dream — where the story only exists in your mind. I needed to see a marker. All I had to cling to were the lone posts and the emptiness.

The Monaco family owned Corona Bakery on Bordeaux Street in Montreal. The three brothers, Donato, Vincenzo and Antonio, worked the long hours required by any bakery. The family attended the Italian United Church of the Redeemer. Vincenzo's son, Michael and Donato's children, Mary and Michael, never doubted that their fathers had been wrongfully interned, and that their internment was the result of an act of revenge by the ousted minister of that church, a certain Bersani. Minister Bersani also happened to be a paid informant for the RCMP.[16] About fifteen years ago Donato Monaco's son, Michael, happened on the Petawawa military camp. I asked him how he felt when he was there:

> I passed there once ... and I stopped at the guard at the door. It's a huge camp, and I asked if the shack was still there, where the people had been interned during the war. And he [the guard] said no. "All you're going to see is pillars of cement. That's all you're going to see. The houses are all demolished." I felt bad. I never went in, but I looked around and saw nothing. It felt like a cover-up. The government had done something wrong and so they destroyed everything. If they had done something they were proud of, don't you think they

would have kept it and allowed people to visit it ... like an attraction? I got the impression they took it apart 'cause they made a mistake.[17]

Despite the fact that Michael was only looking at the military base from the outside and wasn't actually on the site, it still reveals how the place inspired a sense of wrong doing. Michael always knew his father had been wrongly interned, only he never had it confirmed. The "cover-up" by the government, combined with the silence of the internees, has skewed the interpretation of the events. With very limited knowledge to reconstruct "what happened," there's no wonder why family narratives are limited in scope.

It would be easy to attribute the silence to the times, to gender roles and to cultural upbringing. Perhaps the men felt they had to behave according to their roles as fathers. Nor can one ignore how shame may have entered the equation. All these reasons are valid. However, the uniformity of the silence and the commonality of the stories leads me to a different conclusion.

Let's look at what's not there. The events leading up to the arrest and the events of the actual internment are missing in the oral history I was involved in. We know that many fathers told their children that they were "well-fed and well-treated." Teresa Pateras recalls her father, Salvatore, describing it as, "a vacation more than anything else. He didn't have to work, and most of them were with friends."[18] Passerini interprets these stories about making the best of a situation and overcoming obstacles as a self-representation of survival skills.[19] The only account we have from an Italian internee is Mario Duliani's *City Without Women*, in which he describes life at the camp. Roberto Perin has taken issue with Duliani's work and describes it as part of the whitewashing of this event.[20] Although we get a glimpse of camp life, I agree with Perin that it paints a controversially favourable testimony. In fact, this unbalanced point of view is consistent with the testimonies from the children of the internees. Yet in my mind it's inconceivable that everything was fine with everyone. This begs the question, why?

The son of an internee I interviewed strongly believes that silence was something that was imposed on the men. Joe Mastromonaco grew up on Walnut Street in the Montreal working-class district of Saint Henri. His father, Giovanni, worked as *fornaciá* — maintaining the furnaces and the grounds of the wealthy residents in neighbouring Westmount. Joe was home when his father was arrested. "The night that the RCMP came into the house, I remember because it was very noisy and I did not know what was going on. And way back then, there was no 'Gyprock' … there was plaster and they broke the walls to see if they could find arms."[21] Joe had no problem speaking his mind. He is convinced the men were scared to speak.

> Question: Do you think your father told your mother what happened?
>
> Joe Mastromonaco: I don't think he told my mother or he told her lies ... like everything was good. She would have told me.
>
> Question: How do you explain the silence?
>
> Joe: When they went into the camp, they were briefed. And when they left, they were briefed. You know … "if we have any info, if we hear you say … this, this … we will put extra charges on you. You make it sound like everything is perfect."

> I think they were treated badly. They were questioned. When you are questioned, you are tortured. Not everyone in the camp got along. There were fights. Everything was censored. They didn't talk out of fear. My father would tell me that there were squealers in the camp. "We had to watch out." The guy would probably get favours. That's life.[22]

Joe's observations raise questions about the punishment and control systems in place. He is re-positioning the punishment from internment of the body to the control of the mind. Michel Foucault's work on discipline and punishment discusses this very notion and explains how the effectiveness of a penalty can be based simply on the "idea of pain." In other words one doesn't need the actual sensation to prevent a repetition of a crime, just the idea of it will suffice. The use of informants by the RCMP was known by the internees. Many interviewees knew of the informants. According to archival sources, there were fights at the camp and there were suspicions raised as to potential squealers. Considering the pattern, it would be natural for an internee to assume that a surveillance could be in place after release. I know of one instance of a man who was re-interned after almost one year of being released. Regardless of the reason, this would have sent a clear message to the internees who saw the man come back.

There are two documents that I know of that may hold the answer. A former Ukrainian-Canadian pro-communist leader, Peter Krawchuk, wrote a diary about his time in the camps. According to Krawchuk, the men were forced to sign four documents upon release. He describes how the releases were handled in a quick manner and how "they shoved paper after paper at you and told you to sign them."[23]

You signed the "Release Declaration." In it you swore an oath that, having received conditional release, you would not give an interview to a representative of the press or other organization, and that you would not write letters to newspapers or organizations about what had occurred in one or another internment camp. In the document it was further stated that if the signatory broke this vow, he could be interned and dispatched to a camp again. The document signed, a second was pushed at you in which you had to state that you were not carrying any concealed letters, that you would not verbally pass along information about your friends in camp, and that you would not criticize in any manner the authorities, their officials or civil servants. You could be interned anew for breaking this vow. There was still a third paper, an "Undertaking". In it was stated that you would report to a certain civil servant or government official whom from time to time the Canadian authorities would designate, and that you would assent to the laws and regulations which would be especially set for your conduct by competent authorities. The fourth and last paper was a "Route Letter."[24]

I have a copy of the Undertaking and Route Letter my grandfather signed. In addition to the terms Krawchuk states above, the Undertaking also states: "I will strictly abstain from taking up arms against the Government of this country and that, except with the permission of the Officer or Official under whose surveillance I will be placed, I will strictly abstain from communicating to anyone whomsoever any information concerning the existing war or the movements of troops or the military preparations which the authorities of Canada or the United Kingdom …"[25]

These agreements silenced the internees, but they also instilled a fear that once released, they could be "under surveillance," and there would be consequences if they did not abide by the set conditions. Joe Mastromonaco is convinced that there was also a verbal briefing that went along with these documents.[26] If that was the case, it would only have emphasized their conditions. Judging by the silence, I imagine that whatever controls were imposed, they were effective in silencing the men.

Critical assessment of the oral histories of the families must be entered into the evaluation, no matter how they differ from the archival sources. Oral historian Steven High had done extensive work with working-class groups, and cautions us to not dismiss working-class people's recollections as "nothing but nostalgia." High explains how this "serves to depoliticize — and to effectively silence a group of already marginalized men and women."[27] The interviews I conducted in Montreal represent three social classes from various districts in the city. The internment marginalized the families and the silence shaped their experience — before, during and after.

In reality, the internment did not end with the release of the men. In some way the men remained prisoners, the barbed wire followed them. Their punishment was re-positioned from internment to fear. The descendants I interviewed consider their life stories as part of a history that needs to be recorded. Their fathers, on the other hand, were compelled to remain silent. This has left us with public and private silences.

Endnotes

1. The internees were classified as "second-class prisoners of war," according to the Geneva Convention. Bruti Liberati,

Luigi. "The Internment of Italian Canadians," p.83. Trans. by Gabrielle Scardellato. In Iacovetta, Franca, Roberto Perin, Angelo Principe. *Enemies Within: Italians and Other Internees in Canada and Abroad.* University of Toronto Press, 2000.
2. Ibid., p. 6.
3. The Canadian government was aware of fascist propaganda in the country as early as 1923. Italian and Italo-Canadian societies and organizations in Montreal were under the control of The Italian United Moral Front, which was under the direction of the Consul General, LAC RG25, file 5753 54-A (S).
4. Ibid., P.14. In an extract from *L'Italia* newspaper dated June 23, 1924, Italian Consul Brigidi makes it clear that a membership card to the *Fascio* would expedite any official or private documents from Italy that were required through the Italian consulate.
5. General and Confidential Report of the Examining Officer. September 5, 1940, LAC MG30, Vol. 14.
6. The Inter-Departmental Committee files, RCMP, LAC RG18, Vol. 3563.
7. *Past Lives.* Documentary series about Canadians in search of their roots. Bleu Blanc Rouge Productions Inc. Aired on Global Television.
8. Portelli, Alessandro. *The Death of Luigi Trastulli and other Stories.* State University of New York Press, 1991. p. 52.
9. Ibid.
10. Foucault, Michel. *Discipline and Punish: The Birth of the Prison.* Vintage Books Edition, May 1991. p. 45.
11. Interview with Sandra Corbo, October 13, 2011.
12. Interview with Tommassina Visocchi, October 24, 2011.

13. Interview with Josie Visocchi, October 27, 2011.
14. Passerini, Luisa. *Fascism in Popular Memory: The Cultural Experience of the Turin Working Class.* Cambridge University Press, 2009.
15. Interview with Antoinette Palmeri, Columbus Centre of Toronto, ICEA2011.0040.0001.
16. Interim Report of Complaints Arising Out of Internment of Italians. April 28, 1941. PAC MG30, Vol. 14.
17. Interview with Michael Monaco, Columbus Centre of Toronto, ICEA2011.0059.0001. Second interview on October 12, 2011.
18. Interview with Teresa Pateras, October 13, 2011.
19. Passerini, Luisa. op. cit. p. 55, 56.
20. Perin, Roberto. "Actor or Victim? Mario Duliani and His Internment Narrative." In Iacovetta, Franca et al., op.cit.
21. Interview with Joe Mastromonaco, Columbus Centre of Toronto, ICEA2011.0041.0001.
22. Interview with Joe Mastromonaco, October 14, 2011.
23. Krawchuk, Peter. *Interned Without Cause: The Internment of Canadian Anti-fascists During World War Two.* Kobzar Publishing Company, 1985. http://www.socialisthistory.ca/Docs/CPC/WW2/IWC26.htm.
24. Ibid.
25. Personal collection. *Undertaking* dated February 9, 1943, Fredericton Internment Camp.
26. Interview with Joe Mastromonaco, October 14, 2011.
27. High, Steven and Lewis, David W. *Corporate Wasteland: The Landscape and Memory of Deindustrialization.* Between the Lines, 2007, 94.

Filippo Salvatore

Guido Nincheri's Fresco Depicting Benito Mussolini in Madonna della Difesa Church in Montreal

On November 30, 2002 the Honorable Sheila Copps, former federal minister for Canadian Heritage, in a simple but meaningful ceremony that took place inside the Madonna della Difesa (Our Lady of Defense) church located in the heart of Montreal's Little Italy, recognized its historical and architectural value and bestowed upon it the status of a National Historic Site.

Madonna della Difesa was recognized as a distinct parish in 1910 by Montreal archbishop Paul Bruchesi. Between 1918-1919, the church that bears the same name was built. It is a rare, unique monument and is, with Saint-Léon de Westmount church, one of the master works of the talented painter, stained glass maker and architect Guido Nincheri (Prato, 1886 – Montreal, 1973) who had arrived in Montreal in 1912.

At the time a sizable number of the parishioners were from the small town of Casacalenda, Molise, where a few years earlier, in a place named Difesa, the Holy Virgin had appeared. The new church was given the name of Difesa as a sign of devotion.

In the 1920s and 1930s Nincheri covered the walls and the spacious apse vault behind the main altar with frescos, a technique of painting used by the ancient Romans and imitated by Giotto and Quattrocento Tuscan painters. Nincheri's style is overtly reminiscent of both this tradition and of the Pre-Raphaelite style — a school of painting that Dante Gabriel Rossetti founded in England towards the middle of the 19th century. The Difesa iconography is of course religious, but several figures on the vault illustrate episodes of Canadian history, in particular the role played by missionaries in the christening of the native populations.

There is in particular a detail depicting the civil authorities, among them Benito Mussolini riding a horse, painted in 1933 that since 1940 has become a source of controversy. Guido Nincheri was 86 when he died in 1973. His reputation and importance as an artist has grown ever since. He is nowadays considered as the most important practitioner of the fresco technique in painting and as a major figure in the history of figurative and religious art during the first half of the 20th century both in Canada and in the USA. Nincheri's frescos and stained glass windows are found in Montreal, Ottawa, Toronto and in western Canada. In the USA his works can be appreciated at Central Falls, Pawtucket, New Bedford and Woonsocket where he built Saint Anna's church, another of his masterpieces, with its gigantic frescos depicting The Presentation of the Word to the Angels.

Montreal is where Nincheri's most important works, on Canadian soil, are to be found. The first is the parish church of Saint Leon in Westmount. The second is the Chateau Dufresne, a Renaissance-style palazzo (corner of Sherbrooke-Pie IX) built for a French-Canadian family that had almost a monopoly in shoemaking and accumulated a fortune in the first half of the 20th century. The third is the Madonna della Difesa church. Other works by Nincheri are in the church Notre Dame de Villeray, Saint Patrick cathedral and La Chapelle du Sacré Coeur de Jésus.

The common denominator of Nincheri's works is a mix of sacred and profane iconographic and decorative elements, so typical of the Pre-Raphaelites. Inside Saint Leon's church, there is a detail on the apse vault that shows Attila the Hun, riding a horse, being stopped from destroying Rome by Pope Leo brandishing a cross. (This church as well was declared a National Historic Site in 1999).

The Chateau Dufresne caters to what must have been the neo-pagan taste of the patrons who had it built. The palazzo is a carbon copy of an Italian Renaissance or baroque mansion; its walls are covered with lascivious nymphs and satires in a bucolic landscape reminiscent of the Tuscan countryside. It is used nowadays fittingly as a museum.

Inside the Madonna della Difesa there is a really striking, magnificent fresco that covers the apse vault. This church has become known as "Mussolini's church" because of a detail (that of Benito Mussolini riding a horse surrounded by the quadrumviri who had participated in 1922 in the March on Rome, a coup d'état which enabled the Duce to seize power and found the illiberal regime called fascism). This detail was painted by Nincheri between 1930-33 and illustrates the historical and allegorical meaning that was attributed in the very Catholic Quebec of the time to the Patti Lateranensi (Lateran Pact) or Concordato. It was the signing in 1929 of a truce between the Italian State and the Catholic Church which made Catholicism the official religion of Italy and allowed the pope to become the temporal leader of Vatican City.

Benito Mussolini is still viewed in North America simply as a dictator and his name is associated with Adolf Hitler's, his military ally during the Second World War. Between 1922 and 1936 Mussolini's reputation in Canada was the opposite of what remains to the present. He was viewed as a world-class statesman sent by the Divine Providence to defend the western world against the communist threat. Both Canadian Prime Minister W.L. Mackenzie-King and his British colleague Winston Churchill expressed in the early 1930s the opinion that Mussolini was the greatest political leader in the world.

Canadians of Italian origin numbered in the 1930's officially 112.000, and constituted the 12th largest ethnic component of the population. The Montreal Italian community, about 30,000 strong, was then Canada's biggest. Because of the still prevailing social darwinism, Italian/Canadians were considered undesirables, just good navvies, and were the target of veiled and even open forms of discrimination. The prestige that Mussolini enjoyed on the world scene became for them a way to be proud of their *italianità*, until then a source of self-hatred, and most of them established a close link between *italianità* and the fascist régime. It was the officially sanctioned version of reality and identity, especially in the profoundly Catholic Quebec.

The choice of Mussolini as a symbol of the civic authority by Guido Nincheri and its depiction inside Madonna della Difesa church has to be linked to the mystical fervour that the Concordato had produced worldwide, especially in Catholic nations.

Benito Mussolini enjoyed for about 15 years in Canada, then still practically a British colony, in the United Kingdom itself and in the United States of America an excellent reputation. It is only in 1936, at the time of Italy's conquest of Ethiopia, when England's geopolitical interests in the Horn of Africa were threatened by the Italian presence, that Canadian English-language media began echoing Britain's anti-Italian propaganda and using harsh words towards fascism. Quebec's French-language media gave a diametrically opposed interpretation of the Italian conquest of Ethiopia. Mussolini's and Hitler's help to Francisco Franco in the Spanish Civil War and the signing of the Pact of Steel between Mussolini and Hitler in 1938 were turning points for shaping public opinion in English Canada. In 1939 came Germany's invasion of Poland and the declaration of war and the sudden, unexpected defeat of France. This led to Mussolini's June 10 declaration of war to England, France and Canada.

June 10, 1940 remains the darkest day in the history of the Italian presence in Canada. About 700 persons, the élite of the communities from Halifax to Vancouver, most of them naturalized or born Canadian citizens, were arrested and thousands had to report frequently to the police. They were labelled as "enemy aliens"; habeas corpus was suspended; and their civil liberties were disregarded. Italian-Canadians became individuals susceptible of forming a fifth column, of committing acts of sabotage, and since they had publically extolled unpatriotic behaviour by supporting Mussolini, they were considered ready to betray Canada. The Canadian government invoked the War Measures Act, as it had done during the First World War towards Canadians of Austrian, German and Ukrainian origin, arrested the community leaders and put them for years in internments camps.

The image that we still have of fascism, especially in North America, is conditioned by the outcome of the last world war. Fascism and nazism are still equated and condemned. European historiography, especially in Italy, thanks to the research of scholars such as Renzo De Felice, has proven the peculiarities of fascism vis-à-vis nazism and has expressed a less negative judgment of it.

The media in the English speaking world are not yet ready to be so subtle in their view of fascism and still give an apodictic interpretation of it.

Proof of this attitude is the almost hysterical reaction in some quarters — for example, the front page article published in *The Globe and Mail* on August 27 2002 dealing with the Madonna della Difesa church and Mussolini's fresco. Blame was expressed that federal funds were going to be given for the restoration and upkeep of the Difesa. Even some Italian-Canadian historians from Toronto and a respected M.P. from the Toronto area expressed their opposition to making the Difesa a national historical site.

Historically this opposition is explainable but no longer justifiable, if only one cares to take into account the date and the specific context that produced Mussolini's fresco. In order to be historically impartial, the image of Mussolini in the Difesa fresco has to be seen as the expression of Canadian public opinion on Mussolini in 1933, not the one that emerged in 1940. This is difficult to do because history rather than *magistra vitae* is inevitably the version that the winners give of past events. Some people out of coherence, spite, simple ignorance, mental laziness, conformism or self interest, end up accepting or prefer to defend a position that expresses only part of the historical truth.

The vast majority of Italian-Canadians sees nowadays the Church of Madonna della Difesa, even with its Mussolini detail, as part of their own history, of Canadian history.

Travis Tomchuk

Special Agent 203: The Motivations of Augusto Bersani

For Vincenzo Monaco, Monday, 10 June 1940, began as another typically long day of bread deliveries for Corona Bakery — a business he and his brother Donato had started in the early 1930s. He loaded his horse-drawn cart with bread and left the bakery at 7:00 a.m. expecting to complete his route and return by 6:00 p.m. Whether Monaco was aware that Mussolini had declared war against the Allies just after 1:00 pm Montreal time is unknown. At some point along the way, however, Monaco was stopped by plain-clothes officers of the Royal Canadian Mounted Police (RCMP) and taken into custody as a suspected fascist. Unable to return the horse and cart to the bakery, it was left to wander the streets of Montreal. Monaco was taken to Fort Sainte-Jean in present day Sainte-Jean-sur-Richelieu and held for three weeks before being transferred to the Petawawa Internment Camp.[1]

After four months of internment, Monaco was interviewed by Justice James Duncan Hyndman, a former Supreme Court of Alberta judge appointed by the federal Minister of Justice Ernest Lapointe, to review the cases of internees who objected to their internment.[2] When Justice Hyndman asked Monaco why he thought he had been interned, the Montreal baker replied that someone seeking revenge had given authorities false information against him. When pressed further, Monaco told the judge that he believed Augusto Bersani, the former minister of the Protestant Italian Church of the Redeemer to which he belonged, was responsible for his present predicament. This was not the first time that Bersani's name had come up during Hyndman's inquiries. In fact, a number of internees from Montreal felt that Bersani had played a role in their internment. This prompted the judge, who was aware that Bersani was employed as an RCMP informant, to conduct his own investigation into Bersani's credibility as an informant.[3]

Judge Hyndman's suspicion of Augusto Bersani raises important questions regarding the RCMP's selection of informants. As has been well-documented by a number of scholars — most notably Greg Kealey and Reg Whitaker, the RCMP placed more of its resources on the surveillance of the Communist Party of Canada (CPC) than fascist groups during the interwar period.[4] Though the RCMP first noted the presence of Italian fascism in Canada as early as 1923, it did not consider this political ideology to pose the same threat as communism — a position it would maintain even as late as September 1939.[5] In a letter to Norman A. Robertson of the Department of External Affairs, Charles Rivett-Carnac, the head of the RCMP's Intelligence Section, explained that the communists were a greater danger to Canada because they wanted to eliminate capitalism while fascism did not. Further, Rivett-Carnac wrote that "Fascism is the reaction of the middle classes to the Communist [sic] danger."[6] The RCMP's greater emphasis on the CPC meant that officers of this police agency went undercover and infiltrated different branches of the party.[7] It appears as though this tactic was not used during the surveillance of Italian fascist groups in Canada. The RCMP's focus on the CPC led to a reliance on informants from Italian Canadian communities to identify fascists who were potential threats to national and public safety because the RCMP did not have agents of their own directly involved in Italian Canadian fascist organizations. As a result, dubious individuals such as Augusto Bersani were employed to conduct this work. And, in his role as an informant, Bersani wielded a great deal of power and waged a personal war against those who he believed had slighted him.

Little is known about Augusto Bersani's life prior to his arrival in Montreal. Born in Italy, he was believed to have trained in the seminary to become a priest but, for reasons unknown, he did not finish his studies and boarded a ship to New York City. When exactly Bersani arrived in the United States has not been determined though it appears that he may have run into some kind of trouble that necessitated his departure for Montreal in the late 1920s. Once in the city, Bersani began to teach at the Point aux Trembles Protestant School and was later appointed minister of the Italian Church of the Redeemer in 1930. He served as minister until 1938 when he resigned from this position stating health concerns.[8]

After Italy's declaration of war on 10 June 1940, a number of parishioners from the Italian Church of the Redeemer were arrested and interned. This included church elders such as Vincenzo Monaco, Giovanni Fasano, Giuseppe Raco, and Vincenzo "James" Greco. Reverend Domenico Scalera, who had replaced Bersani, was also interned.[9] The allegations against these men included being a fascist or a member of fascist organizations such as the Casa d'Italia, Dopolavoro, and the Italian War Veterans' Association.[10] Giuseppe Raco, for instance, was alleged to be a member of Montreal's Fascio Giovanni Luparini and was "considered to hold very radical views and [be] a convinced Fascist [sic]."[11] Some internees were also accused of having donated gold to Italy and/or made anti-British comments in public. An examination of existing RCMP security reports and the personal papers of Justice J.D. Hyndman reveal that all of these interned parishioners were either informed on by Bersani or believed the former minister had played a role in their internment. Why was this the case? Was this particular Protestant church a hotbed of fascist activity?

Bersani had begun to work as an RCMP informant in 1937 while he was still minister at the Italian Church of the Redeemer. In RCMP security records he was known as S.A. 203 (Special Agent 203).[12] How Bersani became involved in this type of employment is not known. Nor is the amount he was paid for this work.[13] It is also unclear whether the RCMP screened potential informants and what that process might have entailed. As an informant, Bersani was required to provide a report, known as a Personal History File, on those Italian Canadians involved in fascist activities. The information collected on these forms included biographical information about the subject's place and date of birth, vocation, marital status and the number of children he or she had. It also noted their involvement in the Order Sons of Italy or any other so-called "patriotic institutions," such as the Fascio or Dopolavoro, and whether the subject had donated money to the Casa d'Italia or the Italian Red Cross.[14]

Bersani also scoured the pages of the Italian-language press in Canada. In Bersani's collection of personal papers there are hundreds of articles clipped from Montreal's *L'Italia Nuova* and Toronto's *Il Bolletino Italo-Canadese*. The names of Italian Canadians mentioned within these publications are underlined. Bersani did not only focus his attention on the communities of Montreal and Toronto but also much smaller Ontario urban centres such as North Bay and Timmins.[15] Bersani also appears to have cooperated with another informant known as Contact No. 17, but the identity of this person is unknown.[16]

As one of the judges[17] appointed to review the evidence against internees, Hyndman quickly began to question the legitimacy of allegations against the parishioners from the Italian Church of the Redeemer who had been interned. After interviewing Vincenzo Monaco and his character witnesses, Hyndman concluded that Monaco was "a decent, honest law-abiding man incapable of committing subversive acts with which he has been charged." And that "it is my absolute conviction that this man is entirely innocent of any subversive act or intentions, and that justice can only be done by ordering his immediate release from internment."[18]

In two other cases, the evidence provided to justify internment was so unconvincing that Justice Hyndman asked for more information from the RCMP. Michele Tamiglia, for instance, was alleged to be associated with the fascist Party, the Dopolavoro, and the Italian War Veterans' Association. RCMP also believed that he had donated gold to Italy and held anti-British views. During his interview with Justice Hyndman, Tamiglia did admit to being a member of the Italian War Veterans' Association and attending its meetings at the Casa d'Italia. However, Hyndman did not feel this in itself was enough to warrant Tamiglia's internment. The judge interviewed eight others who could testify on Tamiglia's behalf and no proof that the man was a fascist was revealed. As a consequence, Hyndman requested that the RCMP supply him with more intelligence or witnesses to prove the allegations against the man. If no new evidence was forthcoming, Hyndman recommended that Tamiglia be released immediately. The RCMP appears not to have provided further proof against Tamiglia because he was released from Petawawa on 30 March 1941 — two months after Hyndman's recommendation of release.[19]

Nick Jerome was another internee from the Italian Church of the Redeemer whose case was reviewed by Justice Hyndman. Jerome denied any involvement in fascist organizations and, again, Hyndman asked the RCMP to provide him with more evidence. The RCMP forwarded the judge a lengthy report that in Hyndman's opinion "add[ed] nothing of evidential value to the case." The judge then declared: "I am forced to say that I regard [Jerome's] further detention as a rank injustice."[20]

The questionable evidence against parishioners from the Italian Church of the Redeemer and the recurring mention of Bersani during interviews with internees led Justice Hyndman to seriously doubt the former minister's reliability as an informant. This prompted the judge to conduct an investigation into Augusto Bersani in late November 1940 that included the family members of internees as well as non-Italians involved in the United Church of Canada. The exact number of people Hyndman interviewed is unknown but there are surviving transcripts for eight interviews. The oral testimonies reveal much about Bersani's personality and his motivations.

Shortly after the arrests of 10 June 1940, Bersani contacted the families of his former parishioners and feigned concern. He approached Anne Jerome and Filomena Monaco, the wives of internees Nick Jerome and Vincenzo Monaco, and said he would seek their release. In a letter written on Chateau Laurier letterhead dated 18 June 1940, Bersani told Anne Jerome that he was in the city on her husband's behalf. He ended his letter on a positive note by stating: "I have good hopes for you."[21] However, that was the last time Anne Jerome heard from the former minister. In Filomena Monaco's case, Bersani promised to deliver clothing to her husband while he was held at Fort Sainte-Jean. She put together a package that included socks, underwear, a sweater, and a jacket which she gave to Bersani. A few days later Bersani paid Filomena a visit and told her that the clothes had been delivered and that her husband and his brother Donato were doing well. Yet, when Filomena wrote to her husband to ask whether he had received the clothing, his response was that he had not.[22]

But Bersani's act as the caring former minister did not last long. He paid a visit to Mary Monaco, daughter of Donato Monaco, two weeks after her father had been interned. According to Mary Monaco's testimony, Bersani asked if she had heard any news about her father. When Mary Monaco replied in the negative, Bersani stated that all those who had raised a hand against him at the church would be interned.[23] During a similar visit to Filomena Monaco, Bersani was alleged to have said: "Remember when I was put out of the church and how I suffered, well now you are suffering."[24]

Hyndman's investigation also revealed Bersani's controversial behaviour while minister of the Italian Church of the Redeemer — actions that deeply angered members of the church. One incident involved Roman Catholic children attending Protestant schools. Since the Catholic school system in Quebec was francophone, Catholic Italian Canadians who wanted their children to learn English were in a difficult situation. Walter A. Watson, Inspector of Taxes for the Protestant School Board, discovered that there were roughly one hundred Catholic children at Protestant schools in Montreal.

When he asked these students why they were attending Protestant schools they told him that Reverend Bersani had sent them. How Bersani became involved in facilitating this is unclear but he wrote letters to Protestant school principals claiming that Catholic children were actually members of his Protestant church, which allowed them to attend English-language classes. In a conversation with Watson, the principal of one of these schools, whose name was not recorded, described Bersani as a "racketeer" who used his position as minister for his own gain.[25] This suggests that Bersani may have received payment or some other kind of favour for getting Catholic children into the Protestant school.

Unfortunately the sources are silent regarding any repercussions for Bersani regarding this incident.

Bersani was also involved in falsifying the church's Register of Births. By doing so, he could bestow Canadian citizenship to a child born in Italy by changing the child's place of birth to a Canadian town or city. It also appears that Bersani had implicated fifteen-year-old Antonietta Forcillo in this endeavour by having her make changes to the Register.[26] When Bersani was confronted about this irregularity by Reverend Robert George Katsunoff, Minister of the Church of All Nations and Superintendent of the Non-Anglo Mission of the United Church of Canada in Montreal, he simply explained that it had been a mistake.[27]

The most serious charge against Bersani, however, was his inability to prove that Christmas Cheer funds earmarked for the parish's poor was received by them. The first incident occurred in 1936. The elders of the Italian Church of the Redeemer brought this to the attention of Reverend Katsunoff. Katsunoff approached Bersani to determine the veracity of this allegation. He discovered that the majority of vouchers that recipients of the relief were to sign actually contained Bersani's signature. Katsunoff told Bersani that if this happened again he would go to the authorities.[28]

The following year, the payment of Christmas relief was again in doubt. A vote was held by members of the church to determine if Bersani's actions should be brought to the attention of superiors in the United Church of Canada. The majority of voters were in support of this course and the result was conveyed by Vincenzo Monaco to Reverend Katsunoff. The reverend then met with Bersani and demanded that he provide the receipt vouchers which he refused to do. When Katsunoff reported what had happened to the head of the United Church of Canada, Bersani was ordered to produce the vouchers or face the consequences. According to

Katsunoff's sworn testimony, after he delivered the ultimatum Bersani flew into a rage and ordered his secretary to burn the vouchers. The disgraced minister formally resigned from the church in early 1938 citing ill health as the reason.[29]

During the sworn testimonies of Reverend Katsunoff, Walter Watson, and Reverend Munroe, each was asked by Hyndman to comment on Bersani's trustworthiness. None of these men trusted the former minister. Both Watson and Munroe declared that they would not trust Bersani even under oath.[30] Even Italian antifascists did not trust Bersani. Ottawa's Anselmo Bortolotti visited the former minister in Toronto after Bersani had relocated to the city during the Second World War. Bortolotti noticed a file with his own name on it in Bersani's apartment. As the antifascist recounted: "When I pointed out to him that this file could prove a danger if the political situation ever changed, he said in a very unconvincing way that it only contained personal information."[31]

It is difficult to know when Bersani's role as S.A. 203 came to an end. By April 1942, Bersani was living in Toronto and editing and writing articles for the city's antifascist newspaper *La Vittoria*. His role was changed to associate editor in January 1943 and it appears as though Bersani ceased contributing content to the newspaper after that point.[32] Very little is known about Bersani's life after the war. According to Michael Monaco, son of internee Vincenzo Monaco, the disgraced minister turned informant moved to Buffalo, New York, where he co-owned a motel. He would send the Monacos postcards on a regular basis inviting them to stay at the motel. The Monacos, however, never accepted the offer.[33]

The RCMP's use of an informant like Augusto Bersani demonstrates the limits of using paid informants to gather information on others. The documents pertaining to Bersani reveal a corrupt and vindictive person who used his position as a

Protestant minister for personal gain and as an informant for vengeance. Further research needs to be conducted regarding the role played by RCMP informants in the interment of Italian Canadians and other targeted groups during the Second World War. If someone like Bersani was the most prominent or most qualified person to act as an informant, it raises serious doubts as to whether the RCMP followed a screening process or had any criteria for hiring informants. Considering the amount of power Bersani wielded and the number of Italian Canadians on whom he forwarded information, the RCMP shares as much responsibility as Bersani in the unjust incarceration of Italian Canadians during the Second World War.

Endnotes

1. Michael Monaco, personal interview, 23 June 2011, Columbus Centre of Toronto, #ICEA2011.0059.0001.
2. Section 26 of the Defence of Canada Regulations (DOCR), a series of regulations introduced as part of the War Measures Act, allowed an internee to formally object to his or her incarceration within thirty days of being interned. When an appeal was made, the Minister of Justice appointed a judge who conducted an investigation. Government of Canada, *Defence of Canada Regulations* (Ottawa: Government of Canada, 1939) 36. This process included reviewing Royal Canadian Mounted Police (RCMP) security files and speaking with an internee's family, friends, and colleagues. It also meant multiple interviews with the internee. See the James Duncan Hyndman Fonds (hereafter JDHF), MG30, E182, Vol. 14, Library and Archives Canada (hereafter LAC).

3. J.D. Hyndman, "In the matter of the Defence of Canada Regulations and in the matter of Vincenzo Monaco, 40D-269-1-D-751," to Minister of Justice, Ottawa, 3 Dec. 1940, JDHF, MG 30, E 182, Vol. 14, LAC.
4. Gregory S. Kealey and Reg Whitaker, eds., *RCMP Security Bulletins: The Depression Years, 1933-1939*, vols. 1-5 (St. John's: Canadian Committee on Labour History,); Gregory S. Kealey and Reg Whitaker, eds., *RCMP Security Bulletins: The War Series, 1939-1945*, vols. 1 and 2 (St. John's: Canadian Committee on Labour History, 1989-1993); Gregory S. Kealey, "Spymasters, Spies, and Their Subjects: The RCMP and Canadian State Repression, 1914-1939," *Whose National Security?: Canadian State Surveillance and the Creation of Enemies* eds. Gary Kinsman, Dieter K. Buse, and Mercedes Steedman (Toronto: Between the Lines, 2000) 18-34; Michelle McBride, "From Indifference to Internment: An Examination of RCMP Responses to Nazism and Fascism in Canada," MA thesis, Memorial University, 1993.
5. RCMP, "The Organization and Activities of the Italian Fascist Party in Canada," Ottawa, 1937, 13, Canadian Security Intelligence Service (hereafter CSIS), RG146, Vol. 97, File AH-1999/00227, LAC; Reg Whitaker, "Official Repression of Communism during World War II," *Labour/Le Travail* 37 (1996): 137.
6. Whitaker, "Official Repression of Communism during World War II," 137.
7. John Leopold, for instance, was an undercover RCMP officer who infiltrated the Communist Party of Canada in the 1920s. Kealey, "Spymasters, Spies, and Their Subjects: The RCMP and Canadian State Repression, 1914-1939," 25-28.

8. "Evidence of Walter A. Watson," Montreal, n.d., JDHF, MG 30, E 182, Vol. 14, LAC; "Evidence of Reverend Robert George Katsunoff," Montreal, n.d., JDHF, MG 30, E 182, Vol. 14, LAC.
9. These were not the only people involved with the Italian Church of the Redeemer who were interned. Donato Monaco, Nick Jerome (born Nicola Girolamo), Michele Tamiglia, Canio Nicolini, Gennaro Placito, and Costanzo D'Amico were also taken to Petawawa in the summer of 1940. See JDHF, MG 30, E 182, Vol. 14, LAC.
10. The Montreal Casa d'Italia, like its counterparts in other Canadian cities, was an Italian social and cultural centre closely tied to an Italian vice consul. It was home to offices of the vice consul and other associated organizations such as the Dopolavoro and the Fascio Giovanni Luparini. It also provided space for members to play cards, conduct Italian-language courses, and hold band practice. Montreal's Casa d'Italia is located at 505 rue Jean-Talon. The Dopolavoro provided members with recreational activities that could range from various sports leagues to dances and other social events. The Italian War Veterans' Association or Ex Combattenti was comprised of veterans who had served in the Italian army during the First World War.
11. J.D. Hyndman, "In the matter of the Defence of Canada Regulations and in the matter of Giuseppe Raco, 40-D-269-4-D-126," to Minister of Justice, Ottawa, 17 Feb. 1941, JDHF, MG 30, E 182, Vol. 14, LAC.
12. Luigi Bruti Liberati, "The Internment of Italian Canadians," *Enemies Within: Italian and Other Internees in Canada and Abroad*, eds. Iacovetta, Franca, Roberto Perin, and Angelo Principe (Toronto: University of Toronto

Press, 2000) 84. Bersani's identity as S.A. 203 is revealed in the papers of James Duncan Hyndman. In a memo to the Minister of Justice written on 17 February 1941, Hyndman attributed the following quote to Bersani: "In recent times [Giuseppe Raco] has ceased all connections with Fascism [sic] and all his sympathies have turned to the British people and to the allies [sic]. He never held any office in the Fascio nor was he active in any organization." In a second memo dated 15 March 1941, Hyndman quotes S.A. 203 as follows: "[I]n recent times [Giuseppe Raco] has ceased all connections with Fascism [sic] and all his sympathies have turned to the British people and to the Allies. He never held any office in the Fascio nor was he active in any organization." Both the quote attributed to Bersani and the one to S.A. 203 are dated 24 May 1940. J.D. Hyndman, "In the matter of the Defence of Canada Regulations and in the matter of Giuseppe Raco, 40-D-269-4-D-126," to Minister of Justice, Ottawa, 17 Feb. 1941, and J.D. Hyndman, "Memorandum Re: Giuseppe Raco — 40D-269-4-D-126," 15 Mar. 1941, JDHF, MG 30, E 182, Vol. 14, LAC.

13. In an interview, Ottawa antifascist Anselmo Bortolotti claimed that Bersani was paid $100,000 by the RCMP as an informant though this sum is too incredible to believe. Filippo Salvatore, *Fascism and the Italians of Montreal: An Oral History, 1922-1945* (Montreal: Guernica, 1988) 38.

14. Contact No. 17, "Personal History File: Giuseppe D'Amato," 24 Oct. 1940, Montreal, RCMP, RG18, F-3 Vol. 3563.

15. See the Augusto Bersani Papers, Multicultural History Society of Ontario Archives (hereafter MHSOA), Kelly Library, University of Toronto.

16. It is possible that Contact No. 17 is Camillo Vetere, the former secretary of Fascio Giovanni Luparini and editor of *L'Italia Nuova*, who turned informant. However, I have been unable to locate any definitive proof that Contact No. 17 and Vetere were the same person. RCMP, "The Organization and Activities of the Italian Fascist Party in Canada," Ottawa, 1937, 11-12, CSIS, RG146, Vol. 97, File AH-1999/00227, LAC.
17. Justice H.A. Fortier of Quebec was another judge selected to determine whether the detention of internees was justified. S.T. Wood, RCMP Commissioner, to Ernest Lapointe, Minister of Justice, 21 Oct. 1940, JDHF, MG 30, E 182, Vol. 14, LAC.
18. J.D. Hyndman, Ottawa, to Ernest Lapointe, Ottawa, 25 Nov. 1940, "In the matter of the Defence of Canada Regulations and in the matter of Vincenzo Monaco, 40D-269-1-D-751," JDHF, MG 30, E 182, Vol. 14, LAC.
19. J.D. Hyndman to W.R. Jackett, "Memorandum Re: Michele Tamiglia — 40-275," 10 Feb. 1941, JDHF, MG 30, E 182, Vol. 14, LAC and Custodian of Enemy Property, RG117, Vol. 656, File 3850, "Tamiglia, Michele," LAC.
20. J.D. Hyndman to Minister of Justice, "In the matter of the Defence of Canada Regulations and in the matter of Nicola Di [sic] Girolamo (Nick Jerome), 40D-269-4-D-46," 1 Mar. 1941, JDHF, MG 30, E 182, Vol. 14, LAC.
21. Augusto Bersani to Anne Jerome, 18 June 1940, and "Evidence of Anne Jerome," Montreal, n.d, JDHF, MG 30, E 182, Vol. 14, LAC.
22. "Evidence of Filomena Monaco," Montreal, n.d, JDHF, MG 30, E 182, Vol. 14, LAC.

23. "Evidence of Mary Monaco," Montreal, n.d, JDHF, MG 30, E 182, Vol. 14, LAC.
24. "Evidence of Filomena Monaco," Montreal, n.d, JDHF, MG 30, E 182, Vol. 14, LAC.
25. "Evidence of Walter A. Watson," Montreal, n.d., JDHF, MG 30, E 182, Vol. 14, LAC.
26. "Evidence of Reverend Robert George Katsunoff," Montreal, n.d., and L. Colucci, Giuseppe Fasano, and Vincenzo Monaco to Dr. Katsunoff, 26 May 1938, JDHF, MG 30, E 182, Vol. 14, LAC.
27. "Evidence of Reverend Robert George Katsunoff," Montreal, n.d., JDHF, MG 30, E 182, Vol. 14, LAC.
28. "Evidence of Reverend Robert George Katsunoff," Montreal, n.d., and "Evidence of Reverend Lloyd A. Smith, Montreal, 22 Nov. 1940, JDHF, MG 30, E 182, Vol. 14, LAC.
29. "Evidence of Mary Monaco," Montreal, n.d, and "Evidence of Reverend Robert George Katsunoff," Montreal, n.d., JDHF, MG 30, E 182, Vol. 14, LAC.
30. "Evidence of Walter A. Watson," Montreal, n.d., and "Evidence of Reverend William Munroe," Montreal, n.d., JDHF, MG 30, E 182, Vol. 14, LAC.
31. Salvatore, 37.
32. See *La Vittoria*, MHSOA, Kelly Library, University of Toronto.
33. Michael Monaco, personal interview, 23 June 2011.

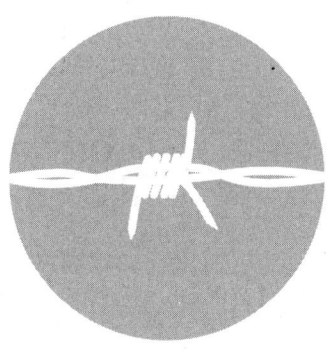

Frank Giorno & James McCreath

Internee 328, Camp Petawawa, June 1940-June 1941

1. James McCreath's Introduction

Of the sixty plus displaced men who were interned in hut number five at Camp Petawawa in June of 1940, none stirred more controversy than the one known as Internee 328.

No other internee residing behind the locked gates and barbed wire fences of this infamous detention centre during the course of the Second World War elicited the undivided attention of Canada's War Cabinet and the Canadian Parliament. Pulled into the web of intrigue that surrounded Internee 328 were: several federal cabinet ministers, a future Prime Minister, provincial premiers, and some of the most prominent judicial and business minds of that era.

I had the privilege of knowing Internee 328 in for the last twelve years of his life, from 1948 until his death in 1960. Internee 328 was my grandfather. How this man withstood the indignities and injustice weighed upon him during his internment, and how he survived to not just live, but prosper again is truly a story for the ages.

Born in the Abruzzo region of Italy in March of 1890, Internee 328 was sent to the new world at the age of fifteen to build a foundation for his family's future. On June 5th, 1905, he passed through Ellis Island in New York City on his way to catch a train to Toronto, Canada. His father had sent him off with the name of a friend who ran a construction business there, and it was in Toronto that he would make his mark on Canada.

Internee 328's amazing life story has never been told to the public before. When author and journalist Frank Giorno contacted me in the winter of 2010 to see if his descendants would be amenable to pulling the pieces of this very complex man's life together for publication, we struck up a working relationship that allowed us to compare and combine our knowledge and research. Internee 328 was born Vincenzo Franceschini. Shortly after his arrival in Toronto, it was suggested that a more Anglicized given name might be beneficial for future advancement. His Irish line boss at the time had two sons, James and Leonard, so Vincenzo Franceschini became "James" Franceschini from that day forth. A few years later, when Vincenzo's younger brother Renaldo arrived, he took the name "Leonard."

James married Annie Lydia Pinkham of Toronto in 1913. Together they had one daughter Myrtle, born in 1921. After Myrtle married future lawyer and international figure skating champion Ralph McCreath in 1946, they raised four children. I am the eldest of those four children, and James Franceschini's namesake.

When James died in 1960, the bulk of his estate was left to our mother, Myrtle. Following her tragic death at age forty-six in 1968, her four offspring eventually took over operation of the family holding company. What we acquired, besides hard assets, was a vast wealth of historical information about James' life in the form of documents, letters, newspaper articles, colour and black and white motion pictures, and most dramatically, two privately commissioned biographies. This wealth of knowledge has come to be known as the "McCreath Family Archives."

This information serves as the basis for telling the story of Internee 328 and enables us to tell the personal side of the long forgotten but extremely relevant story of what happened to one of Canada's most loyal citizens.

2. Frank Giorno's Introduction

It was by chance that I came upon the name James Franceschini. I had volunteered with Heritage Toronto a few years earlier to pursue my interest of local history and heritage. Nancy Luno, the coordinator of volunteers for Heritage Toronto, assigned me the task of researching the notable anniversaries for the year 2006, a task that I embraced wholeheartedly. I went to the Etobicoke Historical Society webpage and came across an entry on Myrtle Villa, which was built in 1906 and became the lake front estate in Mimico for James Franceschini, his wife Annie Pinkham Franceschini and daughter Myrtle Franceschini.[1]

This led me to Harvey Currell's book *A History of Mimico*, which contained information about Franceschini being the founder of Dufferin Construction and also about his internment.

I grew up in the Italian-Canadian community of Toronto and yet knew nothing about this man whose legacy was evident every single day on the streets of the city. I read books about the internment of Italian-Canadians and was disappointed with the lack of solid information about Franceschini. Some of it turned out to be erroneous, such as the assertion that Franceschini was moderately involved in fascist activities in the much hailed book, *Enemies Within*, by leading academics Franca Iacovetta, Robert Perrin and Angelo Principe. Principe, the principal author of the chapter, does not provide any citation to back his conclusion.[2] This research paper will show that Franceschini was not involved in any fascist activities whatsoever.

I contacted James McCreath about the possibility of working together to tell his grandfather's story, after completing five years of research. I pored over old articles in the *Toronto Star* and *Globe and Mail* from 1905 right up to the present; researched documents at the Ontario and National Archives; and had lengthy discussions with John Fullerton of the Canadian Hackney Society. Franceschini was not only Canada's foremost road builder; he was also its foremost breeder and presenter of hackney horses. One of the only accolades ever bestowed on him was his induction into the Hackney Horse Hall of Fame.[3]

In 2008, I paid a visit to the National Archives of Canada in Ottawa and accessed volumes of documents, including the report written by Justice James Hyndman that found Franceschini innocent of all charges of being disloyal to Canada. Until the publication of this essay, the Hyndman report had never been released publically. I read the correspondence between the Orwellian-named Custodian of Enemy Property and Price Waterhouse over the seizure, disposition and management of Franceschini's businesses and financial assets. I learned that at the moment of his arrest Franceschini was one of Canada's largest suppliers of warships and military airport runways for the Canadian Ministry of Supply and Munitions.

Despite Justice Hyndman's finding, the MacKenzie King government and Ernest Lapointe, the Justice Minister and King's Quebec Lieutenant, refused to release him, letting Franceschini languish to the point of almost dying before finally allowing him out for medical care. When they did release him on compassionate grounds, the King government covered up the reasons for his prolonged internment, his innocence, and left a lingering doubt about his lack of guilt by refusing to make public Justice Hyndman's report. This inexplicable act by the Canadian government resulted in a backlash from people who still believed Franceschini could be guilty.

Here, for the first time, is the real story of James Franceschini and how his life was affected by the changing winds of history and the use of that blunt instrument, the War Measures Act of 1914, Defense of Canada Regulations and the absolute power it gave to the Canadian government over the lives of its citizens.

3. James Franceschini: Loyalty and Devotion to Canada

James Franceschini got to know Canada better than most Canadians because of his travels to Quebec, Nova Scotia, Ontario and other provinces on behalf of Dufferin Construction. Franceschini loved Canada because it gave him his career, his financial success and the loves of his life: lovely, bright and dedicated wife Annie, and Myrtle, the daughter he adored so much.

Despite his love of Canada and his contribution to building a modern 20th century nation by helping to upgrade its transportation infrastructure into a bustling highway system that enabled the flow of goods and people by truck and car, and despite his good works and charitable contributions, Franceschini was interned after Italy declared war on the British Empire on June 10, 1940. To this day the complete explanation for Franceschini's apprehension as a suspected "enemy alien" and his prolonged detention, even after he was found innocent, has not been revealed.

Canada in June of 1940 was vastly different than the country we live in today. Having suffered through the horrors of the First World War and the Great Depression, the last thing anyone wanted was to send their loved ones overseas again. But when Hitler invaded Poland in September 1939, the British Commonwealth and Canada were at war once more. Nine months later, when Mussolini signed a pact with Hitler, Canada was at war with Italy.

For thousands of Italian immigrants living in Canada, it was an overnight transformation into "enemy aliens." The seeds of "Italophobia" were quickly sown by racists, bigots, informers, spies, and tabloid newspapers. With the dark clouds of war on the horizon, and the inevitability that Canadian soldiers would soon be dying on Italian soil, the venom ran free and fast.

Within hours of the declaration of war, innocent men were taken from their homes and families, for no other reason than their European heritage. James Franceschini was one of those men, even though his companies were performing valuable service for the Ministry of War. At the time of his internment, Franceschini had lived in Canada for 35 years and had been a loyal Canadian citizen for 27 of those years. He had returned to Italy just once after his arrival in Canada — in 1925 to purchase a home for his father in Abruzzo.

What made the internment of Franceschini a journey into the realm of Kafkaesque absurdity was that, in September 1939, when war broke out between Britain and Germany, he offered Canada's Department of Munitions and Supply the use of his entire enterprises, which included Dufferin Construction and Dufferin Shipbuilding, for the token sum of a dollar. In addition, he accepted the low prices offered by the Department to build four minesweepers. His love of Canada and his fair-mindedness prevented him from doing what some other Canadian, American and British industrialists were chomping at the bit to do — profiting from war. This loyalty to Canada and his desire to see it equipped with minesweepers at a low price may have played a role in his extended internment. Even after he was declared innocent a few months after he was interned on June 15, 1940, it is a distinct possibility that embittered shipbuilding competitors may have pressured Cabinet to prevent his release.[4]

In addition to building the four minesweepers through Dufferin Shipbuilding, Franceschini's road building operations constructed roads and runways for Canada's military airports including the construction of the joint RAF/RCAF training facility at Port Maitland, just south of Dunnville, Ontario.

Another factor may have had something to do with his introduction of modern business practices and his desire to expand his road building operation into Quebec. Franceschini's success was due to his practice of being able to build quality roads, and now ships, at the lowest prices possible. He did this by introducing the latest technology and by vertically integrating his operations so he could control the prices of the supplies and thereby offer his services at prices much lower than his competitors. Most of his competitors were reluctant to invest labour saving technology and they did not purchase their own gravel supply. Franceschini's intention of starting up a cement factory in Montreal to help keep the costs down in his Quebec road building venture also may have played a role.[5]

Although he had put these plans on hold for the duration of the war, many competitors in the Montreal area were angered by what they viewed as an intrusion into their market. The Quebec aggregates industry was angered because they would lose their primary customer Quebec Paving, a subsidiary of Dufferin Construction. The road construction competitors were angered because they could not compete on contracts due to the fact Quebec Paving's vertically integrated operations reduced costs considerably.[6]

4. Arrival in Canada

Franceschini's love for Canada began when in 1905, despite the best efforts of Canada's Minister of the Interior who favoured immigrants from Northern Europe over those from Italy and other southern European nations, the country took in a penniless young man, Vincenzo, from Chieti, Abruzzo. The Minister of the Interior in 1901 informed his deputy minister that "no steps are to be taken to assist or encourage Italian immigration to Canada.... You will, of course, understand that this is to be done without saying anything that will be offensive."[8]

Vincenzo was later joined by his younger brother Renaldo. They became known as James and Leonard, when a friendly Irish foreman bestowed them with the names and that's what the two brothers proudly called themselves for the rest of their lives. They also passed on their names to the second and third generation of nephews — James L. Franceschini and Leonard Jr., sons of Leonard Franceschini; and James McCreath, the son of Myrtle Franceschini McCreath. It was almost a rite of passage for Vincenzo and Renaldo to become James and Leonard. From that day forth, they had irrevocably cut the umbilical cord to their mother country, and placed their destiny in their adopted homeland.

5. Marriage and Citizenship

Annie Pinkham and James Franceschini were married in St. Paul's Anglican Church in 1913 and the reception held at the Pinkhams' home on Chandos Avenue. The year before the wedding, James founded Dufferin Construction with several associates. Dufferin Construction was named after the gritty west end Toronto street where James Franceschini lived at the time of his marriage. The neighbourhood was comprised of working class Scottish and English residents. Italians would soon migrate here from College Street drawn by the industries located along the Canadian Pacific Railway line north of Dupont Street, including Canada Foundry where Franceschini worked briefly. Not only did Franceschini marry in 1913, he also became a Canadian citizen.

6. Dufferin Construction — Master Road Builder

Franceschini became a millionaire before he was 25, thanks to the contracts secured by Dufferin Construction to build roads for the new transportation craze — the automobile. Before companies like Dufferin Construction began building hardtop surfaces, Ontario's roads — dirt, wooden plank, corduroy log and stone and gravel — were virtually unusable, especially in the country side. After heavy rain and during the massive snow melts of spring, the roads would be turned into impassable quagmires.

Franceschini also built roads for internal use by large industrial operations like the other early 20th century miracle — hydro power. Dufferin Construction was awarded the contract to build the roads at Ontario's second major hydro plant in Eugenia. However, the First World War brought an end to road expansion in Ontario and resources were shifted to the war effort overseas.[9]

7. Millions Made, Millions Lost

As quickly as he made his first million by introducing the most advanced road construction equipment — the steam shovel, Franceschini lost it and was forced to sell off his equipment. What happened was that Dufferin Construction grew too rapidly, borrowed to purchase equipment such as the steam shovel and much of the profits that were earned were taken out by his partners so the company had a shortfall and couldn't pay back its loans. The story goes that he was left only a pony which he traded for a team of working horses and a wagon. Franceschini's persistence, perseverance, boundless energy and optimism soon had him back on top of the road construction business. He parlayed an opportunity to dig the foundation for Parkwood, Colonel Sam McLaughlin's mansion, into a contract to build the road system for McLaughlin's new auto plant in Oshawa — General Motors Canada.[10]

8. The New Dufferin Construction — Good Roads Movement

Franceschini restructured Dufferin Construction and he kept tighter control of its executive. Dufferin Construction was reconstituted with a corporate structure that was innovative and foreshadowed the culturally diverse composition of many Canadian corporations of the latter part of the 20th century. James was the President and general manager; his wife the Secretary-Treasurer; and Harry Salmon of Jewish origin the Vice President.[11]

As the age of the automobile took hold in the post WWI era, Franceschini and competing companies played an important role in freeing Canadian farmers from the monopolistic practices of the Canadian Pacific Railway and the Canadian National Railway. Dufferin Construction and its competitors became the agents for implementing the goals and objectives of the Good Roads Movement. This policy of building better roads for its constituents was adopted by all the major Ontario political parties. From the United Farmers of Ontario under E.C. Drury to Conservative Premiers Howard Ferguson and George Henry to the Liberal onion farmer, Premier Mitchell Hepburn, in the Depression ridden 1930s. The policy lasted into the early years of the Second World War.

9. Dufferin Construction Purchases Dominion Shipbuilding Property

As his wealth grew, Franceschini looked for other investment opportunities. In 1924 he purchased the bankrupt Dominion Shipbuilding property on the advice of one of his managers, Thomas Murphy. The property, located on Toronto's waterfront at the foot of Bathurst Street, had gone into receivership and into the hands of the City of Toronto.

Charges of corruption started to fly a few years later as the opponents of Toronto's colourful Mayor Thomas Church accused him of selling the shipyard at a price that was too low to Dufferin Construction and allegedly subjected to corrupt practices by James Franceschini. The original purchase price asked by Church was $30,000. But after complaints by Alderman Gourlay and Colonel W.G. MacKendrick, a member of the Toronto Harbour Commission, Franceschini agreed to pay the higher price of $40,000.[12]

In 1927, a commission of inquiry headed by Judge Denton found Church and Franceschini innocent of wrongdoing. Ironically, the accuser, Colonel MacKendrick, was himself in a unreported conflict of interest because a company in which he had a small interest profited by having MacKendrick on the Harbour Commission.[13]

10. The Purchase of Myrtle Villa

In 1925, Franceschini moved from Dufferin Street and into a large Mimico estate that he purchased for $150,000 from A.B. Ormsby, a manufacturer of metal doors and window frames, who had built the mansion in 1906. The property became known as Myrtle Villa, named after his young daughter.[14]

11. North American Hackney Horse Champion

As a young boy in Italy, it was Vincenzo's job to care for the large draft horses that pulled his father's porcelain wares wagon. He fell in love with those animals, and soon became an experienced hand at training and driving them. Once he had acquired the where-with-all to revisit his equine love affair, he did so relentlessly. To relax and get away from the pressures of running a major road construction, Franceschini took up the aristocratic sport of hackney horse competition and his stable of horses, Dufferin Stock Farms, soon dominated the field. In 1928 Franceschini was among the top Hackney Horse competitors in North America, winning a prestigious competition in Madison Square. His dominant performance merited a write up in *Time Magazine*:

> ... [L]ast week, a coach was pulled around the arena, in Madison Square Garden, Manhattan, by four horses which belonged to Mrs. Frederic Cameron Church, once Muriel Vanderbilt. Three other coaches also rolled around the ring; and the best was judged to be one entered by James Franceschini, a onetime day laborer, out of Toronto.[15]

12. Giving Back to the Community

Franceschini was very generous with his accumulated wealth, supporting the Conservative Party and becoming involved with the Masons. In 1930 when the Shriners held their annual convention in Toronto, the Franceschinis hosted a mammoth garden party reception for 600 guests at their Mimico home.[16]

Likewise Annie immersed herself in good works including the Daughters of the British Empire. In 1937 she hosted a garden tea for the International Order of the Daughters of the Empire under the auspices of the Mimico Chapter.[17]

13. Canada and Fascism

The 1930s were years of economic upheaval. The depression was sweeping across Canada, the United States and around the world.

Everywhere there was fear of social upheaval. Western democracies like Canada, the United States and Great Britain were impressed by the stern hand of Benito Mussolini and how it kept the communists and socialists at bay.

In Canada, the Empire Club, the most formidable of social clubs for Toronto's Anglo-Saxon elite, carried a series of lectures by pro-fascist speakers as well as some offering an anti-fascist perspective such as a speech given by Grattan O'Leary. Among Canada's elite there was fascination with the fascist experiment or the Italian Plan as some called it. If not total and outright support, there was enough interest that the Empire Club featured speeches by pro-fascist Magistrate Alfred Jones, Mario Colonna, Italy's Consul General, and Professor William Sherwood Fox who, though emotionally averse to fascism, could academically praise some of the successes experienced by Italy under Mussolini.[18]

Fox praised Mussolini for upholding Christian moral values threatened by both communists and capitalists alike: "It is my own conviction that, despite many acts of Mussolini and his fellow fascists that we may rightly censure, they were, at least at the outset, truly 'vindicators of moral values' that had been forgotten by Bolshevist and Conservative alike." He heaped adoring praise on the Italian fascists: "Broadly speaking, the Fascists are the best men of the younger generation of Italians, and by the best I mean the best educated, the most self-sacrificing in their patriotism and the most industrious. The organization exists; on the one hand, to oppose and suppress Bolshevism ... There is no doubt that the one human being who is responsible for the stemming of the tide of Bolshevism in its westward flow is Mussolini."[19]

The Empire Club's fascination with fascism continued into 1934 when they invited the Italian Consul General in Toronto, Don Mario Colonna, to give a speech on January 11, 1934.[20] A month after Colonna's Empire Club speech, James and Annie

Franceschini, being the leading notables of the Italian community in Toronto, hosted a reception for Piero Parini, Mussolini's Minister of Foreign Affairs and Responsible for Italians Living Abroad. Parini was treated with great cordiality by the Canadian government and members of the Italian community and his visit was covered warmly by newspapers like the *Toronto Star* and the *Globe and Mail*.[21]

The *Toronto Star* reported on Parini's visit not only in its news section, but also on its social pages. In the society pages the *Star* wrote about the Canadian dignitaries who welcomed Parini to Toronto at a reception at the Royal York Hotel: "Among the guests registered at the Royal York Hotel are: His Excellency Piero Parini, and Mr. Franco Montanari, Rome Italy, Mr. L. Petrucci, Ottawa, Mr. I. Pitbaldo, Winnipeg, Mr. Donald M. Sutherland, Ottawa, Mr. J.H. Thom, Detroit, Mr. A.M. Irvine, Westmount, Que., Mr. T.R. Enderby, Montreal, and Mrs. Irene McKee, Montreal."[22]

During the early to mid 1930s, many public figures like Prime Minister William Lyon Mackenzie King, British Fabian socialists Beatrice and Sidney Webb and George Bernard Shaw sang the praise of Mussolini. But none did so as publically and as glowingly as the former King Edward VIII and his lover Wallace Simpson who had a deep and profound love for fascism. The *Globe and Mail* wrote: "Duke hailed in Italy Gives Fascist Salute to Hysterical Crowds; Responds to tumultuous receptions at Milan and Venice with his arm upraised a la Duce's. Greeted as 'king'."[23]

But Franceschini's good fortune would soon come to an abrupt end. Despite an impeccable loyalty to Canada, Franceschini would be accused by a group of anonymous civil servants, secretive Cabinet Ministers and secret agents, some possibly from within the Italian community.

14. The Arrest and Internment of James Franceschini

June 10th 1940 had no special significance for Franceschini, at least not yet. But that something significant was about to happen was obvious to him, because he was called back from an east coast swing that included a meeting with Nova Scotia Premier Angus Macdonald. During the meeting, a secretary handed the Premier a piece of paper. Macdonald read it, shook his head slowly, then looked up and said to the man across from him: "Mr. Franceschini, it is from Ottawa. Italy has entered the war on the side of the Axis. We are at war with Italy."[24]

The very next day, Franceschini received a phone call from his wife requesting that he come home immediately. She had met with two men at Myrtle Villa who identified themselves as RCMP officers, and who had requested his presence in Toronto. Based on that call and those from his management team at Dufferin Construction, he cut short his trip to Nova Scotia.[25] But what was this all about? No doubt it had something to do with Canada's war effort. Ten months earlier, on September 1, 1939, Franceschini had turned over the use of Dufferin Shipbuilding to the Canadian Department of Munitions and Supply for the token sum of a dollar. In addition, he agreed to the rock-bottom price of $550,000 for constructing naval minesweepers.[26]

Around the time of the incorporation of Dufferin Shipbuilding on March 29, 1940, Franceschini had a most unusual meeting with an individual in Ottawa's Chateau Laurier Hotel. This man, whose name Franceschini would never divulge, identified himself as someone who had been in the shipbuilding business a lot longer than Franceschini. According to Franceschini, this individual said his company had built minesweepers for $750,000, "so what the hell are you doing building them for $550,000? Are you trying to wreck the whole goddam business?"[27] As troubling as this meeting was, Franceschini held firm contracts for Dufferin Construction to build military airport runways, and for Dufferin Shipbuilding to build four minesweepers. At the same time, he had been consulted by the Ministry of War on questions concerning ship production.[28]

15. The Daughters of the Empire and the Conservative Party

There was no mistaking Franceschini's love and devotion to Canada, the country that allowed his talent for road building to blossom and in the process become financially comfortable. On April 23, 1940, a month and half before his arrest, Annie hosted a meeting of the Daughters of the British Empire.[29]

Franceschini had supported his beloved Conservative Party financially and philosophically. He was friends with many of the leading Canadians, including former Prime Ministers, Premiers, industrialists and prominent lawyers. In 1934, the year that he hosted a relatively minor reception for Italy's Foreign Minister, he also hosted a massive political rally for Conservative Ontario Premier George Henry and the Minister of Highways, Leopold MacCauley, at his Dufferin Stock Farm, a rally attended by an estimated 10,000 citizens of Italian heritage. During the picnic, Franceschini exhorted the revelers to vote for his friend MacCauley and the Conservative Party.[30]

"You often come to me for work and other favours," Franceschini told the picnickers. "Then I have to go to some of my best friends so that I can get those favours for you." He had always found MacCauley a square shooter, he said. "If I said to him I want so many Italians to go in my job, he always allowed me to do it. (Note: Government contracts usually specified that 90% of jobs had to go to people of British descent.) I want to tell you to appreciate what he is."³¹

But as Franceschini headed back to Toronto by train, he missed William Lyon Mackenzie King's radio broadcast to the nation. At 10 p.m., King confirmed Italy's declaration of war against Britain, and Canada's entry into that war in support of Britain. He also announced that… "the Minister of Justice had authorized the RCMP to intern all residents of Italian origin whose activities have given ground for the belief or reasonable suspicion that they might in time of war endanger the safety of the State or engage in activities prejudicial to the prosecution of the war."³²

16. Arrest of James Franceschini

Upon his arrival in Toronto, Franceschini was visited by two RCMP Officers. He asked what the purpose of their visit was. One of the officers responded simply that he, James Franceschini, was under arrest and that he was going to be taken to RCMP Toronto Headquarters for arraignment. While being arraigned at RCMP Headquarters on Jarvis Street, Franceschini surrendered personal belongings including:

- a Colt revolver, two boxes of ammunition which he was licensed to carry since the threats against his young daughter in 1933
- three files of correspondence
- one small notebook, one letter and a record book
- his naturalization certificate and his car and driver's license
- one diamond ring (3 diamonds), one stick pin — diamonds and emeralds, one button — diamonds and rubies
- one pair diamond studded cuff links, one cigar lighter, one gold pocket knife and one gold pencil
- $77.50 in cash.³³

Later that day he was escorted to a reception centre in the Automotive Building in the Canadian Exhibition Ground that had been set up as an intake centre for suspected enemy aliens. There he saw a lengthy line of Italian Canadians being processed for shipment to an internment camp located at the military base called Camp Petawawa near Ottawa.[34]

A policeman had previously played an important role in Franceschini's life. Arriving in Toronto, he was to be met by a family acquaintance. But the man never showed. On his own, not knowing anyone else, he sat alone in Toronto's Union Station until a Toronto policeman approached him. Although they spoke different languages, the officer quickly deduced that this young man needed a place to sleep. Franceschini was escorted by the policeman, a dutiful, but kind-hearted officer who even carried one of his bags.

The police officer took him to a rooming house owned by an Italian-Canadian on Elm Street, in what was the original Little Italy in Toronto in the University and Dundas Street West area. It was about a half hour walk from the station where he had arrived by train from Ellis Island, New York. The next day, Franceschini found his first job. He was brought to work at the Canada Foundry Plant located on Royce Street (now DuPont Street) and Lansdowne Avenue.

As he was being processed for internment, Franceschini's mind may have raced to those first moments in Canada. Both times his fate lay in the hands of a Canadian police officer. This time the police officers and the soldiers at the Automotive Building were crass and crude as they ordered the men about, often at bayonet point.[35]

On June 15, 1940, he thought back to how he started with nothing, made and lost millions and made millions again. Now for the second time in his life, all that he had built up for himself, for his family, for his country, was being taken away for something over which he had no control: a distant war involving Italy, the place of his birth, and Canada, his adopted country.[36]

17. Franceschini's Police Arraignment

On the day of his arraignment the *Toronto Star* reported that the usually affable, genial contractor, "whose brown eyes dance like jewels when he smiles", appeared a different man when he walked into Toronto Police headquarters. His cheery, "Hello!" was gone. He looked pale and appeared worried. He was accompanied by an RCMP plainclothes escort. He was photographed and fingerprinted by Detectives Hedley Ashford and Oliver Borland in the fingerprint bureau.[37]

18. Custodian of Enemy Property Confiscates Franceschini's Property

In addition to having his liberty taken away, Franceschini also had his company, properties, and financial assets seized and put under the control of a crown agency with the Orwellian name of "The Custodian of Enemy Property." No charges were read against Franceschini; no conviction was obtained on those unknown charges. Yet the fortune Franceschini had accumulated was taken away.

The *Toronto Star* reported on June 18, 1940 "that all property and companies of James Franceschini, Toronto millionaire contractor, have been tied up by the Canadian Custodian of Enemy Property for the duration of the war, it was announced today. If however, custodian officials said, Franceschini, who is appealing against his internment, can establish that he is innocent and is not an enemy alien and thereby secure his release, the property and companies will be handed back to him. Should Franceschini be kept in internment until hostilities are over, it will depend on government policy or the terms of any treaty of peace as to what disposition will be made of his property and companies. The Canadian Custodian of Enemy Property, who is Hon. Pierre Casgrain, Secretary of State, acts in a dual capacity. He is trustee for Franceschini and also is protecting the interests of the creditors of Franceschini in administrating his property and companies."[38]

A financial survey of the Franceschini's interests was underway by Price Waterhouse and Company but until it was completed an estimate of the value of Franceschini's companies was not available. The custodian had power to wind up any of these companies at any time if he considered it in the public interest. The officials went on to say: "However, it was expected that contracts which Franceschini's companies have for shipbuilding ... for the building of mine sweepers and airports are likely to be completed. D.B. Carswell, the Director of Shipbuilding in the Department of Munitions and Supply, was put in charge of Dufferin Shipbuilding and will oversee the contracts for constructing the four minesweepers."[39]

19. Life in Camp Petawawa

Perhaps the most considerate person Franceschini and the other interned Canadians came to know was the Camp Petawawa Commandant Colonel H.E. Pense. Some guards were described as coarse and cruel, but not as bad as the offensive soldiers at the CNE Automotive Building. Colonel Pense did all he could to see that no man was maltreated. Pense reminded his staff that, strictly speaking, the men were not prisoners and certainly not criminals.

They were internees who in June 1940 happened to be Canadians of Italian, German, Ukrainian, or Russian origin.[40] Yet Pense's civilized and professional behaviour wasn't consistent. For example, when October came and Franceschini began to feel chills, Pense refused a request for a warm blanket.

The internees were ordered out of their civilian clothes and given drab gray prisoners' uniforms with a large red target on their back. They were assigned to work details and lived in military style barracks. Franceschini became the foreman of the road building crew and the spokesman for his barrack, Hut No. 5. During the early months of his internment, Franceschini would pour himself into his work of preparing new roads and repairing old roads. He could often be found working long hours encouraging his crew to work a little harder.[41]

20. James Franceschini Testifies Before Justice Hyndman

Through Leonard's efforts, a team of legal experts was assembled with the help of noted lawyer Dalton McCarthy, long time friend and legal adviser to Franceschini. A lawyer named Forsyth was selected to be his legal counsel when he appeared before Justice James D. Hyndman at Camp Petawawa on July 26th 1940.

Come September, Franceschini was still interned. What was holding up his release? Other men had testified before Justice Hyndman and had been released. Had Justice Hyndman not believed that he was innocent? There was no communication from his legal team, one way or the other. Things got worse when his brother Leonard, who had quarterbacked the efforts to free him, was himself interned in September.[42] This deepened Franceschini's dismay. He worried that Leonard may have been interned because of his persistence in trying to get him out of Camp Petawawa.

Franceschini also worried about the state of his companies. Word reached him that the Custodian of Enemy Property and D.S. Carswell were running them into the ground. The minesweepers were behind schedule and the Custodian of Enemy Property was mismanaging his road building operations.[43] The Custodian had acquired control of all of Franceschini's assets including the cement plant in Montreal. The Custodian took the liberty of selling off the cement making equipment to a competing company. This action rendered meaningless the newspaper quotes in which he gave assurances that the assets of interned men would be held in trust and returned to them if found innocent.

Franceschini's lawyer, Dalton McCarthy, who had strong connections with the Liberal Party, told him in October 1940 that "there was some opposition to his release by certain competitors in the Province of Quebec who are holding things up. These people have started a whispering campaign against you, which has influenced the Minister of Justice, Ernest Lapointe." McCarthy was quoted as saying: "To imprison a man without proving charges against him in order to sell his business from under him while he is in a hapless state is indeed a novel way to get rid of a competitor."[44]

21. Justice Hyndman's Findings

On December 18, 1940, Justice Hyndman presented his report on Franceschini to the Minister of Justice Ernest Lapointe. It is a succinct, five pages long, well written and well reasoned dissection of the flimsy charges against him. However, this report was released only to certain high ranking political individuals, and not to parliament as a whole and certainly not to the general public or the media.

In his introduction to the report he wrote: "Owing to the public interest which has been taken in this case, I have given it, perhaps, more than the usual consideration — I may say that I have never heard of anyone with so many enemies and so many friends. Many articles have been written and published concerning this man, a good deal of which I have read and analyzed, some of which is true, and a great deal imaginary."[45]

Justice Hyndman saw his task as ascertaining whether or not Franceschini, if freed, would be a danger to the Canadian State in view of the war between Canada and Italy. In other words, Justice Hyndman's task was to determine if Franceschini was loyal to Canada, or Italy, to the extent that he would harm Canada to benefit Italy.

22. Charges Against Franceschini

Justice Hyndman listed specific charges against Franceschini as being that he:

a) was associated with the fascist Party and the Dopolavoro,
b) made financial contributions to the various fascist organizations in Canada,
c) "and in view of the above, you appear to be disloyal to Canada."[46]

Hyndman summarized Franceschini's testimony beginning with the story of how he immigrated to Canada at age 15 without money, education or friends. Hyndman said Franceschini's success in the business world had been truly remarkable:

"Starting out as a pick-and-shovel man, he has now reached the stage where he controls the Dufferin Paving Company which, in turn, controls sixteen subsidiary companies doing business in many parts of the Dominion. He considers himself worth seven or eight million dollars. He lives in a palatial home near Toronto, with extensive gardens, and has stables with 70 or 80 valuable show-horses. His hospitality seems to know no bounds and, according to the evidence of some of his witnesses, he seems to take immense pleasure in entertaining his friends and others. His wife is a Canadian of Scottish descent, and he also has one daughter who has been liberally educated and is described as a charming young girl. He is a Protestant in religion, and is a member of the Masonic Order."[47]

23. Hyndman Rejects Claim Franceschini a Fascist

Hyndman noted that Franceschini stoutly maintained under oath that he was not a fascist, and did not belong to the Fascio or Dopolavoro, and in fact knows nothing of fascism or fascist doctrines. Hyndman wrote: "Certain facts appear to be considered as reasonable proof that he is a fascist. For instance, in 1934, he lavishly entertained one, Parini, Minister for Overseas Affairs in Mussolini's cabinet, and on this occasion presented Parini with two fine horses, one of which, at the latter's request, was shipped to Mussolini at Rome. Some of the witnesses herein-after mentioned testified that gifts of horses by Franceschini were not unusual."[48]

Hyndman said that he gave Franceschini's reception and gift to Parini, much consideration ... "and am bound to say that, regarding the time when this occurrence took place, as well as the prominence of Franceschini among the Italians and the conveniences which he possessed for the entertainment of people of prominence, such as Parini undoubtedly was, I cannot justly draw the inference that this was proof of disloyalty on the part of the objector, but ought to be looked upon as a very natural set of hospitality on his part."[49]

24. Franceschini and the Casa D'Italia

Hyndman next considered the allegation that Franceschini had given $15,000 to the building fund of the Casa D'Italia in Toronto. Justice Hyndman dismissed this allegation and its worthiness as evidence: "The alleged proof of this was such that no Court of law in this country would accept." Hyndman reported that a thorough examination of Franceschini's books by the Custodian of Enemy Property failed to reveal any such contribution. Furthermore, the price of the property purchased for the Casa D'Italia was $23,000, according to the Land Titles Office records, and of this, $5,000 was paid in cash, the balance being secured by mortgage: "I am satisfied that Franceschini did not make this gift."[50]

25. The Strange Mr. Vetere

Camillo Vetere was a man whose name surfaced in many of the cases of interned Italian-Canadians heard by Justice Hyndman. Often, accusations made by Vetere led to innocent people being interned. Who was Camillo Vetere? He was a writer for several Italian-Canadian publications, some of which had definite pro-fascist slants. He was also a circulation promoter and advertising salesman for many of the Italian Canadian publications in the Montreal-Toronto corridor. But more than that, Vetere was the secretary for the Montreal Fascio.[51]

Justice Hyndman dismissed Vetere's evidence. Hyndman wrote: "The only serious evidence tending to prove that he gave money to the Casa D'Italia is found in the answer 'Si' (Yes) to a question in a subscription form for a book to be published called 'Oltremare'. The question was: 'Did you contribute to the building of the Casa D'Italia?' — This book was to be a sort of 'Who's Who' amongst prominent Italians in Canada. Franceschini admitted to signing the form, but swore that the various items were filled in by one, Vetere, to complete the essential data of his life ... such as place of birth, age, business, etc., etc. Franceschini's evidence in this respect was corroborated by one, Vistarchi, who claimed to be the originator of the scheme and who accompanied Vetere at the time. On this point I believe Franceschini and Vistarchi. Whether or not he contributed $100 to the Casa D'Italia of Hamilton is a matter of doubt. Franceschini did not deny it, but had no recollection of it. However, in view of the many donations given by Franceschini to all kinds of institutions, if he did contribute this $100, I do not consider it of any serious importance."[52]

26. Hyndman Rejects Other Key Government Accusations

Justice Hyndman also rejected the government of Canada's accusations:

- That he contributed gold to Italy during the Ethiopian crisis.
- That he contributed to the Government of Italy or its agents.
- That being the President of the Italian Chamber of Commerce (in Canada) was proof of Franceschini being a fascist. Hyndman found that the Chamber was established only to promote trade between Canada and Italy. Also the organization was established several years previously and could see no disloyalty on Franceschini's part.[53]

Hyndman also rejected the argument that a decoration or title he received from the King of Italy in 1934 showed he was disloyal to Canada: "The accused explained that this was given him chiefly because of his success as a businessman of Italian origin in Canada and had no political significance so far as he was concerned. He pointed out as well that several other distinguished Canadians received the same honour, including Canon Cody, the President of the University of Toronto, Brigadier-General Mitchell, as well as Mayor Camillien Houde, of Montreal."[54] Hyndman concluded that he was "... satisfied that it has no real significance in determining the point at issue."

After considering and rejecting all the points raised by the government of Canada that questioned Franceschini's loyalty, Hyndman next considered the favourable attributes possessed by Franceschini. Hyndman pointed to Franceschini's generosity: "It is on record before me that he was extremely generous in these donations to all kinds of Societies, regardless of race or religion. Has given generously to Jewish, French-Canadian Roman Catholic and Protestant organizations, and, according to his own account, was continually assisting poor Italians, as well as persons of other nationalities. A statement filed with me by the Custodian shows that over a period of a few years he had made donations of this nature amounting altogether to about $10,000."[55]

Other proof of Franceschini's loyalty to Canada cited by Hyndman was the fact he purchased $300,000 of Dominion of Canada War Bonds of 1939, and within a few days of the outbreak of war, Hyndman noted Franceschini had telegraphed several of the heads of the Dominion and Provincial governments, including Prime Minister MacKenzie King and Premier Hepburn, as follows: "In order to assist in the present national emergency I wish to place at the Government's disposal the entire resources in plant equipment and personnel of the Dufferin Construction and its associated companies. The services of the organization including executive officers and technical staff are available immediately. My personal services in any capacity in which I can be of use are at the Government's call without remuneration." According to Hyndman: "I do not see any reason to doubt his sincerity with regard to this offer."[56]

Hyndman next pointed to the list of witnesses who came forth to testify on his behalf. The list included:

- Hon. Mitchell Hepburn, Premier of Ontario.
- Hon. Victor Marchand, Member of the Legislative Council of the Province of Quebec.
- D.L. McCarthy, K.C. Treasurer of the Law Society of Upper Canada and President of the Canadian Bar Association.
- Robert N. Smith, Deputy Minister of Highways for the Province of Ontario.
- Charles Johnston, President of the Dufferin Paving Company.
- Norman Holland, President of The Brandran-Henderson Co. of Montreal.
- Charles Jules de Baillets, Chief Engineer of the Water Supply Board of the City of Montreal.
- James Ballantyne, head of a large Plumbing and Heating Company in Montreal.
- R.S. McLaughlin, President of General Motors, Oshawa.
- George Campbell, K.C. of Montreal.
- Sir James Dunn.

Justice Hyndman stated: "All of these witnesses were unanimous in testifying that there was no question whatsoever in their minds with regard to the integrity of Franceschini, and that, in their opinion, he is a good, loyal, citizen of Canada."[57]

Finally, Justice Hyndman noted that Franceschini had been in Canada for 35 of his 50 years; that he only returned once to Italy; that he expressed great admiration for Canada and had no desire to go to Italy again. In addition Franceschini made his fortune in Canada and it would be the "height of folly" to jeopardize his wealth and stature to participate in subversive acts against Canada. Franceschini, Hyndman noted, had married a woman of Canadian birth and Scottish ancestry; that he was the father of an only daughter wholly educated in Canada.

Justice Hyndman concluded his report by stating: "In a very careful consideration of the case as a whole, I am satisfied and convinced that this man is not disloyal to Canada, and would not act in a manner prejudicial to the Public Safety or the Safety of the State, and that it would be quite safe and proper to order his release from internment, which I hereby recommend."[58]

27. King Government Refuses to Release James Franceschini

The Mackenzie King government typically released persons that Justice James Hyndman found innocent of the charges against them. Despite having found Franceschini completely innocent of all the charges, Mackenzie King, and his Quebec Lieutenant, Ernest Lapointe, the Minister of Justice, refused to free him.

Why? Because the War Measures Act and the Defense of the Realm Regulations gave King and his government absolute authority to do as they pleased. To this day no credible explanation has been offered by the Canadian government as to why Franceschini was kept interned beyond Justice Hyndman's ruling of innocence.

28. Franceschini's Illness

During the early months of 1941 Franceschini began feeling tired. He couldn't sleep, felt dizzy and his blood pressure swung wildly. Dr. Luigi Pancaro, an interned doctor from Sudbury, noticed that

Franceschini was having difficulty swallowing and then a lump about the size of an egg appeared at the base of his throat. But the camp physicians were indifferent to Franceschini's health. In the spring of 1941, Dr. Pancaro intervened and informed Franceschini that he had cancer.[59] Dr. Pancaro went to the administration building and demanded that a senior doctor from the nearby military hospital examine Franceschini. A military doctor arrived and within a half an hour he confirmed Dr. Pancaro's opinion. The military doctor reported to his superior that Franceschini must be removed immediately from Camp Petawawa and into a hospital for urgent care.[60]

The news of Franceschini's illness reached his office in Toronto and soon the Office of Ontario Premier Mitch Hepburn. Hepburn became incensed. His friend was being allowed to die by negligent camp officers and doctors. Hepburn picked up the phone and called Justice Minister Lapointe. In a brief, angry conversation Hepburn was reported to have warned Lapointe that if Franceschini was not released immediately, he would reveal the real reasons for Franceschini's internment.[61]

On June 21, 1941 Franceschini, still in his internment uniform wrapped in blankets, was rushed by car out of Camp Petawawa to an airfield where he was flown to Toronto and taken to the Christie Street military hospital. Dr. W.E. Gallie, one of Canada's top surgeons and Franceschini's own doctor, C.N. Mooney, worked hard to get Franceschini the best medical care. Mooney was livid at how the Camp Petawawa doctors had neglected him.[62]

Dr. Harold Wookey was selected as the surgeon who would perform the delicate operation. Dr. Wookey had an outstanding international reputation as the finest surgeon for dealing with cancer of the head, neck and esophagus. The surgery would take place at Toronto General Hospital.[63] But Franceschini refused to be operated on unless his brother Leonard was released from internment. The government was in a pickle and even more so if Franceschini died. The entire cover up of Justice Hyndman's finding of innocence; the neglect of Franceschini's health by camp doctors during his prolonged and unjustified detention — all this could explode into a nasty scandal for the government of Mackenzie King.[64] Leonard Franceschini was released from Camp Petawawa on June 27, 1941. The next day, Franceschini was operated on by Dr. Wookey.

29. Cement Making Equipment and Prize Horses Sold

While Franceschini was fighting for his life in June, 1941, the Custodian of Enemy Property was preparing for a fire sale auction of his prize horses and cement making equipment. The Custodian of Enemy Property with its accountants Price Waterhouse kept meticulous details of all the transactions and sales that took place at the Dufferin Stock Farm in Toronto that June 10, 1941, noting the price and to whom the horse or riding equipment was sold.[65]

Among the 28 prize horses sold was Highland Cora, once the dominant North American hackney horse for a price of $15,000. (66) Vindication sold for $2,000, Sir James, named after his friend Sir James Dunn, fetched only $195 and Paddock Lane Marvellous was sold for a mere $90.66 All the transactions were listed on three legal size pieces of paper with the typed names of the Horses and Ponies and description of carriages and riding equipment; and the names and hometowns of the purchasers, some from the United States, others from Nova Scotia.[67]

29. Debate on the Matter of James Franceschini's Innocence

The King government's handling of the Franceschini case and lack of explanations were raised in the House of Commons. These parliamentarians and editorials in the *Globe and Mail* demanded an explanation and they wanted the release of the Hyndman Report. If the Hyndman Report declared Franceschini innocent, why was he still being detained? If he was guilty why was he released? But no clear answers were provided to parliament.[68]

Beginning in February, 1941 and continuing well into 1942, the *Globe and Mail* ran editorials first demanding the release of Franceschini and other innocent men from Camp Petawawa and then demanding explanations for the King Government's continuing incarceration of an innocent man: "Disquieting reports are circulating to the effect that many of the recommendations of Mr. Justice Hyndman concerning the release of persons now held in civilian camps have been disregarded or set aside by the Minister of Justice ... The legal safeguards which protect the common people from persecution and the misuse of authority are a precious heritage which should not be arbitrarily removed from Canada while the people are fighting tyranny abroad."[69]

The editorial concluded by calling for Parliament to "... turn the searchlight of pitiless publicity on the whole system of civilian internment and expose the truth about the fate of the recommendations of Mr. Justice Hyndman after they reached the hands of the Minister of Justice."[70]

On the day of Franceschini's release on compassionate grounds, the *Globe and Mail* issued another hard hitting editorial titled: "Was Franceschini Guilty?" The editorial demanded that the Hyndman Report be made public: "The government has kept its own counsel. It has not taken the people into its confidence, and the public has been left with an uneasy feeling that justice has been travestied in one way or another. It is not necessary that intimate details of the evidence nor intimate details of the judge's report be made public ... It is however necessary for the restoration of public confidence in the impartiality of Canadian justice that the substance of the judge's report in this case be revealed."[71]

After a blistering series of editorials in mainstream newspapers like the *Globe and Mail* and *Toronto Star* about the handling of Franceschini's internment, Ernest Lapointe issued a statement saying he was considering the appointment of a "third advisory committee" to hear cases of persons detained under the Defense of Canada Regulations. To this possibility the *Globe and Mail* replied: "But all the advisory committees in Christendom will avail nothing so long as the Minister of Justice retains complete authority to disregard their advice and to base his final decision, not upon the evidence, but upon the recommendation of subordinates in his department."[72]

Three months after Franceschini's release, Lapointe had still not made public Justice Hyndman's report, leaving lingering questions about Franceschini's innocence on the one hand and grave concern about the mistreatment meted out to an innocent man on the other. The *Globe and Mail* chided the Minister of Justice for failing to heed the recommendations of one of Canada's best legal minds, Justice Hyndman, and instead relying on the advice of his deputy Minister and the Commissioner of the RCMP, who no doubt relied on reports provided by paid secret informants, whose identities were protected by the RCMP and whose questionable information would never be subjected to scrutiny for truth in a court of law.[73]

The closest to an explanation on why Franceschini was kept interned, even though presumably found innocent by Hyndman, was provided by Lapointe to the *Globe and Mail*. Lapointe said he was ultimately responsible for the release of a suspected fascist sympathizer and he did not want to be blamed for releasing someone whom a judge declared innocent only to find the man had perpetrated a serious act of sabotage: "I have worried a good deal about what should be done. If the Judge after having heard witnesses, consisting of the family of the interned man and some others, comes to the conclusion that the man is not a serious danger and should be released, and if the men responsible for the order, the officers of the RCMP and especially those who I trust and in whose judgment I have confidence, tell me on their responsibility that they do not wish to be held responsible for what that man can do if he were left at liberty; then, if I order the release of such a man, and a month or two after such a release a serious act of sabotage is committed, resulting in loss of life, and if such activities can be traced to the man in question, who would be responsible? I would be. The government would be responsible. The judge for whose judgment I would have the greatest respect would not be the one who would be blamed. No: the Minister would be blamed, the government would be blamed."[74]

Lapointe told the *Globe* that his trusted advisors were the Deputy Minister of Justice and the Commissioner of the RCMP; to which the *Globe* responded: "The net result is that justice or injustice is being dispensed not by the court of law, but by the police officials and civil servants who ought to be the servants not the masters of the people ... The most charitable view that can be taken of the whole disgraceful business is that the Minister of Justice has been badly advised by his subordinates."[75]

Many Canadians were concerned that the Minister of Justice may have released a potential threat to Canadian security. Without the release of the Hyndman Report, some fearful Canadians demanded that Franceschini be returned to Camp Petawawa. The *Toronto Star* reported that the All Canadian Congress of Labour voted unanimously to protest Franceschini's release with the Minister of Justice.[76] The *Toronto Star* further reported that Canadian veterans of the Boer War wrote to the Prime Minister: "We most emphatically protest the release of James Franceschini and his brother. We feel that either the government had done grave injustice to Mr. Franceschini and his brother by interning them, or on the other hand, if they were lawfully interned, then the veterans as well as the public have a right to know what were they interned for and the grounds which they were released. And we veterans of two wars feel that such action on the part of the government should not be tolerated when Canada and the Empire have their backs to the wall fighting a common enemy."[77]

30. Franceschini Resumes Control

Franceschini's operation was a success. He recovered and in due time resumed his place at the helm of Dufferin Construction which was contracted to build a portion in Canada of the historic Alaska Highway, needed desperately by the United States military to deliver supplies to its staging points in Alaska for its war against Japan. The praises of Dufferin Construction were heralded at an Empire Club Speech by John R. MacNicol, M.P., on November 12, 1942 on the historic significance of building the highway and the role that Canada played.[78]

The Department of Munitions and Supply however would not return the Dufferin Shipbuilding Company to Franceschini. The *Globe and Mail* reported on April 20, 1942 that the shipyards were purchased from Franceschini for the sum of $975,000 on October 20, 1941 and only revealed the sale under questioning by John Diefenbaker.[79]

Gradually Franceschini's companies, properties and financial assets were restored to him. However, two years after his release, the Custodian of Enemy Property still had not submitted releases to the municipal land titles offices to allow the return of some of

Franceschini's properties. The restorations handled by the Custodian of Enemy Property were quite tardy and messy.

The Custodian of Enemy Property and Price Waterhouse also demanded payment of $54,399[54] or 2% the assets worth $2,719,977[22] that the Custodian of Enemy Property seized from him when he was interned. The Custodian referred to this payment as an "administration fee" for managing his affairs while he was interned. In what was essentially a case of blackmail, the Custodian refused to release their control of $300,000 worth of Canadian War bonds unless Franceschini paid up.[80] Eventually a settlement was reached and Franceschini paid $15,000.[81]

The Conservative Party of Ontario, for whom Franceschini once held a massive rally of 10,000, deserted him and now treated him with distain. Premier George Drew declared during an election campaign that Franceschini would never get another contract in Ontario as long as he was Premier.[82]

Away from the rigours of the business world, it didn't take Franceschini much time to produce winning horses again. By the November 1946 horse competition at the Royal Winter Fair, his horse won top prize in one of the events: "The horse show had a familiar ring to it last night. Grassview Sensation, a chestnut gelding with a white blaze owned by James Franceschini of Toronto, won the five-gaited saddle horse event."[83]

After re-acquiring control of his companies, Franceschini became preoccupied with the building of Dufferin Haven in the Mont Tremblant area of Quebec, to which he would eventually move after selling Myrtle Villa in 1950.[84] Franceschini was brought to the Mont Tremblant area in August 1941 during a low point in his recovery by Mitch Hepburn and J.P. Bickell, an executive with MacIntyre Mining, and chairman of the Toronto Maple Leafs hockey team. The move to Mont Tremblant was made for several reasons, including Franceschini's need for rest and stress free living to restore him to full health. It also allowed him more time to re-establish his hackney horses to prominence.

Franceschini was enshrined in the Canadian Hackney Hall of Fame[85] and so were several horses that he bred including: Dufferin Haven[86] and Dufferin Starlight, winner of every competition in her class in 1966, her novice year in competition and six years after Franceschini's death. Dufferin Starlight also won the Centennial Medal for both the champion harness horse and champion hackney horse at the 1967 Royal.

31. Conclusion

Franceschini was a man who loved his country, and indeed was a main supplier of warships and builder of military airport runways for the Department of Munitions and Supply from September 1939 to June 1940. That Franceschini was wrongfully interned is beyond dispute. The Report of Justice Hyndman rejected every single accusation against him. Despite the absolute finding of innocence, the Canadian government decided to keep him interned, and in the process their negligent treatment of his health concerns almost led to his death. He would have died, if not for the detection of the cancer by Dr. Luigi Pancaro and the intercession of the Premier of Ontario, Mitch Hepburn. A Liberal like Mackenzie King, Hepburn threatened to expose the real reasons this innocent man was held improperly, if he was not released immediately to receive medical treatment.

The fear of fifth column activity was a factor in the way the Canadian authorities looked at Franceschini. Unlike people such as Sam McLaughlin, Mitch Hepburn, Dalton McCarthy and Sir James Dunn, those who made the decision to intern Franceschini did not know him well. They assumed the worst while overlooking the best that he offered Canada. Many Canadians of British stock were strong and impassioned supporters of Mussolini, as seen by the speeches given at the Empire Club, but at least they were British and could be understood. Edward VIII, the former King of England, was a dear and close friend of Mussolini and Hitler. He was spared the hardship of internment and shipped out of the way to become the Governor of the Bahamas. Future Prime Minister Pierre Trudeau during the Second World War held strong fascist and anti-Semitic points of view and took a fancy to driving around Montreal in a Nazi shirt and helmet, but he was never interned.[87]

Also Franceschini's immense ability and personal charm likely scared them. If he could mobilize 10,000 Italian-Canadians to attend a political rally for the Conservative Party in 1934, what else was he capable of? The mistake made by Mackenzie King and Ernest Lapointe was in failing to recognize that all of Franceschini's immense ability was used to make Canada a better place. In answering that question of what else Franceschini was capable of, they forgot to add the key phrase: "What else was he capable of on behalf of Canada?"

This could partially explain the first part of Franceschini's ordeal — his incarceration. However, Mackenzie King and Ernest Lapointe's unwillingness to listen to prominent Canadians who vouched for his innocence — a list that included one of the most enlightened Canadian Justices, James Hyndman; a sitting Premier of Ontario, Mitch Hepburn; two of Canada's foremost industrialists, Sam McLaughlin and Sir James Dunn; Canada's foremost legal expert, Dalton McCarthy; and the editorial staff of the *Globe and Mail* and *Saturday Night Magazine* — indicates that there may have been something else at play in prolonging his internment long after he was declared innocent.

To this day the government has not revealed the reasons or evidence for this. Today one would say that the Mackenzie King government covered up their initial wrongdoing by refusing to release Justice Hyndman's report. The refusal continued to cast a shadow of doubt on Franceschini's loyalty to Canada. The cover up consisted of denying Parliament and the press access to the Hyndman Report. This was followed by obfuscation and tap dancing around the issue by people like future Prime Minister Louis St. Laurent, who took over as Minister of Justice upon the death of Lapointe.

Franceschini always made a distinction between the Canadian people and the Canadian government. Many Canadians came to his defense and fought for his release, and for explanations from the Canadian government on why he was interned in the first place and why his incarceration continued even though the government had a report in its possession declaring him loyal to Canada and innocent of the charges against him. However, others, including leading Trade Unionists and Veterans of the Boer War and a number of conservative newspapers, wanted him to remain interned and were harshly critical of the King government for releasing him even if it was on humanitarian grounds.

The behaviour of the Custodian of Enemy Property can only be described as shocking and bizarre. First by selling off Franceschini's assets including his prize horses and cement making equipment and then for shaking down Franceschini and forcing him to pay a management fee of $15,000 for "looking after" his companies, properties and financial assets in order for the CEP to release Franceschini's other assets. The demand for payment was made even though Franceschini was wrongfully interned and he never requested that this property be managed by a third party.

The unrestrained actions of the Custodian of Enemy Property against Franceschini in June 1941, sadly, foreshadowed the mistreatment that Canadians of Japanese origin received after the mass internments that followed the invasion of Pearl Harbour and after the declaration of war by Canada against Japan in December, 1941.

The Franceschini family has never received an apology — not from the Prime Ministers that succeeded Mackenzie King, and not by Parliament. The Franceschini family has never been offered compensation for the uncalled for sale of assets by the Custodian of Enemy Property that included the Quebec cement plant and cement making equipment and Franceschini's beloved horses.

32. Post Script

In 1960 shortly after Franceschini died at his Mont Tremblant home, Dufferin Construction was sold to St. Lawrence Cement, a Swiss owned company. But the Franceschini family continued in executive positions until the retirement of James L. Franceschini, the son of Leonard Franceschini.

Twenty years after the wrongful internment of James Franceschini, the attitudes towards people of Italian heritage were beginning to change. The massive migration of Italians to Toronto in the Post War 1950s and 1960s led to a larger population base which reached about 500,000 during its peak. There was more of an effort at understanding of Italians by mainstream Anglo-Saxon Canadians and their contributions to improving life in Canada was beginning to be acknowledged.

In 1961 Pierre Berton wrote a column about Italians in Toronto and how Andrew Thompson (MPP, Dovercourt) was spending time living with an Italian-Canadian family on Dufferin Street in the home where James Franceschini once lived before he became a millionaire road builder. Berton hoped that they would be as successful as James Franceschini.[88]

33. Reflections by James McCreath

Resilience, perseverance, and love are the words that best describe my grandfather. After all was said and done, after all the peaks and valleys of his life were exposed and analysed, and after several more cancer operations, he remained true to himself, and to his family. For those of us who knew him, who loved and respected him, he was a once in a lifetime gift. He loved to have fun, he loved to laugh, he loved to enjoy himself, and surround himself with happy people. He would refer to his time in Petawawa as "when I went to college," and he said it with a smile.

When James Franceschini passed in September 1960, his last internment was in Mt. Pleasant Cemetery, in a leafy plot with a horse-shoe shaped hedge. Joining him there in time were Myrtle, Annie, Leonard, and Leonard's wife Teresa: Together forever as a family in Canada.

34. Endnotes

1. Currell, Harvey (April 1967) *The Mimico Story*, 2nd printing, published by the Mimico Library Board.
2. Iacovetta, F., Perrin, R., & Principe, A. *Enemies Within*. University of Toronto Press, 2000, pp. 28-29.
3. Canadian Hackney Hall of Fame (http://www.hackney.ca/hhof/j_Franceschini.html).
4. McCreath Family Archives.
5. McCreath Family Archives.
6. McCreath Family Archives.
7. McCreath Family Archives.
8. Harney, Robert F. (1984). "Chiaroscuro: Italians in Toronto, 1815-1915." From: *Polyphony* Vol. 6, pp. 44-49. Multicultural History Society of Ontario

(http://collections.ic.gc.ca/magic/mt42.html).
9. *Globe and Mail* (Feb. 13, 1914). "Hydro-Electric Extensions to Cost Millions", p. 1.
10. *Toronto Star* (June 15, 1940). "Franceschini Under Arrest Shipbuilding Will Continue to Ensure Completion and Delivery of Mine Sweepers (Photo of Franceschini with cigar in his mouth)", p. 3.
11. Volume 4 Toronto Directory, Suburb, Entry for Dufferin Construction 1926, Franceschini, James, contractor 415 Lake Shore h. P. 1886.
12. *Toronto Star*, (March 16, 1927). "Judge Finds no Corruption in Harbour Land Sale", p. 33.
13. ibid.
14. See Note 1.
15. *Time Magazine* (Nov. 26, 1928). "Sport: Temptation & Friends", http://www.time.com/time/archive/preview/0,10987,732118,00.html.
16. *Toronto Star* (June 10, 1930). p. 26.
17. *Toronto Star* (June 16, 1937). "Hosting the International Order of the Daughters of the Empire," p. 24.
18. Empire Club Speech (Feb. 25, 1932): "MUSSOLINI AND THE NEW ITALY," AN ADDRESS BY DR. WILLIAM SHERWOOD FOX (B.A., M.A., PH.D., LL.D., F.R.S.C.).
19. ibid.
20. Empire Club Speech (Jan. 11, 1934): "ITALY AND WORLD AFFAIRS ADDRESS," BY DON MARIO COLONNA.
21. *Toronto Star* (Feb. 1, 1934). "Italian Emissary Here", p. 1.
22. 22. ibid., p. 36.
23. *Globe and Mail* (June 5, 1937). "Duke of Windsor, Fascist Admirer on his Honeymoon to Italy," p. 17.
24. McCreath Family Archives.

25. McCreath Family Archives.
26. McCreath Family Archives.
27. McCreath Family Archives.
28. McCreath Family Archives.
29. *Toronto Star* (April 23, 1940). "Myrtle Villa Setting for Afternoon Tea Under the Auspices of the IODE", p. 8.
30. *Toronto Star* (June 18, 1934). "Big Party for Conservatives Prior to Elections — Franceschini Picnic Gives Free Beer, Buses and Band," p. 8.
31. ibid.
32. McCreath Family Archives.
33. Archives Canada, RG 178, Interim Container, Franceschini, James (internee), Price Waterhouse Correspondence.
34. McCreath Family Archives.
35. McCreath Family Archives.
36. McCreath Family Archives.
37. Toronto Star, June 15, 1940 p. 3 "Franceschini Under Arrest, Shipbuilding Will Continue."
38. *Toronto Star* (June 19, 1940). "Franceschini Assets Tied Up for Duration Custodian of Alien Property May Release Them If Internment Ends APPEAL LAUNCHED," p. 19.
39. ibid.
40. McCreath Family Archives.
41. McCreath Family Archives.
42. McCreath Family Archives.
43. McCreath Family Archives.
44. McCreath Family Archives.
45. Justice James D. Hyndman (Dec. 18, 1940). IN THE MATTER OF THE DEFENCE OF CANADA REGULATIONS AND IN THE MATTER OF VINCENZO JAMES FRANCESCHINI 40D-4E-179.
46. ibid.

47. ibid.
48. ibid.
49. ibid.
50. ibid.
51. Salvatore, Filippo (1995). *Le Fascisme et Les Italiens a Montreal: une histoire orale 1922-1945*, Guernica Editions, p. 47.
52. See Note 45.
53. ibid.
54. ibid.
55. ibid.
56. ibid.
57. ibid.
58. ibid.
59. McCreath Family Archives.
60. McCreath Family Archives.
61. McCreath Family Archives.
62. McCreath Family Archives.
63. McCreath Family Archives.
64. McCreath Family Archives.
65. Archives Canada Auction Sale, Dufferin Stock Farm Tuesday June 10th, 1941.
66. ibid.
67. ibid.
68. *Toronto Star* (May 5 1942). "St. Laurent defends detention Action in Franceschini Case."
69. *Globe and Mail* (Feb. 19, 1941). Justice by Arbitrary Methods," p. 7.
70. ibid.
71. *Globe and Mail* (June 24, 1941). "Was Franceschini Guilty?"
72. *Globe and Mail* (Aug. 14, 1941). "Mr. Lapointe has Worries," p. 5.
73. ibid.

74. ibid.
75. ibid.
76. Toronto Star (June 24, 1941). "Oppose Release of Franceschini — All Canadian Congress Sends Complaint to Ottawa," p. 11.
77. Toronto Star (July 9, 1941). "Ask Franceschini Facts — South African Vets Send Telegram to PM King," 17.
78. John R. MacNicol, M.P (Nov. 12, 1942). Empire Club Speech.
79. *Globe and Mail* (April 20, 1942). "Paid $975, 000 for Ship Firm Government's Price to the Dufferin Company," p. 2.
80. Archives Canada, Letter to A.H. Mathieu, Assistant Deputy Custodian from Price Waterhouse, September 17, 1941.
81. Archives Canada, World Wide Communications Telegram from A.H. Mathieu, Assistant Deputy Custodian to Price Waterhouse, December 18, 1942
82. *Toronto Star* (June 1, 1945). "Premier George Drew favours competitive road contracts. But not one contract will go to James Franceschini," p. 21.
83. *Toronto Star* (Nov. 1946). "Franceschini back in the saddle resumes horse competitions."
84. See Note 1.
85. Dufferin Haven (http://www.hackney.ca/hhof/dufferin_haven.html)
86. Dufferin Starlight (http://www.hackney.ca/hhof/starlight.html)
87. *The Ottawa Citizen* (June 4, 2006). "Trudeau deconstructed."
88. Berton, Pierre (Wednesday June 28, 1961). "How the Italians Live: How We Have Failed Them." *Toronto Star*, p. 41 6478838224.

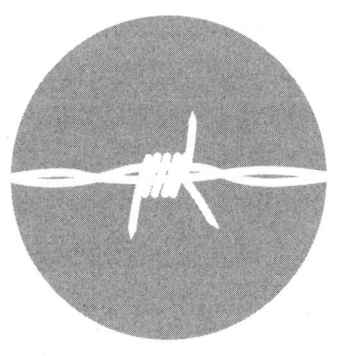

Vittorina Cecchetto

"Don't Speak the Enemy's Language!": The Impact of the War Years on Italian Canadian Identity and Culture

Introduction

When Italy declared war on France and Great Britain on June 10, 1940, the social, political and economic situation of both Italian nationals living abroad and long-established citizens of Italian origin in countries affected by the declaration (including Canada) changed instantly. In the space of a few hours, they were no longer valued members of the community, working alongside other immigrants and members of the "founding ethnicities". Instead they were looked at suspiciously and fearfully as potential "spies and saboteurs," a "Fifth Column" intent on destroying the "English" or "French" way of life.

When disputes between the "new homeland" and the former homelands of immigrants occur, it is easy to assume a stronger link on the part of immigrants and their descendants to these former homelands and to question their loyalty to their new one. This was the situation faced by Italians living in Canada and Canadian citizens of Italian origin during the Second World War (Weinfeld & Massa 2009: 1) when Italy was an enemy nation from June 1940 to September 8, 1943, the date of the armistice between Italy's King Vittorio Emanuele III and the Allies. (But given the existence in Northern Italy of Mussolini's "puppet" fascist government based at Salò and upheld by Germany, the more realistic end date is April 1945.) Because of the imposition of the War Measures Act in June 1940, Italian Canadians faced "officially sanctioned" discrimination, loss of civil rights, and economic hardship. This had a negative impact not only on their physical lives but also on their community identity and culture.

This paper investigates some of the consequences that the trauma suffered during the war years had on the (non) retention of Italian Canadian identity and culture, especially language, in the immigrants and citizens of Italian origin and their descendants. How did those designated as enemy aliens, whether they were interned or left behind to cope with economic hardships and social stigma, come to terms with what their *italianità* had meant and would mean to them once they were released and/or the war came to an end? What was the effect on the *italianità* of those members of the Italian Canadian[1] communities not officially designated as enemy aliens but, by "ethnic" association, subjected to the same discrimination and hardships? What ramifications did this situation have on the manifestations of *italianità* in the years after the war? While the research was carried out in and refers specifically to the situation in the Hamilton, Ontario community, I believe that it mirrors the reality of what happened in other communities in Canada.[2]

From integrated members of the community to pariahs

On August 8, 1935, *The Hamilton Herald* published the pictures and short biographies of seven prominent Italian Canadians (Rev. John Bonomi, Aurelio del Piero, Rev. Charles Mascari, Sam Borsellino, Louis Mascia, Alf Cuomo and Louis Lorenzetti). This was followed by a description of the Italian Canadian pasta company, Cabot Macaroni Mfg. Co. under the headline: "Italo-Canadians Have Helped Build Up Canada. Hamilton points with pride to her citizens from sunny Italy." The article goes on to say:

Today, Hamilton numbers among her most influential and prosperous citizens many Italian-born Canadians who by their industry and perseverance in many walks of life and varied branches of commercial and manufacturing endeavour have materially added to the well being and advancement of the city.

By June 10, 1940, four of the seven "prominent Hamiltonians" praised by the paper would themselves or their family members be declared "enemy aliens," arrested and later interned at Camp 33, Petawawa, or required to report weekly to the RCMP.

As early as 1939, prominent Italian Canadians in Hamilton felt that the community had to publically demonstrate their loyalty to Canada in rallies and speeches, such as those in September 1939 at the Casa d'Italia by Quinto Martini, and by Jerry Ingrassia in June 1940 at the Italo-Canadian Liberal Club (Cumbo 2000: 23-24; Hamilton Spectator, July 25 1981). Or through donations, labour or other contributions to the war effort (Weinfield & Massa 2009: 3). But notwithstanding this public demonstration of loyalty, by the end of the day that the War Measures Act was invoked, 73 Hamilton men had been arrested. Since no one knew why only certain people were being picked up and those arrested were never informed of the charges against them, the Italian Canadian communities in the city — one centred around James Street North and the other around Barton and Sherman — retreated into a world of silence and fear. Italian was not spoken outside the home and, in many homes, English became the sole language of communication. As one person interviewed[3] indicated: "When my father came home from the camp he said that we would be speaking only English from then on. He said that we were not going to be able to be identified by our accent!"

The loss of Italian Canadian identity and culture during the war years

> Language is the key to the heart of a culture.
> — Edwards 1985: 36 (as quoted in Moola 2011)

Most sociolinguists would agree with Edwards that language represents the most important component of ethnicity since it serves not only to transmit the elements of a group's culture within the group but also can be used by outsiders to become part of a community. As Sharifa Moola (2011) indicates: "The loss of language would mean the loss of cultures, identity, heritage, literary traditions, kinship, and so on." Why are languages "lost" or "abandoned" then, if they are so important to ethnic and cultural identity?

One of the reasons can be found in gradual external pressure, what Nancy Dorian (1986: 74-75) calls "tip": "[A] gradual accretion of negative feeling toward the subordinate group and its language, often accompanied by legal as well as social pressure, until a critical moment arrives and the subordinate group appears abruptly to abandon its mother tongue and switch over to the dominant language." For Italian Canadians, that critical moment came with the declaration of war and the need to survive in the "hostile" environment that was created by members of the dominant ethnic communities.

Norman Denison also refers to external pressures to define what he has termed "language suicide," the decision by parents in a speech community to not consider it "... necessary or worthwhile for the future of their children to communicate with them in a low prestige variety ..." (1977: 21). When asked why they felt that their parents had consciously abandoned the Italian language as a form of communication with them and had stopped participating in cultural manifestations in public, many of the interviewees felt that the continuous discrimination suffered by the Italian Canadian community in the years leading up to, then during the war and for a few years after, could be considered strong enough pressure for this switch. Add to this the shame and humiliation of the internment and the strong desire to try to protect them from ever having to suffer the same consequences. For the same reasons, many of the Italian Canadian families at the time decided to "Anglicize" or "Frenchify" their names, either by making them physically resemble the other language — so that *Ardente* became *Ardent*, or the pronunciation of the name was as close to English or French as possible.

The desire to forget what had happened and the almost unanimous refusal on the part of the internees to talk about their experiences in the camps may also be at the root of their switch to English as the language of communication with the children. By no longer speaking in Italian (which would have been the language most used amongst themselves in the camp), this gave them a way of coping with the trauma of their experience. The emotions engendered did not have to be "re-lived" with each re-telling. The term used by many of the internees to talk about the camps — they said that they were "*in collegio*" — is interesting from a connotative point of view. The term in Italian (see the definition in Sabatini-Coletti) is "positive" — a "boarding school" and, because of the expense, usually reserved for wealthy or meritorious students, rather than a "place of confinement" only.

Another immediate result of the application of the War Measures Act was the suppression of Italian language classes offered by the Casa d'Italia, the Sons of Italy or the other associations. In order to help in spreading his fascist agenda outside Italy, Mussolini had instituted free trips to Italy for the children of Italian origin who studied Italian. At least two of the female interviewees indicated that they or someone in their family had been rewarded with a trip to Italy. When the RCMP raided the Casa d'Italia, all language materials were confiscated (along with the building). Italian families who had materials at home very quickly disposed of them, either by burning them or, as another interviewee indicated, by hiding them under some floor boards in an upstairs room.[4]

With respect to cultural manifestations, Hamilton had a long tradition of Italian opera and theatre in the years prior to war. The Italian Philodramatic Society (founded by Dr. Vincent Agro) performed plays from the Italian canon, but also plays written by local playwrights. The Casa d'Italia was home to a number of associations including the Sons of Italy and the Royal Marine Band, led by Alfonso Borsellino (who founded and led a band at Camp Petawawa) and "variety shows" were put on for the community frequently on weekends. Since 1913 the Racalmutese community had celebrated their patron saint's day of Madonna del Monte and, as other groups became large enough, *feste* were celebrated for the different patron saints' days. During these cultural events, communication was effected in Italian, English and sometimes the dialect of the area of origin.

With the decision of many parents to abandon the use of Italian/dialect in the home, this rich cultural heritage began to be lost and would not be revived until the influx of new immigrants started in the post-war period. This situation created a generational "language gap": grandchildren could no longer (nor wanted to) understand and communicate with their sometimes monolingual grandparents. As one interviewee said: "I was embarrassed by my grandmother who only spoke Italian. I didn't want to talk to her." These children would then not transmit their *italianità* to their children, with the result that at least two generations lost their Italian language and culture. It is only the third generation that re-discovers its roots and tries to re-acquaint itself with the culture and learn the language.[5]

Conclusion

There is no denying that the declaration of war by Italy on June 10, 1940 and the invoking of the War Measures Act had a profound impact on the Italian Canadian communities across the country. Not only were a number of men and women interned, without ever finding out the charges against them, but this experience scarred them and their families for at least two generations. Because of the discrimination, the mistrust, suspicion, fear and shame suffered by them, many chose to abandon their heritage and identity, and to assimilate even more into the dominant English or French-speaking community.[6]

But one positive result of this situation was a concerted effort (in some instances subconscious) by the returning internees and those who had been declared "enemy aliens" to "better themselves," to become part of the "power base" so that this could never happen to them again. As William Guyatt wrote in 1981: "Rattle the skeletons in the closet of almost all the professional families of Italian descent in Hamilton … and you'll find a grandfather or a great uncle who was interned." The Italian language, culture and identity in Hamilton was not "lost," nor did it suffer "linguistic suicide." It was just dormant for a while in order to let the wounds of the trauma experienced by Italian Canadians during the Second World War heal.

Acknowledgement

I would like to express my profound gratitude to the following Hamiltonians who willingly shared with me their memories and experiences of growing up during the war years and the effect this had on their Italian Canadian identity, or who recounted to me the stories of their relatives during this period: F. Colangelo, P. & R. Morreale, C. Capponi, J. Ingrassia, M. Romeo, N. Zaffiro, E. Mascia, A. Olivieri, E. Salsiccioli, V. Travale, N. Corrado, M. Goffredo, C. Dorigo and those who wished to remain anonymous.

Endnotes

1. From this point on in the paper, the term *Italian Canadian* refers to both Italian immigrants who were still Italian nationals at the time of the outbreak of war and Canadian citizens of Italian origin who had been naturalized or who were born in Canada.
2. The research carried out by other members of the ICEA (Italian Canadians as Enemy Aliens) project and communicated to me substantiates my belief.
3. Even though these events happened more than 70 years ago, the trauma engendered by the fear and the shame of the internment of friends and relatives still makes those who lived through it unwilling to acknowledge it "publically": many interviewees asked to remain anonymous.
4. The grandchild of one of the Hamilton internees discovered this "treasure trove" of Italian language books — Italian grammar and etiquette books — when the floorboards

of her grandfather's bedroom were taken up in a renovation after his death. They had been hidden for over 70 years.
5. A very honest analysis of his own linguistic situation is given by Ryan Shadford in his MA Thesis *"Has anyone seen my ancestral language?" Italian linguistic suicide and the transmission of the Italian language in Canada, 1935-1947* (Ryerson University: 2009).
6. In the 1980s and 1990s when the issue of redress for the internment of Italian Canadians was again in the forefront, *The Hamilton Spectator* ran a number of Special Articles in which the then remaining internees were interviewed, many for the last time before their passing away, where they finally talked about the emotions and feelings they felt during and after their internment. Please see Works Cited for references.

Works Cited

Brown, Barbara. (1990, Jan. 30). Apology sought for 'outrageous' wartime abuses. *The Hamilton Spectator*

Collegio. (n.d.) In Sabatini-Coletti. *Dizionario della Lingua Italiana*. Retrieved from http://dizionari.corriere.it/dizionario_italiano/C/collegio.shtml

Cumbo, Enrico Carlson (2000). *The Italian Presence in Hamilton*. Toronto: [author]

Denison, N. (1977). "Language Death or Language Suicide?" *International Journal of the Sociology of Language* 12, 13-22.

Dorian, Nancy (1986). "Abrupt Transmission Failure in Obsolescing Languages: How Sudden the 'Tip' to Dominant Language in Communities and Families?"

Retrieved at http://elanguage.net/journals/index.php/bls/article/viewFile/2443/2409

Guyatt, William. (1981, July 25). "The Day They Came for the Italians." *The Hamilton Spectator*

"Italo-Canadians Have Helped Build Up Canada." (1935, August 8). *The Hamilton Herald*

Moola, Sarifa. (2011) *Language Pluralism and Social Cohesion*. Retrieved at http://www.clubmadrid.org/img/secciones/SSP_4_Language_Pluralism_by_Moola.pdf

Shadford, Ryan. (2009). "'Has anyone seen my ancestral language?' Italian linguistic suicide and the transmission of the Italian language in Canada, 1935-1947" (2009). *Theses and dissertations*. Paper 573. Retrieved at http://digitalcommons.ryerson.ca/dissertations/573

Todd, Rosemary. (1990, Jan.18). "Italian-Canadians seek apology for wartime humiliation." *The Hamilton Spectator*

Weinfeld, Morton & Massa, Evelyne (2009). "'We needed to prove we were good Canadians...' A Reconsideration of the Response of Italian and German Canadians to their Wartime Internment." Retrieved at www.surrey.ac.uk/cronem/files/conf2009papers/Massa-Weinfeld.pdf

Wilson, Paul. (1985, Feb.12). "Canada's forgotten Italian wartime prisoners." *The Hamilton Spectator*

John Potestio

The Experiences of Italians at the Lakehead during the Second World War Years

The tragedy that occurred to Italians of Thunder Bay after Benito Mussolini's declaration of war on the British Empire on June 10, 1940 can best be illustrated through the dramatic change in attitude by the mainstream population, the Anglo-Canadians, towards this important segment of the community. Italians had been living in the Twin Cities of Port Arthur and Fort William (the two cities were amalgamated in 1970 to become Thunder Bay) since the early 1880s. During the early decades of settlement at the Lakehead, Italians had experienced a great deal of prejudice, discrimination and exploitation, except for a brief period during the First World War when they found themselves fighting with the Allies.

At a time when Anglo-conformity was the norm in Canadian society, Italians, like many other minority groups, were considered undesirable settlers since they came from a part of Europe whose citizens were deemed to be inimical to British values. The consequence of this harmful attitude resulted in a great deal of marginalization. In the early part of the 20th century, Italians were compelled to live in squalid conditions as the city fathers found it unnecessary to intervene in order to ameliorate the lives of these unfortunate people.[1] Moreover, Italian workers along with members of other minority groups such as Greeks, Hungarians, and others of Slavic background were subjected to such serious exploitation by employers like the CPR that they were compelled to resort to violent strikes in the period 1906 to 1912 in order to achieve some degree of fairness toward their legitimate demands.[2]

Despite these social ills, members of the Italian community managed to integrate successfully into their new country through hard work, finding occupational niches and establishing businesses that bore witness to their entrepreneurial skills. In addition, in order to cushion their sense of anomie, Italians founded two churches in 1912: St. Anthony's Church in Port Arthur and St. Joseph's Church (later to become St. Dominic's) in Fort William. They also founded two fraternal organizations: the Principe di Piemonte Society in Fort William (founded in 1909) and the Italian Mutual Benefit Society in Port Arthur (founded in 1929), as well as the *Cooperativa di Consumo Operaia* (1920) (Workers' Cooperative of Consumers).

In what can be considered a historic irony, the accomplishments of the Italian community over the years were recognized in an editorial written in the Port Arthur *News-Chronicle*. The writer went even further and acknowledged the loyalty of Italians to Canada at a time when war clouds were beginning to appear on the horizon. The editor wrote:

> ... [I]t is noticeable that in a city like Port Arthur no word or comment or criticism of the Italians is ever heard. As a matter of fact the thought that they might have some sympathy for the old land and antagonism for things British never occurs. Their loyalty to things Canadian and their good taste have been such that it is the common thing for Canadian people to discuss the international situation with Italian residents without thought of the possibility that they might be sympathizers of Mussolini.[3]

Less than a year later, the Canadian Government and a significant number of mainstream Canadians at the Lakehead reversed their attitude and relationship to Italians in a manner that betrayed their earlier outlook. It was as if Italians in Thunder Bay in the span of one year had undergone a transformation that defied logic. The reality was that the majority of Italians in the Lakehead wanted nothing more than to continue their considerable effort to improve their lives and contribute to the development of their communities, despite the fact that their homeland was at war with Canada.

What happened to hundreds of Italians in the months following the declaration of war is indeed a dark page in Canada's history. The designation of Italians as enemy aliens wounded them deeply, particularly those people whose children were born at the Lakehead, many of whom had volunteered in the Canadian Armed Forces.[4] Joseph Brescia and Rino Albanese, both of whom were volunteers in the Canadian Army, made this point abundantly clear in the interviews and preliminary discussions the author had with them.[5] According to police records, there was only one man from the Lakehead who was interned: Giovanni "Joe" Maltese, a braggadocio whom the authorities considered dangerous because of his openly sympathetic views on the fascist government of Italy.[6] A far greater number were compelled to report regularly to the RCMP after they were fingerprinted. Once again, Joseph Brescia recalled the humiliation he felt when a supercilious officer interrogated him.

A great many individuals also felt the pangs of discrimination and prejudice and the contumely of many people in the community who now saw Italians as enemies. In 1940, Primo Fabio, a young man who had emigrated to Fort William with his family at the age of seven, was seeking an apprenticeship in a welding course fully expecting to be accepted. The principal dashed his hope, however, when he replied: "Do you think that we should give you this position now that Mussolini has declared war on us?" Needless to say, Fabio was rankled by the insensitive taunt of the bureaucrat who could not rise above the political discord of the time. Undaunted by the provocative response, Fabio answered resolutely if not menacingly: "What does this have to do with me? I am here now. Mussolini is over there." Within a week Fabio got his reply: He was awarded the apprenticeship.[7]

That same year Helena Baratta remembers her husband telling her that she was no longer considered to be a Canadian citizen. She had come to Port Arthur in 1924 with her family as a six-year-old and, as far as she could remember, she had always been a Canadian citizen. Bewildered, Helen asked why she would be no longer considered a citizen. To which her husband replied that, since he himself was not yet a citizen of Canada, she had forfeited her citizenship when she married him. Baratta also recalled that a hydro meter reader who entered her home with an air of superciliousness sarcastically remarked that "Italians jumped on the wrong horse this time." Cowed and humiliated, perhaps even realizing that Italians were indeed on the wrong side, she could not muster the courage to silence the man.[8] Even belonging to an Italian organization was deemed suspicious by Anglo-Canadians as John Defeo, a second generation Italian Canadian, found out when he was called a fascist by a co-workers simply because he was a member of the Principe di Piemonte Society.[9] Little wonder then that, with such experiences as described above, many Italians felt as Jim Bruni did — that they had to "walk very softly."[10]

Fear and shame also gripped Italians at the Lakehead. Helen Strawson (nee Aquino) remembered many young people of high school age who attempted to hide their ethnicity. Her older sister who did some house-cleaning work for the well-to-do was contemptuously dismissed from a particular job because, in the words of her employer, she was "Aitalian."[11] Norma Mortellaro, who later became the Italian Consular Agent at the Lakehead, remembered her family burning Italian books and magazines that might appear suspicious to the authorities.[12] Emilio Marino, a community leader, businessman, municipal councillor and Italian Consular Agent, was under constant police surveillance. On one occasion, the police showed a "little muscle" by forcing Marino to take down the Italian flag which was flying in front of his house.[13]

Almost three-quarters of a century later, it is difficult to ascertain whether Italians as a community were surprised by the actions taken by both government authorities and members of mainstream society. After all, the enmity displayed towards Italians was not universal. There are numerous examples of empathy and leniency towards the plight of a community at odds with its host society. Doris Pomanti and Jim Bruni both lived on Secord Street, then the heart of the Italian community of Port Arthur. Both recalled that there were no major incidents of reprisal against Italians after the declaration of war. At times, even the law enforcement officers displayed unusual leniency and understanding as was the case with Rino Albanese's father. When Giovanni Albanese, a resident of Port Arthur, informed the police that he could not afford the bus fare to Fort William for his monthly reporting, the RCMP officer accepted his statement. Luigi Petrone, a naturalized citizen, was exempted from future reporting as the officers knew him as a foreman of city maintenance crews.[14]

And yet, even before the declaration of war, there were signs that, despite the calm, stormy weather lay ahead. In the winter of 1940 the Italian Mutual Benefit Society had requested a room in St. Joseph's School from the Separate Board of Education in order to teach Italian to children. In March the society received a letter from the Board which stated that permission was granted, but in the last paragraph of the letter the Board admonished the society that it reserved the right to rescind the decision at any time it saw fit. The Board also added that the teaching will be non-political.[15] As Rino Albanese and Catherine Giardetti recalled, the class was well attended by both children and adults, the latter being non-Italian individuals like Giardetti herself who wanted to learn the language of their Italian spouses. Their recollection also underscores the arbitrariness of Canadian authorities once Italians were seen as enemy aliens. After the declaration of war, the class was cancelled without explanation with a simple posting of a notice on the bulletin board of the school.[16]

These are only a few of the many examples of how the war years affected the personal lives of Italians at the Lakehead. But the injury went beyond individuals. Italian associations were also impacted. When a mob of Canadians led by a "prominent" citizen took to the streets to march towards the Italian hall of Fort William bent on causing some damage, the police had to intervene to prevent a potentially humiliating and dangerous situation.[17] Indeed, both Italian organizations, the Italian Mutual Benefit Society and the Principe di Piemonte Society, were keenly aware that some elements of mainstream society regarded them with suspicion and distrust. In fact, even before Italy's declaration of war, the Italian society in Port Arthur was worried about the potential impact that hostilities between Italy and the British Empire might have on the entire community. At a special meeting of the society held on September 6, 1939, the following resolution was adopted unanimously:

> Be it resolved that the members of the Italian Mutual Benefit Society of Port Arthur, be loyal to the British Empire, and abide by the laws of our Canadian Government and pledge ourselves to be loyal British subjects.
>
> We sincerely hope that the good relations between our native land and our adopted country will forever remain.
>
> Be it further resolved that a copy of this resolution be forwarded to the Right Honourable W.L. Mackenzie King,

Honourable C.D. Howe and the Mayor and Council of the City of Port Arthur.[18]

As the months passed and as the potential for war between Italy and Britain became palpable, the anxiety of the Mutual Benefit Society grew in degrees. On May 21, 1940, only a few weeks before war was declared, the society sent a letter to the mayor of the city, C.W. Cox. It stated:

> At a regular meeting of the Italian Mutual Benefit Society, held last night, the war situation in Europe was discussed and considerable concern was expressed over the rumours that Italy may at any moment enter the war against the Allies, notwithstanding the fact that the Italian people, the Italian Royal Family, and His Holiness Pope Pius XII, are definitely against it.
>
> A resolution of loyalty to King George VI, and British Empire, which was passed at a meeting last September, was unanimously reaffirmed.
>
> The meeting gave what a spokesman described as unmistakable evidence that whatever happens, the Italians of Port Arthur, will stand solidly behind the Dominion Government in its war effort.
>
> It was also resolved to send copies of the resolution to G. Taylor, Chief of Police, Hon. W.L. Mackenzie King, Prime Minister of Canada, Hon. M.F. Hepburn, Premier of Ontario, and Hon. C.D. Howe, Minister of Transport and M.P. for Port Arthur.[19]

As necessary as these resolutions might have seemed to the Italian Mutual Benefit Society at a critical time, its subsequent actions were likely intended to further confirm its loyalty to Canada. On

July 4, 1940, a motion to purchase a Union Jack for the hall was approved. Less than a year later, the society decided to enter a float in a Victory Loan Parade. The hall was also made available on several occasions to the Auxiliary Society of the Canadian Legion, the Finnish Auxiliary Society, the Princess Beatrice IODE Society and the Rebecca Lodge Society to raise funds for the Canadian Red Cross and for the war effort. In June 1941, the society bought a $100 Victory Bond and planned a meeting with other Italians in the city to buy more bonds. By the end of 1942, the society had spent $500 on Victory Bonds. That year, too, the society approved several resolutions to hold smokers for the Red Cross.[20]

The Principe di Piemonte Society in Fort William took a similar plan of action in order to display its loyalty to Canada. The society raised funds to purchase war bonds. It also held weekly dances the proceeds of which would be used to purchase War Savings Stamps. By the end of December 1944, the society had purchased $2,604 worth of War Bonds. Periodic contributions were made to the Canadian Red Cross. It even sent donations to help the victims of the London bombings. In 1943 a $100 gift was sent to the Canadian Government as a contribution to the country's war effort.[21]

That the Italian organizations exhibited a great deal of anxiety about how their role within the Italian community would be perceived by the Anglo-Canadian world should surprise no one. Indeed when one looks at the reaction of the local newspapers during the critical week of June 10 — June 17, 1940, one is left with the impression that dark clouds were gathering on the horizon for Italians at the Lakehead. An editorial for June 11, was titled "Italy amongst the Gangsters." Some of the rhetoric would raise eyebrows today, but in 1940 it must have hurt Italians deeply. The editor wrote:

> ... [T]he pages of history will record nothing more cowardly and contemptible than the conduct of Italy... In true gangster fashion Italy chose the moment of her neighbour's [France] preoccupation and distress to drive this stiletto into her back ...²²

Words like "gangster" and "stiletto," the latter term implying a propensity to use the weapon, were handy stereotypical descriptions of the behaviour of Italians which italophobes had used regularly in the past when Italian immigrants were considered undesirable settlers to Canada. Now those old ghosts had come back to haunt Italians. Seventy years later, it would be difficult to assess how Italian people would have felt in reading these lines or hearing about them. But it is not difficult to imagine now how the recipients of these calculated insults would have felt.

During the subsequent weeks after the declaration of war, the Italian community continued to be subjected to a barrage of articles that underscored the precarious situation in which Italians found themselves. In addition to a constant reporting on the theatre of war, the newspaper also featured what must have been worrisome articles for the Italian community. New headlines causing further alarm amongst Italians appeared almost daily: "Several Hundred Italians under Arrest" (June12); "A Wide Arrest of Italian Aliens"(June 13); "All Italians Must Register" [the article stated that only Italians over the age of 16 were required to register] (June 15); "Collect Guns, Explosives from Lakehead Italians, Germans" (June 17); "To Cut Relief from Italians?" [the article reported that Ontario relief officials would not help non-naturalized Italians] (June 17).²³

The headlines in the Fort William newspaper were no less disquieting for the Italian community. The day after the declaration of war, the *Daily Times-Journal* featured an article titled "Canada Standing beside Allies against a New Foe." On June 12 a front-page headline read: "Dangerous Italian Elements in Canada Nabbed in Swift Raids." The following day another headline appeared: "Many Prominent Italians Caught in Police Toils [in Toronto]". In the interest of fairness it should be noted that the *Daily Times-Journal* also posted an article that in all likelihood reflected the real situation within the Italian community of Fort William. In a much more conciliatory tone than in previous articles, the paper reported that the local police had made no arrests in the city and that it had not experienced any trouble.[24]

In addition to reporting on the backlash against Italians of the Lakehead during the first week after the declaration of war, the local newspapers focussed on the reaction of community leaders on the question of loyalty towards Canada and the British Empire. The two spokespersons for the Italian community were Frank Charry (Cerra) and Hubert Badanai, both residents of Fort William, but also well known and respected by Italians in Port Arthur. Charry had been a long-time president of the Principe di Piemonte Society (1932-1943) and a City Councillor from 1933 to 1943. Hubert Badanai was a prominent businessman and rising political star who would later become mayor of the city (elected in 1951, 1954 and 1958) and a Member of Parliament (arguably the first Italian to be elected to this position in 1958[25] and re-elected in 1962, 1963 and 1968). These two men were held in high esteem in both the Italian and non-Italian communities and would therefore be regarded as the "voice" of Italians at the Lakehead.

Though these two leaders used different approaches, their aim was to ensure Canadians that Italians at the Lakehead remained loyal to Canada. On June 10, 1940 The Fort William *Daily Times-Journal* reported that Frank Charry had stated that Italians "view with disgust and deepest regret the actions of Premier Mussolini and affirm their loyalty to the British King and Empire."[26] No doubt, Charry was likely motivated by the possibility that a statement of this kind, made public, would calm the turbulent waters through which the Italian community was navigating in these troubled times. Badanai had the same end in mind, but the means to achieve it was somewhat extreme and likely meant to shock and to have greater resonance within mainstream society. On June 12, 1940 the Port Arthur *News-Chronicle* reported that Hubert Badanai, then a City Councillor, presented a resolution to Council recommending to Fort William Italian organizations, "that they delete from their activities any reference to Italy or to the Italian Government."[27]

We do not know how the community received this news. Likely it did not produce the desired effect because of its exaggerated message. We do know, however, that the Fort William City Council rejected the resolution, no doubt mindful of negative consequences that its approval would have generated. Nevertheless, we can speculate that such a draconian measure — the complete dissociation with their culture and identity — would have been a lot to ask of Italians let alone monitor its compliance. We can only speculate, of course, as to whether Badanai acted alone on this issue or whether he consulted with other Italian community leaders. We can assume, however, that, given the war hysteria of the time and all the consequences thereof, this resolution reflected the panic that many Italians must have felt.

It would take several years before life for Italians at the Lakehead returned to any semblance of normalcy. One of the factors which contributed to this was the repatriation of dozens of war veterans of Italian descent. All of them had fought in the war as Canadians fighting for Canada. Some of them had made the supreme sacrifice. This was a fact that could not be easily ignored by mainstream society. Indeed, the veterans themselves were conscious of the significant contribution they had made to Canada's war effort. Some of them were even aware of the irony that they found themselves in while at the front. As a veteran of the Royal Canadian Navy, Alfred Petrone, then a young man who later became a well-known lawyer, businessman and community leader, put it this way: "While I was in mid-Atlantic on a war ship, my father was reporting to the RCMP as an enemy alien."[28]

It was fitting that a woman — a mother — paid tribute to the dozens of Italian Canadians who had proven their loyalty to Canada as volunteers or draftees in the Canadian Armed Forces. In February 1946, at a testimonial for Italian Canadian veterans organized by the Ladies Auxiliary of the Italian Mutual Benefit Society, Luisa Petrone, Alfred Petrone's mother, spoke on behalf of the ladies of the society. She described the veterans as "brave soldiers who, as heroes of the Dominion of Canada, suffered all the perils of life, fighting bravely, first as children of God, and then as good Canadian soldiers."[29] Luisa Petrone, like hundreds of other parents at the Lakehead, understood well that these soldiers were *Canadian* soldiers. Indeed, a number of the volunteers had even faced the possibility that in joining the Canadian Armed Forces they could be fighting against their brethren in Italy, as was the case with Dave Fiorito.[30] Still, many of them thought it was their duty to volunteer. Fred Bragnalo who was wounded in action in the Normandy Campaign fighting with the Royal Winnipeg Rifles in 1944 recalled that he joined the army in 1942, as he put it, "in defence of my country which was Canada."[31]

Like Italians and Italian Canadians in various other cities in Canada, the Italians of the Lakehead community were subjected to a number of injustices during the turbulent Second World War period. Italians in Port Arthur and Fort William were victims of prejudice, discrimination, taunts, and name-calling — all as a result of the actions of a government in Italy that, with a few exceptions, had very little to do with their lives in Canada.[32] Nevertheless, they became embroiled in the Canadian government's harsh response to Mussolini's decision to join the Axis Powers. The arbitrariness and hasty response by Mackenzie King's government to a non-existent threat by the Italians in Canada was dictated more by war hysteria than any real danger that the community might pose to Canada's war effort. The arrest, internment and the declaration of Italians as "enemy aliens," coupled with the fingerprinting and the weekly reporting to the RCMP, had a profound effect on both individuals and organizations. The shame, embarrassment and humiliation, though mitigated somewhat by a few thoughtful Canadians, ethnic and neighbourhood solidarity,[33] and the hundreds of Italian Canadians who either volunteered or were drafted into the Canadian Armed Forces, lingered for a long time. Many Italians had difficulty affirming their identity for years to come. Indeed, a number of Italian immigrants who settled at the Lakehead in the 1950s found many "old Italians" (*vecchi italiani,* that is, those who had settled here in previous decades) to be aloof and indifferent to things Italian, an attitude that undoubtedly had its genesis during the difficult years when too many Italians were considered "enemy aliens."

Endnotes

1. See *Report on Preliminary and General Social Survey of Fort William,* March, 1913 and *Report on Preliminary and General Social Survey of Port Arthur,* March, 1913. Also see Roy Piovesana, *Italians of Fort William's East End* (Thunder Bay: Institute of Italian Studies, 2011).

2. Jean Morrison, *Community in Conflict: A Study of the Working Class and Its Relationship at the Canadian Lakehead, 1903-1913*, unpublished M.A. Thesis, Lakehead University, 1974, p. 12.
3. The Port Arthur *News-Chronicle*, August 28, 1939.
4. One hundred-sixty individuals (90 in Fort William and 70 in Port Arthur) had volunteered or were conscripted in the Canadian Armed Forces. The larger number in Fort William can be accounted for by the larger Italian population in this city.
5. Interview with Joseph Brescia, May 31, 2011. Interview with Rino Albanese, June 14, 2011.
6. RCMP Records at LAC: RG 18, F-3, Vol. 3563, Part 5, Minister's Order List.
7. Interview with Primo Fabio, November 19, 2001. Rita Van Brundt, an interviewee for the project "Italian Canadians as Enemy Aliens: Memories of World War II," also recalled discrimination against Italians as she mentioned her own father's being overlooked for a promotion in his job primarily because he was Italian. Interview with Rita Van Brundt, June 7, 2011.
8. Interview with Helena Baratta, March 29, 2003.
9. Antonio Pucci, "The Italian Community in the Fort William East End in the Early Twentieth Century," unpublished M.A. Thesis, Lakehead University, 1977, p. 288.
10. Interview with Jim Bruni, March 8, 2002.
11. Interview with Helen Strawson, October 22, 2001.
12. Interview with Norma Mortellaro, April 30, 2002.
13. Interview with Norma Mortellaro.
14. Penny Petrone, *Breaking the Mould*, (Toronto: Guernica, 1995), p. 201.

15. *Letter from Separate School Board, Port Arthur, to Joe Dallas,* March 29, 1940.
16. Both Giardetti and Albanese recalled this incident in the interviews the author conducted nearly ten years ago as part of the research for the book *The Italians of Thunder Bay.* It is interesting to note that Rino Albanese mentioned this incident during the interview for the project "Italian Canadians as Enemy Aliens: Memories of World War II."
17. Pucci, p. 301.
18. *Minutes of the Italian Mutual Benefit Society,* September 6, 1939.
19. *Minutes of the Italian Mutual Benefit Society,* May 21, 1940.
20. 20. John Potestio, *The History of the Italian Mutual Benefit Society* (Thunder Bay: 1985), p. 49.
21. See Pucci, pp. 289-290.
22. Port Arthur *News-Chronicle,* June 11, 1940.
23. Port Arthur *News-Chronicle, June 10-June 17, 1940.*
24. Fort William *Daily Times-Journal, June 11- June 14.*
25. Historical references to Badanai being the first Italian Canadian to be elected to Parliament abound. However, it should be noted that Quinto Martini, another Italian Canadian from Hamilton, was elected as a Member of Parliament in the 1957 election.
26. Fort William *Daily Times-Journal,* June 10, 1940.
27. Port Arthur *News-Chronicle,* June 12, 1940.
28. Interview with Alfred Petrone, November 24, 2004.
29. Speech made by Luisa Petrone to the Ladies Auxiliary of the Italian Mutual Benefit Society, February, 1946. Document can be found in Penny Petrone's papers at Lakehead University.
30. 30. Joe Fiorito, *The Closer We Are to Dying* (Toronto: McClelland and Stewart Inc., 1999), p. 168.

31. Interview with Fred Bragnalo, April 21, 2003.
32. There is little evidence of fascist activity at the Lakehead. On one occasion when Emilio Marino, the Italian Consular Agent, attempted to have the Principe di Piemonte Society and the Italian Mutual Benefit Society join the Order Sons of Italy, an organization with strong fascist leanings, he was rebuffed and received scant attention.
33. Frank Sabatini and Doris Pomanti grew up in the heart of the Italian community, an area that was home to people of many other nationalities. Both individuals felt that there was a great deal of ethnic solidarity during the war years, a situation which, in their opinion, cushioned the blow to the Italians who were now considered enemy aliens. Interview with Doris Pomanti, April 18, 2003. Interview with Frank Sabatini, March 8, 2002.

Adriana A. Davies

The Black-Shirted Fascisti Are Coming to Alberta

1. Italian Patriots in a Foreign Land

Italian immigration to Alberta began in the late 19th century. Individuals and family groups, comprising mostly men, began to arrive to work in mines, forestry camps and the railways. As the West developed and immigration was encouraged by the Government of Canada, Alberta and British Columbia, interconnected as they were by geography and resources, became destinations. The men who came were largely workers from agricultural regions or towns, and passports stated their occupation as *bracciante*, that is, labourer. For many, the goal was to make money and, then, return to Italy to live. Some even returned to fight in Italy in the First World War, returning to Canada to work after it ended. For others, the beauty and opportunities of the land enticed them to send for wives and children, as well as the extended family, and to make a new start. Oral history interviews done in 1973, 1983 and 2001-02 reveal all of these motivations.[1] In the period 1970 to 2000, with Government of Alberta funding, many communities produced history books recounting the personal histories of local families. Based on oral histories and family histories, it is possible to tell the story of Italian settlement in Alberta. By the early 1920s, Italian communities existed in the Venice-Hylo region of Northern Alberta; the cities of Edmonton, Calgary and Lethbridge; and the coal mining areas of the Rocky Mountains and Drumheller. In all, the Italian population of Alberta likely numbered only about two or three thousand.

In Italy after the First World War, communist and fascist supporters fought both rhetorically and physically for the hearts and minds of citizens. In 1922, Benito Mussolini became Italy's fortieth Prime Minister and with him came a resurgence of patriotism and a vision of a heroic national identity based on the ancient Roman past. Mussolini's desire to propagate fascist beliefs to Italians abroad coincided with the Government of Canada's initiative to attract agricultural settlement. According to historian John Zucchi, in 1923, Italia Garibaldi, the granddaughter of Giuseppe Garibaldi, visited Canada to promote the formation of Italian agricultural colonies. Garibaldi and her brother are interesting figures because they link the founding of Italy with fascism.

Manitoba Italian-community historian Stan Carbone in *Italians in Winnipeg* cites a memorandum to file from F.C. Blair, Department of Immigration and Colonization dated Ottawa, 6 February 1923 describing a meeting with Garibaldi. It states that Garibaldi arrived in Canada on December 4 [1922] and expected to sail from St. John on February 10 [1923]. Besides meetings with the federal government, she had meetings in "Winnipeg, Regina and districts, Montreal, the mining districts of Northern Ontario, Toronto, and various points in the Western Provinces, not including British Columbia."[2]

Both *The Edmonton Journal* and *The Calgary Herald* report on her visit fully and it is made clear that she is promoting both fascism and agricultural colonization. In the January 9, 1923 *Journal*, there is a picture on the front page with the following caption: "Signorina Italia Garibaldi, who is visiting Canada in the interests of the fascisti movement in Italy. She is the granddaughter of the famous liberator, General Garibaldi. She is in Edmonton today." The article headline trumpets:

Men Who Overthrew Communists in Italy Would Bring Wives and Families to Alberta Farms

Miss Italia Anita Garibaldi Tells of Black-Shirted Fascisti, Many of Whom Are Eager to Settle in Western Canada

The black-shirted Fascisti are coming to Alberta.

Not for conquest and bloodshed — not for new principles and new ideals — not to overthrow governments and establish something more modern in this most modern of countries — but coming simply to till the land.

With their wives and families, these men who fought a war in the clouds from 1915 onward, waist-deep in the snow of their native Alps, they are coming, fresh from stirring contact with pioneers from the four corners of the earth, to adopt as their future home this land where the skilled and trained agriculturist may be always sure of a living.

The twin themes of the article are that northern Italians are "a good type of settler" and also the "romantic career" of Italia Garibaldi:

> In 1912, Signorina Garibaldi served as army-nurse with the Italian volunteer forces in the Balkan war; after which she was sent to Rio de Janeiro [sic] to start Red Cross committees among Brazilian ladies. When Italy entered the war in 1915, she returned to Rome to take charge of one of the Red Cross city hospitals. In the following year, 1916, she was assigned to a field hospital on the Carso, returning in October 1917 to Rome for leave of absence she undertook the work of organizing a home for refugee children.

Continuing her hospital work Signorina Garibaldi was later in France with the Italian Army corps, which served there. On the Argonne front in 1914, two of her brothers were killed, of the other five, two were seriously wounded while serving during the war in the Italian army. During the last German offensive on the Marne, stationed at Epernay, she followed the Italian troops to the French frontier which she crossed after the armistice into the zone of occupation in Belgium, there during the influenza epidemic caring for the sick until March, 1919, when she took up the work with the Italian peace delegation in Paris.

The article goes on:

Dealing with the Fascisti movement, Miss Garibaldi related the conditions which existed at the end of the war, when her country was in the throes of socialism, when war decorations were torn from the tunics of the soldiers of Italy in the streets of her cities; when factories and estates were taken possession of by the Communists, and when chaos reigned until the everyday people, rising as did the same people of old under the first Garibaldi, swept the forces of Communism before them, and established in the new Italy, a new and democratic government, under Mussolini.

With the laborers giving one hour's work free each day to the new government, and the school children contributing their mites the success of the new government was assured claimed Miss Garibaldi, and it was these same people, who were now coming to western Canada to take up land.

The Edmonton press lionized her. The placing of fascism strongly in the anti-communist camp further endeared her to her audience. Finally, her being a part of a military family and reference to the Communists' attacking veterans would have had her audience eating out of her hand.

Members of the Italian community who heard her speak, and those who met her, would have had no doubt that Italy's star in international politics was rising and they too were a part of this. All they needed to do was to help establish *fasci* in their own communities. This was the logical conclusion.

On January 10, 1923, she visited Calgary and the *Herald* reported:

> Granddaughter Noted Garibaldi Visiting Calgary
> Is Investigating Possibilities of immigration Into Canada Italians Anxious to Improve circumstances
> Outlet for Surplus Population Of That Country Must Be Found
>
> From the narrow mountain ledges of Lombardy where toil wrung peasants painfully carry baskets of earth to get another foot of land whereby the fruits of the soil may be coaxed for their sustenance; from the plains of Venice where every yard of ground is regarded as treasure, and where intensive cultivation has reached the heights of an art, known only in densely populated countries; from these places are looking toward Canada thousands of farmers who hope, if plans in their behalf materialize, to seek their fortunes in Canada, and apply their agricultural art, not to a narrow strip of ground, but to at least a quarter section, a wealth of land, which to them would be far beyond the dreams of avarice.

The article makes it clear that she is an ambassador for Mussolini:

> For the purpose comes Miss Anita Italia Garibaldi, granddaughter of the famous Garibaldi, and a lieutenant of Mussolini, the leader of the Fascisti in the recent revolution which seized control of Italy, and placed Mussolini with the reins of government in his hands. Miss Garibaldi has been sent by the government of the country to inquire into conditions in Canada, and take back with her the information, which will be disseminated throughout Italy by articles from her pen, public addresses and pamphlets from the government.

She continues emphasizing that Italians will make good settlers and describes them as "a thrifty people, a people of a nation with the best ideals, they will come here endowed with gifts which, in the great melting pot of the west will aid in building the new nation of the world." One wonders whether she was the first to use "the great melting pot of the west" phrase, which in the latter half of the nineteenth century came to dominate dialogue around the diversity of both the US and Canadian populations.

She also met with Minister of Agriculture the Hon. George Hoadley and heard first-hand about efforts to promote colonization to a new irrigation district in southern Alberta. In the December 31, 1922 issue of the *Journal*, an article titled "More Settlers, Mixed Farming Alberta Slogan: Southern Farmers Who Have Cut Out Wheat Game Are Making Success" reports on a conference in Lethbridge on December 21 in which Minister Hoadley leads the discussion on "preparations of lands, handling of water and farm programs connected with the Lethbridge northern district, which will produce for the first time in 1923." Involved are representatives from various organizations including the Dominion Experimental Farm, Lethbridge, and the Brooks C.P.R. farm. He reports that bankers in Calgary and other financial institutions are prepared "to assist any sound agricultural enterprise."

Zucchi mentions that, as a result of her trip, fascist locals were set up in Toronto, Winnipeg and Montreal. He does not mention Alberta likely because he was not aware of these sources.

2. The Beginnings of Fascism in Alberta

Italia Garibaldi's visit set the context for the establishment of *fasci* by members of Alberta's Italian community. While a number of oral histories refer to the existence of *fasci* ascribing participation in them to "hotheads," there seems to have been a "collective amnesia" about this chapter of Italian immigration history after the Second World War. This is understandable; for the interviewees, this was a troubling chapter of their lives involving both fear and shame. When they were interviewed in the 1970s and 1980s, this experience was behind them and considered best forgotten. In addition, the interviewees were all elderly so whether the "holding back" of information was intentional or the result of memory loss (or both), the evidence that I had discovered in my earlier research was largely circumstantial with the mention of few names and events. This changed in the period 2000-02 when I began research and writing of key articles for *Celebrating Alberta's Italian Community* website.

Researching the history of Venice-Hylo, the agricultural colony established in 1914 under the leadership of Italian consular agent Felice De Angelis, I found specifics of meetings of the local Fascio.[3] A member of that colony Tony Bonifacio writes:

> In Italy Benito Mussolini had come to power and control of the country and ruled under the banner of the (Fascio) Fascist party a regime that the wealthy did not appreciate, but the poor were much in favor of. The Mussolini rise to power in Italy had a strong effect on some Italians in Alberta, and it began in Calgary. Antonio Rebaudengo organized and founded the Fascist party in Calgary, and having known about the Italians in Venice through Rudolph Michetti, he came to Venice. With Rudolph Michetti, Efisio Manca, and Benedetto Colli the Fascist Party was organized, and formed in Venice. All the Italians became members, got their membership card and were quite proud of what had transpired.[4]

He indicates that the club had about 40 members. Gisella Biollo, daughter of O.J. Biollo, writes in her family history:

> November 25, 1925-Pietro Colbertaldo [from Edmonton], Antonio Rebaudengo and Gafolla [Iafolla, according to Rebaundengo's internment letters] from the Fascist headquarters in Calgary, came to Venice and the Fascio de Venice was officially organized. It was like a club where the members met once in a while as a get-together with never any harm done. Although the organization was allowed in peace time, during the war it was considered a threat to the Allies.[5]

With respect to fascism in Edmonton, there are no written sources; however, there are a number of references in oral histories. For Calgary, there are two keys published sources: John G. Fainella's paper "The Development of Italian Organizations in Calgary"[6] and Antonella Fanella's brief discussion in her book *With Heart and Soul*. Fainella cites an interview with a local Italian (the footnote stated this was done in August 1974), who was extremely well informed about fascism in Alberta. Fainella writes:

> Ovindolo Onofri suggests that a Fascist promoter was active in Calgary in 1922 and formed a Fascio complete with all the fascist symbols, and the beatings for dissenters. The black shirt tactics had to be somewhat moderated in the Canadian environment. For example, a heated encounter in the Riverside consular office between Onofri and the fascist promoter eventually resulted in an attempted appeal by the former against the latter for police protection. Onofri tried to reason with the man and recounts how he admonished him: "You see that with force no one wins? You may win momentarily because you are strong. This is not Italy, that with force either you become a Fascist or you get the 'oil'; here we are in Canada."[7]

Though Fainella does not name the "Fascist promoter" or the individual involved in the "heated exchange" in the Riverside consular office, this is almost certainly Antonio Rebaudengo, who served as the Italian consular agent in Calgary, and who would later be interned. Fainella further notes:

> The *Fascio* in Calgary seemed to have existed as a separate organization outside of the *Giovanni Caboto Loggia No. 8*. The sources did not reveal the extent of the Fascist membership among Calgary's Italian community; yet it seems probable that it was considerable though not as pervasive as in other parts of the country.[8]

He also provides the following information about the Edmonton and Lethbridge *fasci*:

> Edmonton was the provincial centre of Alberta's Fascist organizations which reported and sent dues to the national headquarters in Montreal. As late as 1926 a convention of all Fasci in Alberta was held in Calgary under the direction of a special envoy of the Italian party, a *Sottotenente della Milizia* by the name of Gottad. In 1927, the Lethbridge Fascio was broken up due to internal sabotage.[9]

And:

> Southern Alberta's fascist organizations seemed to have experienced considerable internal opposition right from their onset and apparently never achieved the status and level of activity of sister organizations in the United States or eastern Canada.[10]

It is likely that Fainella had seen the article published in *The Calgary Herald* of Wednesday, December 8, 1926 titled "Alberta Fascisti Forge Firm Ties Through Province," which he does not cite but it is cited by Antonella Fanella. She writes:

> During the 1920s and the 1930s, there was also an active Fascist party in Calgary called the *Fascio*. It seems to have existed outside the *Giovanni Caboto Loggia*, but it is not known whether it was a chapter of the Canadian Union of Fascists. Little is known about the activities of the Fascio, but it was probably more of a social club, whose members admired Mussolini and the glory he was bringing to Italy, than a political organization. At a convention in Calgary in 1926, the *Fascisti* outlined their objectives: among other goals, they sought to improve the well-being of Italian immigrants in Canada and to promote a better understanding of Italo-Canadian culture.

Claims that it was a subversive organization are doubtful, since Italians are apolitical by nature. In fact, at the convention members pledged to "love, serve, obey and exalt the Dominion of Canada and to teach the obedience to and respect for its constitution and laws."[11]

It is interesting that Fanella describes the Calgary Fascio as "more of a social club" since this is what interviewees in various oral histories stated. She goes on to make an untenable assertion that "Italians are apolitical by nature" and that is why fascism did not get a firm hold in Calgary. She does refer to the internment of Antonio Rebaudengo, and asserts that he was the only internee from Alberta. In fact, at the time that she wrote, I knew of two other Alberta internees: O.J. (Oliva John) Biollo and Rudolph (Rodolfo) Michetti both from Venice-Hylo.[12] Since Fanella's thesis and book were focused on Calgary's post-WWII immigration history (that of her own parents and their peers), her lack of focus on fascism is understandable. Perhaps for both Fainella and Fanella it was too soon to write about this painful chapter in the community's history and with the children of internees still alive, it would have created tensions in the community.

On May 30, 2011, at the Glenbow Archives I was able to access the December 8, 1926 article in *The Calgary Herald*, and also found two others published in subsequent days. The second article challenges assertions in the first piece and is followed by a third, rebuttal piece. These reveal that at least a segment of the Italian immigrant community had very strong beliefs and attitudes with respect to the *fasci* in Alberta. The convention was not reported in *The Edmonton Journal*.

The article names the officers of the new entity and the delegates to the Calgary convention. This information is crucial to an understanding of Italian fascism in Alberta — who was involved determined how the party evolved and, ultimately, the context for enemy alien designation and internment in the province. It is also fair to say that almost all, if not all of the founders had heard Italia Garibaldi speak in December, 1923, though she is not referred to in any oral history interview.

The Herald article states:

Alberta Fascisti Forge Firm Ties Through Province

Black Shirts of Italy Have Strong Organization in Four Centres of Alberta — High Aims of Organization Are Discussed At Annual Meeting Held in Calgary — a Provincial Federation Formed

The Black Shirts of Italy, Mussolini's Famous Fascisti, are represented in Alberta by an organization that has sections in four communities and aims within the next year to represent the seven thousand Italians who make their home in Alberta.

Pledged to the principles of the Fascisti, delegates representing more than two hundred of their comrades have just concluded the first annual provincial convention of the Alberta Branch of the order.

Form Provincial Body
The convention saw the formation of a provincial federation in which sections in Calgary, Edmonton, Lethbridge, and Venice, Alberta are represented. Following the general meeting held in the Variety Theatre on Sunday, delegates from the Fascist sections met in the I.O.O.F. hall on Monday and completed the organization of their provincial body.

F. de Angelis, royal Italian consul at Edmonton, was elected provincial president. I. Rader, consul for Calgary and Lethbridge, vice president, and A. Rebaudengo, Calgary, secretary. The executive consist of representatives from each of the existing sections.

Delegates Present
Those in attendance as delegates were: A. Michette, Venice; P. Colbertaldo, P. Butti, Edmonton; M. Sestini, Edmonton; A. Gottarolo,[13] Edmonton; O. Anofri, Lethbridge; P. Credico, Lethbridge; I. Rader, A. Rebaudengo, E. Sgreni, Calgary.

An "O. Anofri" from Lethbridge is listed as one of the delegates and, undoubtedly, this is a typo for "Onofri," who was John Fainella's primary and only source. This would explain why he is so well-informed. What is surprising is that he agreed to be interviewed by Fainella in 1974 and provided him with quite detailed information. It is noteworthy that the Dante Alighieri Society, based in Edmonton, started its provincial oral history project in 1973 interviewing pioneers in centres including Edmonton, Calgary and Lethbridge.[14] It is likely that this initiative inspired and motivated Fainella to begin Calgary Italian community oral histories.[15] This was thirty-two years after enemy alien designation came into effect on June 10, 1940.

The article mentions that a flag for the Calgary Fascio was dedicated, the first in the province, and notes that the organization's intention is one of service to "their own countrymen who come to this province as immigrants." The article points out that they are strongly anti-communist and describes their objects:

> The objects of the Alberta Fascisti, according to the organizers are summarized in the following points.
>
> "To serve with loyalty and discipline the idea of society based upon religion, the nation and the family, and to

promote respect for law, order, hierarch and traditions of the race.

"To love, serve, obey and exalt the Dominion of Canada and to teach obedience to, and respect for its constitution and laws.

"To vigorously oppose all theories and ideas that tend to subvert or disintegrate the nation, religion or the family.

"To educate the inhabitants of Canada of Italian birth to become good Canadian citizens and to encourage and impress on the Italian non-citizens the full performance by them of the duties that the hospitality of Canada imposes upon them.

"To assist Italian immigrants and employ all lawful means to safeguard their interest so long as their interests are in harmony with those of the nation and their rights in respect to employment and their relations between employer and employe[e].

"To promote a better understanding of Italo-Canadian politics, economy and culture.

"To promote athletics."

The language, as can be seen, echoes that of Italia Garibaldi. The convention concluded with a banquet hosted by the Calgary Fascisti in the Hudson's Bay Restaurant. The article is accompanied by a head and shoulders picture of the "royal Italian consul" Mr. De Angelis in military uniform with the caption "Royal Italian consul at Edmonton, who was elected provincial president of the Alberta Fascisti at their convention in Calgary." De Angelis was the founder of the Italian agricultural colony in the Venice-Hylo area of Northern Alberta, which was visited by Garibaldi. Two Albertan internees would come from that settlement.

In August, 2011, Antonella Fanella told me that there was a restricted photograph in the Rebaudengo Collection in the Glenbow Archives that purportedly represented the executive of the Fascio. It was one of the photos gifted to the Archives by Mario Rebaudengo, Antonio and Angelina's son, in 1997. I obtained this photograph and noted that the date of December 6, 1926, in hand writing on the photo, confirms that it is a representation of the founding of the Alberta Fascio. The men pictured are the founders whose names are listed in the article and the majority is wearing fascist or military uniform. While Angelina Rebaudengo was able to destroy any records associating her husband and others with fascism, after his arrest and internment in June, 1940, she apparently could not destroy this iconic photograph. It symbolized pride in Italy, hope for the future and also involvement in an international movement that linked the Italian community with the rebirth of Italy promised by Mussolini. In her oral history interviews, Angelina notes that her husband was a strong anti-communist.

The following day, on December 9, another article appears titled "Many Italians Against Fascisti, Says Alex Picco: Lodge Official Declares no Need for Movement in Canada: Urges Italians to Retain Citizenship: Alleges Intimidation in Attempt to Secure Memberships."[16] It is clear that Alex Picco approached *The Herald* and presented a strong, dissenting argument, which the paper considered worthy enough to publish. Picco's stance demonstrates that the issue had caused dissent in the Italian community beyond the altercation between Onofri and Rebaudengo in the Riverside consular office. The article basically presents all of the points made by Picco and is cited below in its entirety:

> That the reports of the Fascisti movement, its aims and objects, as they were expounded at a meeting on Sunday, were not given to the press correctly is the statement of Alex Picco, grand deputy of the Giovanni Cabot Lodge, which is a fraternal, but not secret society among Italian residents of Canada.

In the course of an interview with The Herald, Mr. Picco declared that at the meeting on Sunday, Mr. Rader who occupied the chair, stated that the Fascisti were going to fight to the last drop of blood in their veins to gain control over the non-Fascisti and that they would mark the name of the Fascisti movement on the big prairies of Canada.

"The Fascisti movement in Canada has been formed, undoubtedly, for the purpose of encouraging Italians to retain their Italian citizenship," Mr. Picco declared. "There are many Italians here who are Canadian citizens and desire only to live in Canada."

Mussolini Anti-Democratic
"In Italy, Mussolini found it necessary to abolish all societies and lodges, and to do away with the democratic principles of government including the election of mayors, aldermen and members of parliament," Mr. Picco continued. "He set up a dictatorship. These procedures are not necessary in Canada. The large mass of Italians in Canada are very good Canadian citizens, pleased with the law of Canada and its government, and they have no desire to support any movement which may advocate for Canada a government such as they now have in Italy.

At the Sunday meeting, also, according to Mr. Picco, Antonio Rabandengo [sic], secretary of the Fascisti party, declared that all those who do not belong to the Fascisti Party are idiots and stupid.

Alleges Intimidation
According to Mr. Picco, the Fascisti movement has between 12 and 18 members in Calgary but the leaders are now trying to increase their enrolment by methods of intimidation, by

stating that unless they join the movement their property in Italy will be confiscated.

That the church does not approve of the formation of the movement on the present foundation in Canada is evidenced by the fact, Mr. Picco declared, that three weeks ago Rev. Father Buchini, of the Roman Catholic Church, refused to dedicate a flag for the members of the movement. Rev. Father Buchini refused, he declares, stating that if he were in Italy he might support the Mussolini form of government, but while in Canada he was a Canadian and therefore has no desire to bring in any controversy among the Italians residing in this country.

Fascisti Press Insulting
"The Fascisti press of Montreal has been very insulting to Italians who do not care to support the movement here," Mr. Picco declared. "Libelous statements were issued and we tried to take legal action against the publication. Although our lawyer advised us that we might get damages we have not sufficient funds to prosecute. At any rate, in view of the fact that the articles appear only in Italian, they have very little effect."

The sub-headings in the article are significant because they suggest that being a supporter of fascism challenges key principles of Canadian life: "Mussolini Anti-Democratic," "Alleges Intimidation" and "Fascisti Press Insulting." By 1926, a few members of the Italian community in Canada had begun to see the negatives in Italian fascism, as they had in Italy.

Picco is articulating the very strong anti-fascist position taken by some of the fraternal orders in the US and Canada. These were particularly entrenched in mining communities in Alberta and British Columbia. Lodges in Alberta included the Loggia Leonida Bissolati No. 5 of the Ordine Indipendente Fior D'Italia (OIFDI), which appeared to have existed from the period 24 January, 1916 to 24 January, 1926 in Lethbridge; the Giovanni Caboto Loggia in Calgary (which Picco mentions and which, according to Mario Grassi, was established in 1918); and the Società Italiana di Mutuo Soccorso, Confederazione Columbiana [Italian Society for Mutual Relief, Columbian Confederation] in Coleman.[17] The OIFDI was headquartered in Fernie but had a branch, the Cesare Battisti Society, in Nordegg, Alberta. These societies are referred to in a range of oral history interviews.

On the 11th December, 1926, a third article appeared in *The Herald* titled "Fascisti Backing Present Form of Canadian Gov't: Respect for Laws of Canada Being Taught, Declares Italo Rader, Answers Statement Made by A. Picco: Seventy-five Per Cent. Of Members Are Canadian Citizens, Leader Says." Vice President Rader is quoted as rejecting Picco's assertions "in toto." Noting that he does not want to prolong a newspaper debate, Rader states:

> In conclusion we would point out that 75 per cent of our members in the city of Calgary are Canadian citizens. Of those who are not yet naturalized, most of them are unable to take out papers as they have not been here for the full period of five years.

The first *Herald* article mentioned that the "delegates represent[ed] more than two hundred of their comrades" as well as "represent[ing] the seven thousands [sic] Italians who make their home in Alberta." The number of Italian residents in Alberta is exaggerated to suggest the power of the Italian community. (At the time of internment in 1940, the federal government lists the population of Albertans of Italian descent at just over 4,000.)

For the historian, the debate in *The Herald* is invaluable because it not only provides a date for the formation of the Alberta *fasci* but also the names of the people involved and their attitudes. It is clear that the formation date is very early indeed, even with respect to the rest of Canada, and can be directly attributed to Italia Garibaldi's visit.

Endnotes

1. The author helped to design and implement the "Italians Settle in Edmonton" oral history project in Edmonton, in 1982-83, as a part of the planning of the 25th anniversary celebration for Santa Maria Goretti Parish. As the Edmonton President of the National-Congress of Italian-Canadians (as well as Alberta Region), from 1986-92, she became involved in the request for an apology from the Government of Canada for internment during World War II. In 2001-02, as the creator of the *Alberta Online Encyclopedia* (www.albertasource.ca), she developed the *Celebrating Alberta's Italian Community* Website, a multimedia website that explores Italian settlement in Alberta in a national context. Excerpts from various oral histories appear on the site and all of the key essays including the fascism and "Internment" articles were written by the author.
2. According to the Ellis Island website an Italia Garibaldi arrived in New York on September 14th 1924 from the Port of Napoli. She is listed as single and 38 and her last place of residence is listed as New York, New York.

Retrieved July 27, 2011, URL: http://www.ellisisland.org/search/passRecord.asp?MID=08174181810237759168&FNM=ITALIA&LNM=GARIBALDI&PLNM=GARIBALDI&CGD=F&first_kind=1&last_kind=0&TOWN=null&SHIP=null&RF=5&pID=600655010009
Cited by Stan Carbone from a document in the Provincial Archives of Manitoba, p 100.

3. The primary source of information about this Italian agricultural colony is *Hylo-Venice: Harvest of Memories*, published in 2000 by the Hylo-Venice History Book Committee.
4. Bonifacio, an unpublished history of Venice titled "Venice Alberta 1914: The Pioneers and Others that Lived There," c1990s, p. 40.
5. Adriana Davies, "Fascism" essay in the *Celebrating Alberta's Italian Community* website from the Gisella Biollo family history, Hylo-Venice: Harvest of Memories (Hylo: Rose Country Communications, 2000).
6. John G. Fainella, "The Development of Italian Organizations in Calgary," *Alberta History*, vol. 32 (Winter 1984), pp 20-26.
7. Fainella, p. 22.
8. Fainella, p. 22.
9. Fainella, p. 23.
10. Fainella, pp 22-23.
11. Fanella, pp 43-44.
12. In August, 2011, a fourth internee, Giovanni Galdi, a miner from Nordegg was found on federal government lists and, shortly after, a fifth, Emilio Sereni.
13. The question arises whether A. Gottarolo is the "Gottad" mentioned in Fainella's quote from Onofri: "As late as 1926

a convention of all *Fasci* in Alberta was held in Calgary under the direction of a special envoy of the Italian party, a *Sottotenente della Milizia* by the name of Gottad."
14. Extracts of the taped interviews and transcripts are available on the *Celebrating Alberta's Italian Community* website. Retrieved June 23rd, 2011, URL: http://wayback.archiveit.org/2217/20101208162732/http://www.albertasource.ca/abitalian/people/dante.html
15. Fainella completed his Masters' thesis *Cultural Background and Italian Settlement in Calgary* at the University of Calgary in 1975. Howard Palmer at the University of Calgary in the late 1980s was also undertaking oral histories with ethnocultural communities including the Italian community culminating in his book *Peoples of Alberta: portraits of cultural diversity*, published c1985 by Western Producer Prairie Books.
16. "Many Italians Against Fascisti Says Alex. Picco," *The Calgary Daily Herald*, Thursday, December 9th, 1926.
17. Genieve Rizzo's family history mentions that her Father, Frank Alampi, and others founded the Società Italiana di Mutuo Soccorso, Confederazione Columbiana [Italian Society for Mutual Relief, Columbian Confederation]. She also mentions that she joined the Società Stella d'Italia [Star of Italy Ladies Society] in Coleman.

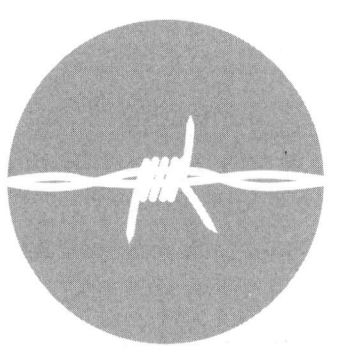

Antonella Fanella

The Rebaudengo Family

Antonio Rebaudengo (1892-1982) was born in Piozzo, Cuneo, Italy. He married Angelina Ceresero (1900-2000) in 1920. Angelina was born in Coassolo, Italy. In the spring of 1922, Antonio, Angelina and their infant son Mario (1921-2000) arrived in Calgary, Alberta. They settled in the Bridgeland/Riverside district of Calgary and Antonio, who was a machinist, was hired by the Canadian Pacific Railway (CPR), Ogden shops. Like many immigrants who came to Canada in the early part of the 20th century, the Rebaudengos found it difficult to adjust to life in their new homeland.

The Italian community was quite small (.3% of the population) and Roman Catholic southern Europeans were not welcomed by the city's largely Anglo-Saxon population. Life was hard and there were virtually no services available to help immigrants. Angelina remembers: "Neither one of us were happy here. I cried everyday for months, asking God to help me."[1] Angelina's prayers were soon answered. She and Antonio eventually adjusted to life in their adopted home. Many of the Italian migrants were from Piemonte and soon a Piemontese Society was formed which Antonio and Angelina joined. The Rebaudengos began to volunteer their time helping Italian immigrants settle in Calgary. Antonio also wrote articles on the activities of the Calgary Italian community for Italian newspapers in Toronto and Vancouver.

Antonio was also the head of the Fascio, an active fascist party founded in ca. 1922. Little is known about the activities of the

Fascio but it was probably more a social than a political club. At a convention in 1926 in Calgary, the Fascio outlined its objectives. Among other goals, it sought to improve the well-being of Italian immigrants in Canada and to promote a better understanding of Italian Canadian culture. At the convention, members pledged to "love, serve, obey and exalt the Dominion of Canada and to teach obedience to and respect for its constitution and laws."[2] While Antonio was proud of his heritage and made no secret of his admiration for Mussolini and the glory he was bringing to Italy, he was also loyal to Canada. So much so that, on July 31, 1931, he became a Canadian Citizen.

Around 1936, Antonio was made an honourary agent of the Italian Consular Office. Though Antonio held official title, it was his wife who actually performed the duties. Not only did she carry out the necessary consular duties, she also met new arrivals at the train station, reunited them with family members, filled out government forms, and helped them to find housing and employment. Her services went beyond the call of duty. She helped women with marriage preparations, and even assisted women during their pregnancy and childbirth. Life for the Rebaudengos was blissful. Little did they know that across the Atlantic a storm was brewing that would tear their family apart.

On June 10, 1940, Benito Mussolini declared that Italy was entering the Second World War as an Axis partner. That same day, Canadian Prime Minister William Lyon Mackenzie King announced that Royal Canadian Mounted Police (RCMP) had been authorized by the Minister of Justice to arrest anyone who engaged in activities deemed to be dangerous to the security of Canada. Italian immigrants who became naturalized citizens after 1929 were declared to be "enemy aliens" and had to turn in their firearms and register with the RCMP.

On the evening of June 12, the RCMP showed up at the Rebaudengos' small bungalow in Bridgeland and arrested Antonio. Before being taken away, Antonio asked permission to say goodbye to his wife. During the embrace, Antonio whispered in Angelina's ear: *"Distruggi tutto!"* Angelina knew what Antonio was referring to. Later that night, she burned all the documents relating to the Fascio, including the names of the members.

After Antonio's arrest and detention, the RCMP searched the home on two occasions and interrogated Angelina on numerous others. Over and over, they demanded that she tell them the names of the other members. She steadfastly refused. Angelina believed that, if the RCMP had known the names of the other members, they also would have been arrested. As a result of Angelina's silence, Antonio was the only Calgarian to be arrested. Antonio was only an honourary counsul, hence he did not have diplomatic immunity. He spent the next three years in the Kananaskis, Petawawa and Gagetown internment camps. Angelina and Mario were not arrested but as enemy aliens they had to register with the RCMP.

The official reason for Antonio's internment was his "pro-fascist activities and sympathies." While it is true that Antonio had been a supporter of fascism, his arrest seems to have been based more on hearsay from those who disliked him personally rather than concrete evidence that he engaged in any activities that could have been considered a threat to the security of Canada. Antonio's bewilderment is revealed in a letter to his family:

> 16 September 1941
> Dear family,
> Today I have received your much appreciated letter, dated September 12. I will get immediately to the point; first of all I must tell you that the judge was perfectly aware I was a

fascist when Fascism in Canada was legal, namely before June 12, 1940, the day in which all so-called subversive associations were dissolved and therefore I was not against the law of this country; the judge knew I had cooperated in the collection of gold for the homeland in 1936 and knew other facts regarding my activity which continued until June 12, 1940, as I have always stated, that is to say while it was permissible ... Furthermore having behaved as a law abiding citizen during twenty years of life in this country it should be sufficient proof that I have never contravened the law. That the gentlemen of [word omitted] demand their victims, even innocent victims, is not surprising for the hatred is personal; I know those people and among them are the two bosses I often mentioned to you and who upset me at work. You are right not to have any illusions on what effect the letters of support may have on the new committee examining the files, unless they wish to be impartial.[3]

In an effort to get Antonio released and to counteract the negative letters written by Antonio's detractors, Angelina and Mario wrote letters to government officials. They enlisted the help of MP George Ross as well as family and friends to attest to Antonio's strong moral character and lack of criminal record. Despite their efforts, the response from Ottawa was the same: Antonio's imprisonment would continue, though they held out a glimmer of hope by stating the case was under review.

In 1942 the Rebaudengos' son Mario turned 21 and was drafted into the Canadian army. At first Mario thought it was some sort of mistake. How could an "enemy alien" be drafted into the Canadian army? Mario reported to the military office thinking that they would realize their error and he would be sent home. However during the interview, it was suggested to Mario that, if he served in the armed forces, it could lead to his father being released from the internment camp.

Mario was willing to do anything to help his father's case and agreed to enter the army. He was stationed in Gagetown at the same time his father was interned. He took the opportunity to visit his father in the camp although he was dismayed to learn that he would have to wear his uniform during the visit. The irony of the situation was not lost on Angelina who remarked: "Imagine my son in the [King's] uniform going to visit a prisoner of war who was his own father."[4] When Antonio saw his son wearing the uniform of the country that had imprisoned him for his beliefs, he broke down.

As it turned out Mario's decision to join the army did nothing to help his father get released and Antonio started to lose hope. In a letter to his family dated April 5, 1942, he wrote:

> ... Do not delude yourselves, treachery and lack of humanity have fertile soil here. If you only knew how many injustices take place, nothing could surprise you anymore. Leaders of political parties go free since they can pay a lawyer; those with a proven criminal record, those without family, a job, money, fixed residence, they too go free. Here gentlemen, family men, hard working citizens are imprisoned without a way out; look at my case: I am fifty years old, I can strongly claim never to have been involved in a fight, I have no criminal record, in twenty years in Canada nobody ever saw me drunk, I never lost, without a reason, a day of work, I was never involved in Canadian political parties, and yet I am labeled dangerous, in the wrong because according to them I think differently from the ruling classes; twenty years is not enough to demonstrate that I respect the law and I am mild-mannered.

•••

> But can they explain why in Canada there are eighty thousand Italians and in the last two years no subversive or violent event has occurred? They would like us to believe that the dangerous ones are interned and yet half of the internees have been released and nothing has happened; how do they explain it?
>
> I am happy that [word omitted] member of Parliament, H. Ross [sic] has shown interest in my case, [but] my letter of January 20 has not yet been answered by Ottawa.[5]

Angelina remained undeterred and continued to lobby the Canadian government for her husband's release. The news that other internees had been released from the camps filled her with hope and she believed it was only a matter of time before Antonio would be released as well. She reasoned that the Canadian government could not keep an innocent man in prison. Antonio was a kind, hardworking, gentle soul, not a criminal. Once the government was convinced of that, she would have her loving husband home and they would be a family once again.

Her hopes were crushed when she received a letter sent from the Department of Justice dated February 23, 1943, informing her that "… an Advisory Committee recently reviewed your husband's file and in view of the information disclosed thereon, including letters from yourself and your son to him, is not prepared to alter the recommendation previous made, namely, that his detention be continued."[6]

Left alone, stripped of her family and of any source of income, Angelina became very depressed. She was shunned by some in the Italian community — often the very people she had assisted. They would cross the street to avoid her and turned away when she entered a grocery store. A co-worker at the Hudson's Bay demanded she be fired because she didn't want to work with a "fascist dago."[7]

Over time, the physical and mental stress took its toll. In April 1943 she developed scarlet fever and nearly died. Yet throughout her ordeal Angelina refused to give up the fight for her husband's release. One evening, as she listened to a radio broadcast in which Prime Minister MacKenzie King promised that the mothers and spouses of Canadian servicemen would be looked after, she decided to take matters into her own hands. Earlier that day she had been denied the wartime allowance given to the mothers of servicemen because she was an enemy alien. She had been denied relief for the same reason. An angry Angelina wrote Mackenzie King a letter calling him a liar. In her letter to the Prime Minister, she asked to be put into an internment camp so that "at least I can eat." She demanded and to her surprise received the allowance.[8]

Antonio was finally released from camp on September 25, 1943, seventeen days after the Italian government announced it had joined the Allies. After Antonio was released, he returned to his job with the CPR and, along with his wife, continued to assist Italian immigrants in Calgary. He never spoke again of his ordeal. His only thoughts regarding the internment are recorded in the letters he wrote to his family. Incredibly, Angelina harboured no harsh feelings toward the Canadian government. Neither did their son Mario who summed up the wartime experience as follows: "We were called 'dago,' 'Mussolini,' ' fascist.' We tried to ignore it. We were the minority. We were the aliens. War was not on our side."[9]

Endnotes

1. Rebaudengo, Angelina. Interview, February 23, 1987. Glenbow Archives.
2. Fanella, Antonella. *With Heart and Soul: Calgary's Italian Community*. Calgary: University of Calgary Press, 1999.
3. Angelina and Antonio Rebaudengo fonds. Glenbow Archives.
4. Rebaudengo, Mario. Interview 23 July 1985. Calgary Italian Club.
5. Rebaudengo fonds.
6. Ibid.
7. Rebaudengo, Angelina interview. See note 1.
8. Ibid.
9. Rebaudengo, Mario interview. See note 4.

Raymond Culos

Italian Canadian Enemy Aliens Sent to Kananaskis*: Chapter Six of *Injustice Served*

The second wave of internees sent to the camp at Kananaskis near Banff, Alberta, included 27-year-old Erminio (Herman) Ghislieri. He and his brother Fred were among 18 men ushered aboard a special CPR train on a warm summer's night in 1940. The group was being transferred from the Immigration Building in Vancouver.

Like the enemy aliens who had made the journey less than two months earlier, Ghislieri and his associates were confined to specific Pullman cars and fettered to their seats for part of the trip. In spite of their anger and frustration, an air of guarded optimism prevailed. As the whistle signalled departure, the train chugged slowly through the rail yards and along the southern exposure of Vancouver's Burrard Inlet. Ghislieri made a concerted effort to clear his mind of the events surrounding this most bizarre experience. His thoughts turned to the exciting prospect of how he and his brother soon would be reunited with their father already behind barbed wire at the POW camp.

The stop at Seebe, Alberta, was a brief one. In chain-gang formation, the men stepped off the train and climbed onto waiting military trucks. Although the 11-kilometre ride to the camp was uneventful, Herman felt a sense of exhilaration at seeing the nearby hills on which he had often skied during the time he was employed at the Banff Hotel.

It was 10 a.m. as they approached the gates to their forced exile in the majestic mountainous expanse of the Rockies. The detention facility presented quite an imposing site: high barbed wire fences, search lights, armed guards. The high level of anxiety felt by the new inmates was somewhat diminished as the army vehicles neared the gates. They were met with a chorus of rousing cheers from the German internees! The Nazis had orchestrated a demonstration in honour of their Axis partners. The Germans bellowed patriotic songs while giving the Nazi salute in defiance of the armed guards whose attention had been diverted by the arrival of the new prisoners of war. The Italians were incredulous.

Once in the triangular compound and past the commandant's quarters, the Italians were marched to the quartermaster's building. This was conducted under the surveillance of armed guards, including those manning the observation towers. After turning over their personal effects, each of the internees was searched and then given a uniform. The government issue garb comprised a pair of blue denim jeans, shirt, underwear and socks plus a jacket. On the back of the jacket was sewn a 13" red circular image simulating a target.

"Fred and I had our reunion with Dad and our friends, then we were issued identification disks. Mine was number 538," Herman Ghislieri stated nostalgically. "Next morning, the new recruits marshalled on the parade grounds, answered roll call, and had a look around the complex. The camp was built as a triangle. The prisoners' barracks started from the north and came south in rows. In the western part of the compound there was a kitchen, ablution huts and latrines. In the southern tip of the triangle was located an office for the camp prisoners' spokesman and a guard room. In the south-eastern corner there was the isolation hut called the 'cooler.' In reality it was a jail inside the wire fence for those who broke camp regulations.

"The camp's population of 795 prisoners comprised 25 Ukrainians and other Communists, 47 Italians, with the balance being made up of Germans. Integrated among the German-Canadians was a crew of 50 or more nationals from a captured German merchant ship. A similar comparative percentage mix was reflected in the nationals assigned to each hut.

"In my hut we were 12 men. There was Ennio Fabri, the lawyer, and his father, Alemando, the sculptor, and Piero Orsatti, the singer. Also with us was Santo Pasqualini, the baker, and Angelo Ruocco, the tailor, along with Fred Lenzi from Summerland, and Carlo Casorzo, Fred and me from Vancouver. Oh, yes Frank Federici, who was released within a very short time, was with us, too. Most of the rest were Germans.

"Max Bode, a congenial German from Saskatchewan, was the prisoners' senior camp leader with Ennio Fabri representing the Italians. These leaders communicated the commander's orders, directives, and general information to the individual hut leaders who in turn briefed the others."

Herman went on to say that conditions at the camp were not difficult for young men. "At times it was very much like a picnic, especially when we got to play soccer. We had our huts — bare, but with cots, army cots — and blankets. We used to maintain the units ourselves. At one time we were, I would say, about 18 to 20 per hut. The facility was run like a military camp. There was morning inspection, you know, when the commandant came in to expect. Your bed had to be made just so but it was no hardship."

In describing the various chores and assignments that were required of each internee, Herman stated: "If you started on sanitation, it would be for one month. You then would go on kitchen

Herman Ghislieri, sketch by fellow internee, Guido Casini

duty for a month. This would be followed by a month's stint on the cleaning detail. You could also volunteer for the work gang assigned to detail in the adjacent wooded area, but only if you so wished. This assignment would take you out of the camp enclosure right into the forest to trim trees, etc. It was like a regular forestry camp's clean-up detail.

"The hut leader, a position which alternated every six months, assigned me to fetch wood for the hut's two drum stoves. I also was required to remove and clean the latrine pails kept inside each hut for emergency use, and to serve on the clean-up detail. The prisoners were in complete charge of the maintenance, kitchen, work schedules, and social activity planning."

No Italians attempted to escape Kananaskis. However, a lone German gained his freedom briefly by exiting through a tunnel under the kitchen to the outside fence.

"He was a baron, very arrogant and a real Nazi. I think he acted out of some sense of bravado because he was highly regarded by his fellow Germans," Herman said. In three days the baron was back.

The guards serving at Kananaskis were of the Canadian Home Guard. Many of them had served in World War I. The guards as a group were relatively easy going and enjoyed playing cards and drinking wine with the gregarious Italians. There was a medical officer, however, who was "a prejudiced son-of-a-bitch." Allegedly Dr. Gillespie, who had a serious altercation with Bruno Girardi, so infuriated some of the Germans that one night when walking to the camp infirmary he was accosted, grabbed and beaten. In fact, a number of the Germans from Calgary apparently threatened him by saying: "If not his year, next year. We'll get you!" The commandant's reaction to the alleged attack on one of his officers was swift but only mildly punitive. He ordered that the normal

11 o'clock curfew be withdrawn in favour of confining all inmates to their huts every evening for two weeks.

The day began with a gong at 0630 hours precisely. After making their beds to military standards and visiting the ablution huts, the men would assemble in the dining room at 0700. After the first of four daily parades and inspections, duties were assigned and the prisoners went to work until 1130 hours. The duties included clearing the wooded areas adjacent the compound, trimming trees and working in the forestry camp. These assignments represented no physical hardship to the prisoners who were paid 20 cents a day in compensation. They were issued yellow paper chits which they could use to purchase items in the camp commissary. Lunch was at noon and dinner at 1750 hours.

The evenings and Sunday were free for recreational activities, handicraft workshops or for writing correspondence. Each person was permitted to write four letters and four postcards every month but the length and content of each was subject to rigid rules and censorship. Pasqualini made beautiful small furniture items including jewellery boxes. Once back home, he and others including Nino Sala proudly displayed their artistic creations.

Not everyone, however, was of the same mind. For example, Fred Ghislieri stored his items in a duffle bag and placed it in the attic of his home. It was years later before the items were shown to his children. Oliver Marino, too, did not want to be reminded of those days when his freedom had been denied. While at camp, he made himself a suitcase. It remained in the attic of the family home undisturbed until his wife Nellie died in 1982. His daughters Gloria and Elain subsequently discovered that the suitcase contained some old dental plates and two receipts. One was given to him for the nine dollars that he had in his possession at the time of his arrest. The other was issued for five dollars, his pay for working out in the bush at twenty cents per day.

Fred Tenisci, an accomplished musician, was among the POWs from Trail. While in the camps he met and befriended Antonio Rebaudengo, who allegedly was associated with those who founded the Fascio club in Venice, Alberta, in 1925. Before being arrested for allegedly being a member of the Circolo Giulio Giordani, Tenisci worked at COMINCO. He also operated a shop for religious items in his off hours. According to his son Leonard, Fioravante (Fred) had been tipped off about the RCMP coming to arrest him. This heads-up information gave Fred sufficient time to contact his pastor and friend Fr. Settimo Balo to whom he entrusted the store's inventory.

Tony Cianci, 60 when detained, later likened life at Kananaskis with being on a grand vacation. Food was in abundance and Italian groceries, ordered by family members, often would become menu items. Cianci, the hut's barber, loved to eat the delicious Italian meals prepared by Nino Sala and Emilio Muzzatti and devoured more than his share of Santo Pasqualini's pastry specialties. After light duties, he would play cards or a game of bocce with some of his older friends.

"Cianci used to cut my hair in the concentration camp [sic]," recalled Bruno Girardi with a smile. "He was a number-one guy, eh, number-one funny guy. I told him, you and I are going to decorate the camp around. I put you in charge, I said, I am your assistant. We approached the guard and I said, my partner and I have to go out and get a [Christmas] tree. Good idea. The Bow River was here, so we sat down, had a drink, smoked cigarettes, and slept."

Girardi also regarded his stay in the camps as being a holiday, but only when compared to the hardship experienced by the wives and children left grieving at home. While he was in Kananaskis, his wife Emma had been refused health-care attention. The medical doctor in question obviously was acting on his own when he dismissed her right to medical service. Apparently he objected to the fact that she was the wife of an enemy alien.

Dora Ruocco had been an executive member of the Italian Ladies' League or Lega for 12 years. She was shocked and mortified that the society for which her husband Willie Ruocco had laboured so unselfishly for so many years should suspend his membership because he had been interned. In an apparent retaliatory move, she resigned her position as the Lega's secretary of finance. Her husband, miffed, puzzled and terribly hurt by the Sons of Italy Society's precipitous actions, arranged for his son Andy to return items to the society which had been held in safekeeping at his Europe Hotel offices. The items included furniture and an old piano which originally was purchased for use by the society's Italian Language School, circa 1930. A month later, the piano was sold to the Sacred Heart Parish for the nominal amount of $35.

A few weeks before the RCMP arrested Ruocco, Angelo Calori died. The 80-year-old owner of the Europe Hotel had been a much revered pioneer leader of the Italian community. Ruocco, as executor of his former father-in-law's estate, attempted to administer the provisions of Calori's will from Kananaskis. This proved to be a difficult assignment. He managed, however, with the help of Ennio Fabri, who provided legal advice and handled much of the estate's correspondence. Fabri also had a vested interest in the disposition of the assets of this will as his mother-in-law Rosa was Calori's step-daughter. Calori's other daughter Lina, who predeceased him, had been married to W.G. Ruocco.

Santo Pasqualini also benefitted from Fabri's generous cooperation. In this case, the former baker was confronted simultaneously with a bankrupt business, agitating creditors, and most importantly with a critical situation at home. During this highly stressful period, Fabri's professional counsel and assistance proved extremely beneficial.

Speaking in sympathetic tones, Herman Ghislieri recalled part of the Pasqualini family's crisis: "I was very close to Santo because I used to write some of his letters when we were in the camps. Yes, and he was quite a good friend, being an *ex-combattente*. He would do anything for Dad, you see. Santo used to come to our house, sometimes being accompanied by Alice. So, before I was released [from Petawawa], I promised Santo I would go and see his wife. He worried about Alice because she was sick and at that time a patient in the old Vancouver General Hospital. When I saw her, I was amazed to see her in that condition. So, I spoke to Father Bortignon and said, what can be done because that's no place to keep this woman. She needs better care than that."

Life in the internment camp also had its exciting moments. Rivalry existed between the Italians and Germans, but basically it was friendly in nature, especially in those early months of the war. When the Germans challenged the Italians to a game of soccer, a team was quickly formed.

"Bruno and Attilio Girardi, Fred and I and a couple of others could really play soccer," Herman stated. "The team was made up of eight because the field wasn't big enough for 11 players on each side. Anyway we beat them. They couldn't swallow that Germans had been beaten by the Italians, you know. They never asked us to play again."

"In fact, the relationship between our two groups deteriorated in the following months. The Nazis at Kananaskis no longer could abide Italians. This was because Italy's armed forces would not fight for Hitler, particularly in Greece where they were beaten, and in Albania and Africa."

In 1941, Kananaskis became an exclusive German prisoner-of-war camp. As a result, all non-German POWs were transported by rail to Petawawa near the Canadian military base of the same name. The camp was located about 160 kilometres north of Ottawa, on the Ottawa River between Pembroke and Chalk River.

The Italians from Western Canada immediately sensed a difference in attitude between themselves and their *paesani* from Quebec and Ontario. Among their new compatriots were high-profile professional people accustomed to getting their own way. Although basically a good element, it appeared to Herman Ghislieri to be tinged with "a little bit of the Mafia." A few of the rich Italians had become camp work-foremen and actually hired people to do their bidding. These underlings would shave them, cook and serve their meals, and do their camp chores. The authorities seemed oblivious to this arrangement or at least turned a blind eye to it.

This situation and atmosphere proved quite a change for the group from Kananaskis. They had come to appreciate the solitude and ambience of the Rocky Mountain forests. Moreover, they soon missed the laid-back manageable arrangement which existed between themselves and the guards. Petawawa represented more bustle and, in terms of sheer numbers, it was akin to the difference between the quiet of a village and the fast pace of a city. The prevailing structure of the Petawawa camp, influenced by Italians who enjoyed special status and privilege, wasn't of their choosing.

In *Dangerous Patriots,* authors William Repka and Kathleen M. Repka provide quite an insight to this social contrast. They quote Bruce Magnuson, a former prisoner at Petawawa, as saying: "There were also Italian Fascists from Montreal and Toronto. It was interesting when we were on work parties, people like the millionaire Franceschini, the Montreal [sic] industrialist, and Mascioli, the big construction millionaire from Timmins, were the foremen. The wealthy Italians were also able to get certain privileges. They could pay people to do their chores in the camp."

However, there were certain amenities at Petawawa which represented an improvement for those relocating from Alberta. For example, the camp boasted a hospital staffed by eight doctors, some of whom were drawn from among the 600 to 650 Italian internees. In addition, accommodation afforded more privacy, with bathrooms attached to each hut. These larger facilities accommodated 50 men instead of only 12, which was the case in Kananaskis.

Bruno Girardi provided this take on the origin of internment camps as well as outlining his perception of the differences in facilities at the two POW camps: "English people, as good as they are, are the rotten bastards of the world. Let's be honest about it. Internment camps were invented by the British.

"At Petawawa we had less privacy because of the size of the bathrooms. Each comprised 10 toilets that were attached to the individual huts. This is because we were about a thousand people — maybe 10 sections of 10-hole toilets — all sitting down together. We were in full view of one another and could discuss the issues of the day as we went about our business. It wasn't a problem; you get used to it. At the camp we were able to see doctors, dentists and everything. It was better than a university. Anything you wanted to learn, you could go and talk to someone.

"We were about 650 Italians and maybe a hundred Germans. Most of the rest were French Canadians, including Camillien

A work detail of internees is escorted by military guards back to Camp Petawawa (National Archives of Canada).

Houde, the former mayor of Montreal. His problem was he was against conscription."

Friction between the Italians and Germans continued as the war progressed. This included arguments and fights over which group, for example, would have the dominant influence in the kitchen. The resulting frustration occasionally was mitigated in the boxing ring. A few Italians tended to take on all comers, winning their share of the matches. Notwithstanding, there were a couple of memorable losses to the German side. One in particular involved a fellow by the name of Clark who finally vanquished the Italian champ.

Herman Ghislieri gave this account of the fight: "Among the Italians housed in another hut was a young swarthy boxer with broad shoulders whose name I don't recall. However, he was of the Graziano type: a brawler. He could fight, let me tell you. But maybe he was out of shape when he challenged this Clark who was about 20 pounds lighter. They put up a ring outside. It was in the afternoon. For the first couple of rounds this Clark, all he could do was just stand up, see, because this [Italian] guy was a tough fighter. He was strong, but later in the rounds he started to weaken. And this Clark, he was a smart boxer, started to pummel him. They went ten rounds and this guy was nothing but pulp. The German really gave him a beating."

* Excerpt from the book by Culos, Raymond, *Injustice Served: The Story of British Columbia's Italian Enemy Aliens During World War II*. Cusmano, Montreal: 2012, reprinted by permission.

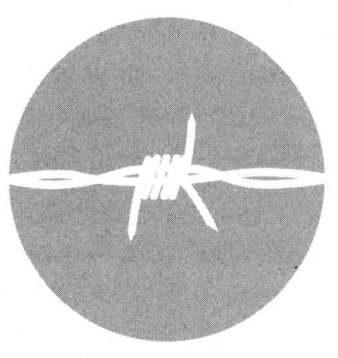

Jim Zucchero

Internment and Duliani's *The City Without Women*: A Case Study for Multiculturalism in Canada

In *Canadian Society in the Twenty-First Century,* Harrison and Friesen suggest that a society is a large social group that shares the same geographical territory and is subject to the same political authority and dominant cultural expectations. In 2012, multiculturalism has become a hallmark of Canadian society. But the compatibility of one's cultural heritage, beliefs and practices with the dominant cultural expectations of Canadian society is one real test of the viability of Canadian multiculturalism. Considering the long history of Italians in Canada and their contributions to Canadian society, the internments of the 1940s stand out as a particularly problematic event. However, those internments can provide important insights into the development of multiculturalism in Canadian society, and developments within the Italian Canadian community. Although multiculturalism would not be introduced in Canada as official government policy until 1971, examining the internment of Italian Canadians provides a useful case study of how multiculturalism has worked for one ethnic group in Canada. Mario Duliani's writing about the internment of Italian Canadians brings into focus in unique ways the convergence of several key features of the Italian emigration experience in Canada; namely: ethnicity, language, and political authority.

I take Duliani's text *The City Without Women* as the focal point for this discussion of the evolving sense of Italian ethnicity in Canada. I assert that the internments of the 1940s, and the subsequent response of Italian Canadians (individually and as a community) is a microcosm of the wider experience of this group; it illustrates significant changes in their self perception, and important developments in their social agency. The story of the internments and their aftermath marks the movement of Italian Canadians from enemy aliens and victims of state authority to agents of social change and loyal defenders of rights and freedoms that are among the defining features of Canadian society. In the intervening seventy years, members of this ethnic group have gone from being prisoners of war camps suspected of plotting espionage and acts of terror, to being engaged social activists seeking accountability, social justice, and due respect for the rights and freedoms provided for by law. Despite a difficult past, Italian Canadians have emerged from this experience as worthy defenders of the rights and responsibilities that are central to Canadian society and its model of multiculturalism.

Duliani was a prominent member of the Italian Canadian community in Montreal, working as a journalist and director of a local theatre company, when he was arrested and interned in June of 1940, shortly after the start of the Second World War. He spent forty months in internment camps, in Petawawa, Ontario and Fredericton, New Brunswick and, as Roberto Perin points out, "distinguished himself by being the only internee, Italian or otherwise, to write a first-hand, book-length account of his confinement" (*Actor* 312). In 1945 Duliani published a French language text entitled *La ville sans femmes*; the following year an Italian language version was published as *Città senza donne*. However, nearly fifty years would pass before an English translation of the text would be made available, finally, in 1994, as *The City Without Women*. Duliani's text clearly depicts the deeply problematic relationship that some Italian Canadians had with authorities in the Canadian government and security forces in the 1940s. It also illustrates that those internments have had a deep and lasting effect on both personal and collective identity for some Italian Canadians.

My analysis of Duliani's text takes the idea of authority (and an attitude of ambivalence toward that authority) as the focal point for understanding the internments themselves, Duliani's writing about the experience, and the subsequent response of Italian Canadians. This essay examines three main topics: first, political dimensions of interment are considered. It was an extreme example of the absolute authority of the state being exercised against individuals who were perceived to pose a threat or the potential of a threat to the welfare of loyal citizens and their social security. Second, some sociological dimensions of the internments are considered; specifically, how authority was exercised within the camps; how was the prisoner/jailer tension managed, and what might that suggest? Finally, from the perspective of literary analysis, what have been the effects of Duliani's text being issued in different languages at different times? Especially, what effect has the translation of the text into English had on responses to it?

Historical analysis of Duliani's text has tended to focus on questions of historical accuracy and the political implications of internment. A literary approach can extend the discussion of his text in quite a different direction. My analysis focuses on the relationship between the text as a literary record, collective memory, and ethnic identity and how the relationship between these shifts over time. Duliani's text has become a literary monument, a form of commemoration that elicits strong, varied responses. Its meaning evolves over time, across generations, in different social and political climates to render different meanings. Its reception is difficult to measure, in part because it is complicated by matters of language and translation, which I will discuss. Examining the reception of the text (including sharply polarized responses within the Italian Canadian community) demonstrates that ideas about ethnicity in Canada are changing and that the Italian Canadian community has developed a different status and orientation toward authority, in this case the political and legal authority of the state. At the time of the internments of the 1940s Italian Canadians collectively were submissive and accepting of the state's authority; their response to internment (as it is conveyed in Duliani's text) is marked by a tone of lament and regret but above all by a sense of resignation.[1] In contrast, the campaign on behalf of Italian Canadians to seek redress over the wartime internments suggests that the Italian Canadian community now has a very different orientation toward what it perceives as the abuse of authority by the state.[2] The campaign for redress demonstrates agency on the part of the Italian Canadian community; it manifests a proactive stance that questions how the authority of the state was exercised. These actions convey resistance and indignation toward past treatment. In the end, examining Duliani's text within the context of the Italian Canadian community, and within the broader context of Canadian literary studies, may reveal as much about contemporary Canadian society (especially our tendency to reconsider our orientation toward our past and our ideas about ethnicity), as it does about its enigmatic author, Duliani, or the lives of his fellow internees.

I argue that the most striking feature of Duliani's text and the key to its interpretation is its tone of ambivalence. Ambivalence is embedded in the text: in its literary form; in the images of ethnicity, memory and authority that it presents; and in responses to the text among historians, literary critics, and those in the Italian Canadian community. Ambivalence also characterizes Duliani's own response to the experience of internment. He makes statements that are contradictory and which have the effect of unsettling interpretation of his text. I examine his statements about internment and how they have been interpreted by critics as another aspect of how internment engages the dynamics of authority. I begin with the ambivalence of genre in the text as a primary feature that opens into other problems of ambivalence.

The Ambivalence of Literary Genre and Duliani's Position

The problematic ambivalence of genre in *The City Without Women* has been noted by both historians (Perin) and literary critics (Mazza, Stellin). In fact, the ambivalence of the genre of the text, and the difficulty of establishing Duliani's position (in terms of his political affiliations and activities) has been a focal point for debates concerning this text and internment in general. The central issue of contention is between those who see Duliani as an apologist for the Canadian state (Ramirez) and those who contend that Duliani and many of his fellow internees were far less innocent of wrongdoing than they would have us believe.[3] Critics have posed the question: was Duliani a cagey actor or a hapless victim, innocent of any wrongdoing or malicious intent? Are we to approach *The City Without Women* as "novel or historical document"?[4] The text can sustain both kinds of analysis. Its richness derives, in part, from its resistance to being slotted neatly into one category or the other. The problems of examining the historical accuracy of Duliani's account are (as Perin notes) best left to historians; however, examining the literary merits of the text opens up a wider range of questions about its effects than those he suggests. For example, not all literary analysis of the text has as its objective the vindication of Duliani and his political reputation, or a desire to confer on Duliani's text the status of "a classic in Canadian letters"(313). Rather, the text functions as a cultural signpost with personal and collective significance. I am most interested in the text as a constructed representation of the past, for what it suggests about historical memory. My interest is in examining the images the text presents and their effects over time, in different contexts, how these recorded memories and the 'holes in memory' work and rework the past, and condition the present and the future.

The City Without Women is a hybrid in terms of its literary genre. As a man of literary pursuits Duliani seems keen to address the issue of his book's genre. He begins: "The pages that follow are neither a 'journal' nor a 'memoir'. Rather, they constitute a 'documentary novel', that is, a true human chronicle whose threads of reality the imagination has embroidered into narrative ... This book therefore relates a 'lived' story" (3). Clearly, this blending of literary genres — of documentary and novelistic functions — complicates the reception and interpretation of the text. An approach that considers both historical and novelistic features points to the broader implications of this text for the Italian Canadian ethnic community, beyond questions of its author's integrity or his intentions. The blending of literary genres is another way in which Duliani's text resists authority; it transgresses across the lines of several literary genres: memoir, diary, novel and documentary. This blending of genres may have been a conscious strategy on Duliani's part; a strategy for positioning his text that would, on one hand, appeal to those who were sympathetic but also mitigate against his critics, by allowing him to resort to its "imaginative" elements as a means of avoiding criticism. This ambivalence highlights one of the problems of a text that is part historical record, part fictionalized account: the representation that emerges from the text becomes, to a very considerable extent, the collective memory of the events described. Quite literally, as those who experienced internment first-hand die off, the written record of those events takes on increased importance and is relied upon to reconstruct events, and determine their long term effects on the Italian Canadian community and Canadian society. Ventresca suggests: "During the campaign [for redress], the 'story' of political innocents hurt by a vindictive wartime state effectively became *the* 'story' of *all* Italian internees" (378). This status places the focus on the relationship between Duliani's text, collective memory, and the "ethnic" identity of Italian Canadians today — especially on how this relationship evolves over time.

The ambivalence and tension present in the hybrid genre of the text are echoed in the author's stated responses to the experience of internment. For example, Duliani claims, to be entirely accepting of the severe measures taken against him; and yet, he is full of regret at his unfortunate fate and laments his loss of liberty deeply. He offers his personal reaction to internment, and expresses his view clearly and emphatically: that the actions taken by the Canadian government against him and the others interned were justified; regrettable and difficult to manage, to be sure, but above all they were, in his estimation, justified and necessitated by the political and historic events of the day — the need to protect the greater good of the nation and its citizens in a time of war. In fact, as if to emphasize his commitment to this position, he places statements to this effect at the outset and conclusion of his account. He states: "The internment measure taken against a certain number of enemy subjects or Canadian citizens whose origin was in enemy countries seemed wholly justified by the political and military situation of the moment when it was taken. Before the tragic circumstance of war ... a government has the supreme obligation to safeguard the order and security of the entire nation ..." (4). In Duliani's view, the responsibility of the state to its citizens is the single most compelling issue; the risk of erring, in such a way as to produce disadvantage and hardship to a few, is an acceptable risk. In the debate over this text in recent years, there has been much speculation that this opinion may have been expressed for diplomatic or pragmatic reasons, that it was merely prudent for Duliani to express such views at the time. His reference to "the military situation of the moment" contextualizes internment as an extraordinary measure that must be interpreted in light of the events occurring at the time. (This view, that extraordinary times call for extraordinary measures, still holds currency for many.)[5] It is clear from his comments that, at that time, one's country of origin was seen as sufficient basis for the government to take action against "citizens whose origin was in enemy countries" (4). This issue, the question of the close association between nation of origin, ethnicity and treatment under the law, has become considerably more complex in recent years.

As Duliani notes, the ethnic identity of Italian Canadians (and various other nationalities) was the basis for their internment. He refers to "country of origin" or "nationality" as the reason for his internment and that of others imprisoned. In my reading of his text I would suggest that ethnicity was the basis for the actions taken against these individuals. This distinction is important because it highlights the fact that the concept of ethnicity has evolved as a more complex phenomenon than nationality, as it was conceived in the 1940s. Today migration (and often multiple migrations) makes "country of origin" more problematic as a means of ascribing ethnicity. Duliani's own case, his having been born in Istria, illustrates the point.[6]

The dilemma for the state concerning internment is one of balancing of civil liberties with the duty to provide security. Today there is far greater emphasis that this is a duty owed to all citizens, regardless of their ethnicity or country of origin; this responsibility has been enshrined in the Charter and in the law of the land. In the 1940s, however, different ideas and standards prevailed. Duliani sets out the problem in measured tones:

> It may then happen that in the execution of this duty some error, some blunder may occur. It is natural that at the time when the error or blunder occurs, the individual who has to suffer for it may find it hard and bitterly difficult to swallow. But in the middle of the collective drama that a world war can be in modern times, how much can the destiny of the individual weigh?
>
> Let this be the proof that the ex-internee, once freed retains no resentment or grudge for what he's had to mistakenly endure.
>
> He knows that at the time when his internment was decided, appearances, more than hard evidence, worked in his disfavour.
>
> Today, having demonstrated vividly that he never committed anything, either acts or words, against this Canada whose guest he was, he accepts what has transpired. This at least is my own feeling! (5)

Significantly, Duliani characterizes those interned as "guests" in Canada; his doing so fails to recognize that many of those interned were not merely visitors or migrant workers but were, in fact, landed immigrants or native-born Canadians, people whose citizenship was Canadian and who counted Canada as their home. Their treatment clearly conveys that they were not regarded as equal under the law and they did not enjoy the privileges that they were due as Canadian citizens. He offers the anecdote of a traveller who arrives at a border station; everyone must display his or her luggage for inspection and, while one may indicate that they have 'nothing to declare,' the officials of the state reserve the right to impose delays in order to conduct a more thorough search and verification. He notes: "This is the law, and we're to respect the law" (5).

This statement suggests that acceptance of the law and submission to it was expected, a 'given', something taken for granted and not open to question or challenge. Duliani's statement places a clear emphasis on deference to authority here. It invokes the image of the poor southern Italian peasants who were resigned to their lot in life, powerless against the authority of their feudal lords. However, my analysis of the text demonstrates that those interned were a resourceful lot and less deferential in managing their internment than Duliani's statement might suggest. Duliani's statement — "we're to respect the law" — offers no suggestion that the inherent justness of the law should be evaluated, or that examination of how the law was applied and executed was or should be given consideration.

But this image of deference and assurances of innocence on Duliani's part are not upheld consistently. He repeatedly proclaims his innocence of any wrongdoing, only to later retract his own words and undermine the credibility of his own position. Toward the end of his account, as he rides the train to freedom following his release from the internment camp, there is a curious turnabout. He offers the following statement: "I open the notes I have made in this journal over the past forty months and read at random what I've written. I begin to deny everything I have written" (155). These lines have a profoundly unsettling effect on the entire narrative; they cause the reader to call into question the genuineness of all of what is written, what the author previously claimed to be "a true human chronicle" (3).

Every work of biographical writing (and more so autobiography) poses the problem of attempting to distinguish fact from fiction; how much of what is set out is accurate and how much has the account been embellished for effect, or simply from the slippage that characterizes human memory? Here the authority of personal memory — that is, its reliability — is called into question and cast in the light of ambivalence. Duliani acknowledges this problem openly with his statement of denial and his qualification of his own narrative: "Usually, when we reread what we've written, at a certain distance, we realize that we no longer think the same thoughts. Still it doesn't mean that we did not think them once" (155). His comment emphasizes the dynamic nature of personal identity. It is difficult to know precisely how to interpret his statement. Is it a renunciation of a mistaken personal political orientation (as a fascist sympathizer), or is it a renunciation of his prior assurances of innocence of any wrongdoing, now that he is once again free?

Perhaps it is evidence of his ambivalence about his own internment. Historians will continue to debate this matter; but what it does demonstrate is the author's own shifting orientation to the past, and the necessity of interpreting his work and the history of internment with the same wariness. Duliani suggests: "The interest of a personal journal may consist precisely in that it shows a sequence of successive truths. Journals of this kind are like a series of instant photographs. Here the image resembles us there it does not. Or, if this photograph no longer resembles us, it once did resemble us" (155). His comments, about the images in the text and about his own reliability as narrator, stress ambivalence and unsettle his text. They complement and compound his statements about the ambivalence of genre in his text. The author's positioning of himself and his text as fundamentally ambivalent represents two ways in which his text resists authority: first, he does not submit his text as fitting a distinct literary genre; second, he claims and later disavows claims to transparency. His statement, that some images resemble us and others do not, highlights that his internment chronicle is useful because it presents constructed images of the Italian community at a point in time, in the 1940s (images that may or may not be accurate). In the next section I focus on some of those images of community in the internment camps as profoundly ambivalent toward authority; specifically, I examine the ambivalence with which Duliani portrays memory and authority for internees in the camps.

The Ambivalence of Memory and Authority in Internment

Duliani's chronicle describes in detail what those interned experienced. Much of his account focuses on memory and social organization within the camps. He emphasizes that the most difficult aspect of that experience was not the material conditions under which they were required to live, but rather the psychological hardship caused by extended absence from their families and by not knowing how long they would be deprived of their liberty. He states: "The principal trauma for the internees pivoted around this fact [separation from family]. It is what justifies the title of this book. After all I've witnessed in this Camp, let no one characterize men as unfeeling beings, insensitive to Love!" (4). This motif of the pain created out of loneliness and isolation recurs frequently, like a refrain, in the text: "[T]he pain of separation from our loved ones ... proved an insufferable burden to us all" (18).

Duliani's reference to the title of the book bears consideration. It may have been selected to draw attention to the peculiar nature of life in the internment camps and how life there differed from conditions for others, notably Japanese-Canadians who were interned in mixed gender camps, sometimes as families. As Duliani conveys it, the deprivation of family life (including contact with women) was one of the most difficult circumstances of life in internment and a defining feature of their experience. Why was this so? Because as well as the physical deprivation it entailed, it also symbolized being cut-off from the emotional depth of family life the internees had enjoyed in civil society. Duliani emphasizes that the principal source of anxiety was psychological trauma that hinged on the uncertainty of their predicament (and the uncertainty of any pending release). Those interned were victimized by their lack of information; conversely, the authority of those who kept them captive was secured by their privileged access to information. In the dynamics of internment, information equals power equals authority.

Memory is central to *The City Without Women*. I will examine how memory functions in relation to internment from several perspectives: as it was experienced by internees according to Duliani's reflections on this theme; the collective memory of the Italian Canadian community about internment; and the impact of personal family memories and stories on my approach to this subject. The ambivalence of personal memory for those interned is vividly conveyed in many passages in the text. Similarly, the shame and ambivalence the internees felt is reflected in the collective memory of later generations of Italian Canadians. I will consider specific examples of the ambivalence of personal memory for internees and demonstrate how that ambivalence toward memory reflects a broader ambivalence toward authority. The ambivalence of the internees toward memory and authority in the camps is reflected in the ambivalence of collective memory of internment, represented in the response of the Italian Canadian community, and especially in responses to Duliani's text.

Memory among the Internees

According to Duliani, nowhere were the tortuous effects of internment more apparent than in the way that it sharpened the memories of those who were interned. He repeatedly suggests that their suffering was brought about primarily by their "ethical disquietude", the fact that none of the men interned had committed any act of treason; they had merely made the mistake of expressing outwardly their sympathy for a government that had later declared war on Canada. Another major source of angst is the impossibility of knowing how long they will be required to endure this isolation and deprivation; Duliani notes:

> And a man who has left his wife and children behind to fend for themselves reflects: "If only I knew I'd be here for one, two, three months even, I might yet be able to endure it, but how much more time will I have to spend in here before I'm free to go and look after my family?
> And this is the brutal, inhumane cause of the general moral malaise in the Camp — the indefiniteness of our term of imprisonment. (21)

These conditions, not surprisingly, produce a "nerve-racking state of mind" and many respond "with a sort of internal revolt and ill will" (21). Duliani describes in great detail the downcast state of mind of those interned. Their small social gatherings become their primary means of trying to combat the difficult mental conditions they face; they meet casually in their barracks and attempt to replicate their usual social interactions over watery coffee and biscuits (17). Invariably their conversations gravitate toward reminiscence of their loved ones and they "begin to unstring the rosary of [their] memories" (17).

They worried greatly about the welfare of their wives and children and some were tormented by the thought that they might be suspected of having betrayed their country. Duliani's description clearly conveys the sense that the loss of dignity, even more than the loss of freedom, was the hardest blow to withstand. He is stoical in his response to the psychological hardships brought on by internment. He notes:

> Despite our floundering the only way to save ourselves is to keep ourselves afloat by keeping our spirit high. This psychologically agonizing test can prove beneficial for this reason alone. The experience can transform the weak, nervous and irascible men into worthy men capable of resisting misfortunes and surmounting life's great difficulties. In life all is a matter of perception. We must embrace this life. We must allow that we are here for a valid purpose ... What we suffer most here is memory itself. (53)

History and the past are visited upon those interned in the form of personal memory as an ambivalent force that both comforts and torments. This is the heart of the matter: the persistence of memory, its capacity to both sting and soothe; to act at times as a balm, and at other times as a burr. The image of memory and incidents that Duliani relates through his chronicle, which is itself a "remembrance of things past," highlight the different and often conflicting roles of memory, its capacity to cause pain and its important function in helping to consolidate identity. So, for example, when he describes the plight of the labourer who left five children at home and laments that the youngest does not remember him anymore (52). Or when he suggests that it is good to "taste the bitter joy of once more resisting an attack of remembrance" (53). Such pleasures, surely, are only available to those who "suffer memory"; for those interned memory functions as both a lifeline to the things that matter most in their lives, and a curse — the relentless and inescapable presence of what is absent. Of memory, Duliani says simply: "[O]ur brains are permeated with it. The value of the past has radically increased — that is what assails us. At moments the nostalgia for a landscape, a face, a voice, bursts in our heart — and chokes us" (53).

Duliani's two professions are relevant to how he tells his story. As a journalist he was trained in determining public interest in a story and in crafting narrative that would engage the interest of readers. As a theatre director he was skilled at dramatization, communicating ideas and emotions through the effects of rhetoric, details of narrative and the staging of scenes.[7] These professional skills might easily heighten suspicion that his account of internment was embellished for effect.[8] Analysis of *The City Without Women* indicates that his literary and theatrical talents were often used to great effect. Many of the scenes Duliani relates have a visual and conversational quality that draws them close to theatre and allows the reader to imagine them being set on a stage.

Perhaps for some interned "enemy aliens" the separation from loved ones was so excruciating because it was analogous to and replicated, at an emotional level, the pain of separation from their homeland, the mother country they had left behind to settle in Canada. So the pain of internment was, in a way, like being rejected by an adoptive parent.

The memory of internment retains this ambivalence for the Italian Canadian community today. Historical memory, including such dark episodes as the internments of the 1940s, can be a catalyst to consolidating identity, a reason for commemorating the past. It can be a signpost against which to measure forward motion, social progress, and the agency of this ethnic group in becoming the masters of their own destiny and contributors to the development of a strong and genuine multiculturalism in Canada. But memory can also be a cause of pain for some, even after the passing of many years. (Some of the essays and creative works in these volumes attest to this.)

The Dynamics of Authority in Internment

Just as memory functions in complex and ambivalent ways in the text, the dynamics of power and authority in the camps is also shown to function in complex ways that emphasize ambivalence. The social organization the internees create, amongst themselves and with camp officials who oversee them, provide ways of addressing issues of authority and the loss of liberty, power and control that internment imposes. Their interactions with guards and prison officials, which are described as fairly congenial, become a means of breaking down the rigid lines of authority. Structures of power become fragmented and are negotiated at an interpersonal level, on individual terms. In real terms these "arrangements" that made life manageable, on both sides of the equation, represented an example of *"arrangiarsi"*: getting by, making do, finding ways to negotiate terms that made the adverse circumstances of life in internment more bearable.

Duliani dedicates a chapter to describing relations between the internees and camp authorities. He suggests that "between the two disparate castes a special symbiotic relationship developed" (141). The title of the chapter, "Prisoners of the Prisoners", clearly suggests that there was a shared sense of oppression at work. Duliani notes the oppressive nature of the work the guards were required to undertake: "Whenever you saw the wearied soldiers making their monotonous rounds around the Camp, you could have thought it was they rather who were the prisoners: watching over us day and night, observant of our every move, responsible for us every minute" (141). He describes one episode in detail:

> In Petawawa, our first guards were a group of young soldiers who conducted themselves also in a gentlemanlike manner. I remember one day when a soldier who escorted us into the bush sat down beside me:
> "I am not supposed to converse with you," he said. "We were told you were a dangerous lot. But I can see for myself how far from the truth that is."
> And as we sat there engaged in this cordial exchange, without warning my interlocutor jumped up and cautioned under his breath:
> "Careful, here comes the sergeant." (142)

This scene describes the informal breaking down of the lines of authority between the guard and his prisoner, merely in the service of genuine human relations. The breaking of formal protocol and official regulation is significant because it requires that both parties trust each other for their mutual benefit. In effect, they operate under their own unofficial and unspoken code of conduct and, by their collusion in this, they undermine the official protocol and rules of conduct they were expected to abide by. Duliani suggests that this level of mutual understanding was the norm and not the exception in the camp, particularly in relations between the inmates and the camp's internal guards.

It is noteworthy that the internees adopt distinctly democratic practices to establish some kind of collective identity for themselves: each of the twelve barracks delegated a "hut leader" to represent their interests to the camp spokesperson, an individual elected by secret ballot to act as their official intermediary with the military command. "Universal suffrage reign[ed] among the internees" (23), we are told. Ironically, these alleged fascists appear to have developed a system of self-governance and representation that replicated the very same democratic values championed by their captors, and which they were said to abhor.

Alberto Melucci has written about the ways in which the bonds of solidarity are strengthened by adversity. The ways in which this adversity motivates social action are relevant not only in considering the plight of the internees, but also in relation to the problem of internment as historical event. My discussion of the collective memory of internment and responses to that collective memory (the campaign for redress) extend the application of Melucci's point: that adversity can strengthen the bonds of solidarity and promote social action. Before I consider critical responses to Duliani's text and the effects of internment on the collective memory of Italian Canadians, I will demonstrate how issues of language and translation have complicated the transmission of his text and affected its reception.

Language, Translation and Authority in *The City Without Women*

Issues of language and translation are central to a discussion of *The City Without Women* and have a direct bearing on the reception of the text by different audiences. What is the relationship between the language of the text, the order and timing of translations, the purpose and effects of the various versions, and their respective impact on the Italian Canadian community? What is the significance of the fact that Duliani published the book first in French (in 1945), then quickly followed it with an Italian edition, *Città senza donne*[9] (in 1946), but stopped at that? Did the lengthy delay of nearly 50 years before the creation of the English translation have a significant effect on the reaction of the broader Italian Canadian community to internment? In his introduction to the English translation Antonino Mazza suggests that the primary reason *The City Without Women* "hardly figures in Canadian letters is due largely to a controversial allegation surrounding its author, which has discredited the book and also undermined the request of Italian Canadians for just reparations" (xvii). Mazza is alluding to questions that persist concerning Duliani's political sympathies and speculation over his supposed involvement with fascist organizations in Canada, allegations which have been suggested but never proven, or disproved, conclusively.

On this matter I would disagree with Mazza on several counts: first, I believe it is not the author's questionable political orientation that has inhibited interest in the text but rather the lack of availability, until 1994 at least, of an English translation of the text, a situation that Mazza himself remedied by creating an English translation from the French and Italian texts. Second, rather than inhibiting the reception of the text and interest in it, I would argue that much of the critical attention the text has received has been generated by historians around precisely the issue of Duliani's character — his integrity, trustworthiness and motivations (see Ramirez and Perin). In point of fact, the question of the author's integrity and genuineness has not deterred but heightened interest in his account (arguably to the exclusion of other important critical concerns, at least from a literary perspective). Mazza claims that the impetus for providing an English language version of Duliani's book was not so much an effort to vindicate the author (although clearly much of his introduction to the English translation is directed toward this purpose) as it was intended to have a positive effect on the broader issue of rehabilitating the reputation of the Italian Canadians interned as a group.[10] Mazza's English translation was intended to contribute in positive ways toward the larger matter of addressing the long term harm done to the Italian Canadian community as a result of those internments and the lack of widespread awareness of actions taken by the Canadian government of the day. Mazza states:

> As relevant as the final verdict on Duliani himself might be, however, the impetus to reissue this unique book in English comes from a deep conviction that the repression of innocent Canadians during the war, which violated individual rights and freedoms and ravaged the collective life of Italian Canadians, did tremendous harm to participatory democracy in Canada. *The City Without Women*, in so far as it is an essential chronicle of those events, ought to take its distinctive place in the Canadian literary canon. (xix)

Mazza and those involved in the campaign to seek redress for Italian Canadians interned are justified in their indignation over the internments; however, it would be difficult to provide conclusive evidence that they caused "tremendous harm to participatory democracy in Canada" as he claims.[11] It would be hard to demonstrate conclusively Mazza's assertion that internment "ravaged the collective life of Italian-Canadians" (xix); nonetheless, I am deeply interested in seeking ways to effectively evaluate the impact of internment (and the effects of Duliani's literary text) on the collective identity of Italian Canadians and how they have been perceived in Canadian society.

    What is suggested by the fact that Duliani originally wrote his book in French, then provided an Italian translation, but not an English language text? In part, the decision to publish initially in

French and then in Italian was a practical choice, since he was fluent in both those languages.[12] French and Italian versions also likely served Duliani's purposes: to ease his transition back into Quebec civil society. Since the vast majority of his intended audience in Quebec were literate in French,[13] he wrote and published a French edition first, in 1945. The following year he provided an Italian version, presumably to reach those members of the Italian community who could not read French.[14] But there would have been little need for him to produce an English language translation for his Quebec audience in 1945. Also, it is very likely that Duliani was incapable of producing an English translation on his own, and that he lacked the financial resources required to do so had he wanted to. Nowhere in the critical materials about Duliani and his writing is there any mention of his proficiency in English.[15] Likely then, both Duliani and the Italian community lacked the financial resources needed to produce an English text at that time. Furthermore, as Pivato notes, an English text, in all likelihood, would have received a very cool response in English Canada, at a time when anti-Italian sentiments still ran high and rehabilitation of the Italian image was just beginning.

It is difficult to ascertain with certainty why there was a lapse of nearly fifty years between the publication of the French and Italian language texts and the English translation. The availability of the text in French and Italian but not in English would have determined the reading audience for the book. The appearance of the English translation in 1994 suggests that the Italian Canadian community experienced considerable self-reflections and developed a sense of agency during the latter half of the twentieth century. Certain individuals (including Mazza) and groups (like the National Association of Italian-Canadians) felt it was important to revisit the history of internment, to gain wider recognition of the facts, and seek public and political accountability in the form of an apology and redress. These facts are evidence of a significant shift in orientation toward authority on the part of Italian Canadians from that described in Duliani's chronicle.

Reaction to Duliani's Text and Internment

The original French and Italian language texts received little critical attention from the Quebec literary community and even less in the broader Canadian literary establishment. What interest they did generate was almost exclusively from Italian historians interested in Italian fascism abroad (see Luigi Bruti Liberati's *Il Canada, l'Italia e il fascismo 1919-1945* (1984) and essays by Mazza, Perin and Ramirez). One discussion of the literary features of Duliani's French text *La ville sans femmes* appears in an essay by Susan Iannucci entitled "Contemporary Italo-Canadian Literature" (in *Arrangiarsi: The Italian Immigration Experience in Canada* (1989)).

Her analysis relates Duliani's text to a canonical work — Susanna Moodie's *Roughing It in the Bush*, and to one of the traditional unifying themes of Canadian criticism — the garrison. She also recognizes in Duliani's text the familiar theme of immigrant displacement and isolation and traces it to the psychological effects of inhabiting a homogeneous ethnic neighbourhood, the so-called "Little Italy" of many Canadian cities that becomes home to significant numbers of Italian immigrants.

Monica Stellin also emphasizes immigrant displacement in her literary analysis of the Italian text, *Città senza donne*, in an essay published in 1996. She relates Duliani's text to classic migration literature by highlighting images of travel, isolation, and hardship in his account of internment. In Stellin's view, internment, as it is portrayed by Duliani, "can be viewed as a powerful existential metaphor of the conditions Italian immigrants had to face with respect to their isolation and enclosure within the limits of their own communities, as well as vis-a-vis the surrounding Canadian society" (129). She notes the similarity between the image of internment life "without women" and conditions endured earlier by many Italian men, as immigrants living in small, isolated ethnic communities without women or families. These are valid points; however, emphasis on features of the immigrant condition in Duliani's account can elide issues of ethnicity and political dimensions of internment that emphasize the dynamics of authority. Stellin concurs with the widely held view that his book was "aimed at rehabilitating [Duliani's] image in front of the francophone community to which he belonged, as well as the Canadian authorities" (127). Finally, she suggests that readers familiar with "how tragic life had been in other concentration camps in Europe" might find it difficult "to consider the Canadian experience in the rather benign light [Duliani] wants us to" (128). Conversely though, the description he provides of life in the Canadian camps is so far removed from the real horrors of life in many of those other camps in Europe that it can have the reverse effect. It can minimize the reader's sympathy and make us even more suspicious of the broader claims of those who would use internment to seek to "rehabilitate" the ethnic identity of Italian Canadians.

Apart from this analysis by Iannucci and Stellin to the French and Italian versions, there was very little critical reaction from the literary community in Quebec to Duliani's internment chronicle. This apparent lack of response from critics to the French and Italian texts suggests that the rate of cultural transmission in Canada as a whole, its impact and the social effects it generates, is a direct function of the availability of the work in the dominant language of the culture — in English. Put another way, the language of the text determines, to a great extent, its cultural "authority" in the sense of its impact.

Pivato sees Duliani's French language text as an "early example" of a work that attempts to break down barriers that translation highlights, "barriers, both visible and invisible — walls, the separation of time, social restrictions, cultural differences, psychological problems and personal prejudices" (129). He sees both political and apolitical dimensions in Duliani's writing — an attempt "to break through his isolation in the camps and to communicate once again to the larger society" (129). The Italian language text is further evidence of the author's attempt to reach out to those in his own ethnic community and provide a sense of "justification for their treatment in this country during the war" (129). Finally, Pivato notes that "the language barrier kept the author's views from reaching the rest of Canada" and he believes that in the years immediately following the war it would likely not have been well received (130).

When Mazza's English translation of the text was released in 1994 it received a very positive review from Mark Thompson in *The Globe and Mail* (April 9, 1994 C19). His review suggests that with the passage of those many years the suspicion toward Italian Canadians that was so prevalent in the 1940s had dissipated and been replaced by different attitudes, namely a far greater sense of vigilance toward protecting civil liberties in Canada, including those of ethnic minorities. (The question of which ethnic minorities remains.) The shift in views about ethnicity in Canada is underscored by the opening lines of his review: "What if Canada went to war against Britain? Would our government designate all new Canadians of British ancestry "enemy aliens"? ... Should we, arbitrarily, arrest white Anglo-Saxon males, without warrants, and intern them indefinitely at Petawawa without laying charges? Just a thought — but such idle fantasies put in perspective Canada's lamentable treatment of Canadians of Italian descent during the Second World War" (*Globe and Mail*, April 9, 1994, C19). The prospect of anyone posing such a question in the wake of the War seems unfathomable; but the passage of time and shifting sensibilities toward ethnicity and rights make doing so now possible, even instructive. In recent years the English translation of *The City Without Women* has attracted some further attention (see Salvatore's *Ancient Memories, Modern Identities* (1999)), but it can hardly be said to have assumed a "distinctive place in the Canadian literary canon" as Mazza hoped it would. Still, the appearance of Mazza's English translation has exposed the issue of internment to a new generation of Italian Canadians.

The City Without Women and the Collective Identity of Italian Canadians

There are important connections between internment, Duliani's chronicle and the translations of it, and the sense of collective identity that Italian Canadians share today. Why do some Italian Canadians continue to pursue the issue of internment and redress? Why does it still matter? Because the cohesiveness of this group as an "ethnic community" is breaking down, being slowly eroded and slipping away. The changing conditions in which Italian Canadians now live help to identify why Duliani's text means different things now than it did when it was first published in 1945.

I find evidence of this in the radically different purposes for which the various language versions of the text were apparently generated. When it was first published in French and Italian, the content and tone of lament in Duliani's texts would likely have served to promote some measure of reconciliation for those who had experienced internment. The consensus among critics is that he intended those texts to assist in smoothing over difficult relations between Italian Canadians, Canadian authorities (in government and police), and the Canadian public, immediately following the war. The preface to the first chapter, entitled "To Know and Understand Each Other", speaks directly to that purpose. Duliani's justification of internment and his apologetic tone strongly suggest that his goal in offering his account of internment is to move forward and rehabilitate relations by setting aside the events of the recent past. He paints internment as an unfortunate, difficult ordeal but he suggests that its effects should not be seen as insurmountable. (Others have noted that his depiction of Italian Canadians interned as "model immigrants" might also have been intended to promote Italian Canadians collectively and to improve the perception of them (see Ventresca)).

Conversely, Mazza's comments concerning the provision of an English language text suggest that his English translation is intended to have exactly the opposite effect: to cast new light on old events in the hope that this backward glance will cause people to reflect on what took place, recognize the lasting harm done, and take steps both to "set the record straight," to rectify the situation, and to learn from the errors of the past. In 1994 Mazza wrote: "The publication in English translation of Mario Duliani's *The City Without Women* could be a timely opportunity to reflect upon the impact that sustained "ethnic" balkanization in Canada may already be having on the nation's future" (xvii). In the "post-911" era, and in light of continued concern over the issue of "ethnic profiling" in Canada, Mazza's comments now take on new meaning. For Duliani, the literary text was an exercise in memory and writing whose purpose was reconciliation and rehabilitation. Mazza's purpose was to recover an episode from the past and expose it as a means of moving forward in very different ways. His English translation is an important expression of agency and a radically different approach to the past as being vital to present and future understandings of Italian ethnicity in Canada.[16] It suggests that the past, including painful and shameful episodes, must be acknowledged to move forward; however, the pain and shame he exposes belong to Canada, not just to Italian Canadians. Many in this ethnic group can relate direct incidents of prejudice and bigotry based on their ethnicity; others have experienced a deep sense of shame which they associate with their ethnicity.[17]

The appearance of an English translation of the text has raised awareness about internment among a younger generation of Italian Canadians, but it may also expose the perceived need by leaders in the Italian Canadian community (or at least by those leading the movement seeking redress) to seize upon historical events as a means of consolidating an ethnic identity. The painstaking research undertaken by historians who attempt to determine Duliani's ideological orientation is justified precisely because some members of the Italian Canadian community continue to invest so much in the issue of the internments. Some maintain that those internments play an important role in how they define themselves as members of an ethnic community. These issues make it important to consider the effects of personal memory, vernacular history, and the critic's "self-location" as dimensions of the complex relationship between internment, ethnicity, and understanding how collective memory is formed and reformed in contemporary Canadian culture.

Personal and Family Memory in the Internment Puzzle

Attempting to assess the impact of the internment of some 600 Italian Canadians during the 1940s on the Italian Canadian community today is problematic; is it possible to quantify and measure such a strange occurrence or its effects projected over time? Personal accounts suggest the impact was devastating for some whose lives were directly touched, but those effects cannot be the same for subsequent generations. Here, I find it useful to consider my own position and personal experience as an academic of Italian ancestry. (Other Italian Canadian scholars — Pivato, Loriggio, and Di Cicco, for example — have commented on ethnicity being at times "inside" and at times "outside" the object of analysis.) I reflect on my own experience, my "self-location" (to borrow Kamboureli's term) and try to discern how it fits into this puzzle. I had no knowledge of the internment of Italian Canadians before I began to pursue this topic as an academic interest. My initial orientation was informed by the usual academic standards; I set out to conduct scholarly research and tried to be "objective" in my approach. For me, the impact of the internment of a few hundred Italian Canadians in the 1940s has been relatively small. I do not feel fundamentally formed or deformed by it. I do not feel that internment affects how I think about being of Italian heritage. It does not make me particularly sad or angry to think about it; I think about it as a historical event.

Then, I began to make inquiries within my own family about the memory of internment. I discovered that there were personal family stories connected to these events that I had been unaware of, and these stories had an impact on me. For example, my Aunt

Mary told me that she remembered studying Italian as a young girl at the Casa d'Italia in Toronto at this time, and she recalled digging a deep hole in the backyard of the family home in Toronto and burying the medals she had earned by her hard work and aptitude, because of fears that the RCMP might enter their home at any time, search it and find those prize medals, conclude that her father was a fascist, and throw him in jail. Stories like that make the fear that I have read about in historical accounts (like Bagnell's *Canadese*) seem a great deal more real. When she recounts stories about being told to burn all the Italian books in the house, I can sense the genuine terror that gripped her as a young girl, at the prospect that her father (my maternal grandfather) might not arrive home one evening after work. These personal memories and stories help me to understand another dimension of the history of those events and the durability of their impact on both personal and collective memory. Apparently, her fears were not unfounded; Luigi Bruti Liberati has noted that: "A special effort was devoted to the surveillance of schools for teaching Italian. The books used in these schools were subjected to intense study by officials of the RCMP, who were concerned that Canadian youths were being educated according to principles that were foreign to the British democratic tradition" (Liberati 79).

Another relative, my Aunt Lena (now deceased), described the anxiety and hurt that crushed my paternal grandfather on the morning when he arrived at his fruit store in downtown Toronto and found the store windows had been defaced with anti-Italian graffiti and anti-fascist slogans — ironically, at the same time that his only son (my father) was serving in the Canadian Forces overseas. The relating of such stories — painful memories that must be coaxed out of reluctant witnesses to history — helps me to comprehend the lasting impact, the emotional residue of ethnic profiling on that generation of hyphenated Italian Canadians. This emotional residue, I would submit, is a form of "authority" — the intangible but very real effects of the influence of history and memory.

Such vernacular history is prone to the same kinds of distortion, possible manipulation, and misrepresentation as any other historical document. It too needs to be investigated on questions of accuracy and reliability. Still, such memories become embedded and they can assume enormous weight. They become hyper-real and can assert a profound impact on the development of personal identity and collective ethnic identity. Such memories also become part of collective memory when they are transmitted informally, as in this case.

Still, their experience was not mine (at least not directly) or that of my peers. So I might be led to conclude that the broader impact of those events and the stories related to them probably is relatively minor for most Italian Canadians of my generation. But these events and the personal stories connected to them do not exist in a vacuum; their meaning evolves and changes. Their significance cannot be the same for those who experienced those dark days as they are for those of us who have followed. So, their experience becomes mine in a strange and interesting way — not mine personally, but mine collectively, through memory, history and ethnicity. The family stories, related only when requested, coaxed out of reluctant or reticent witnesses to history, reveal some of the "holes in history," some of what gets forgotten in official records unless they are recorded in stories, written or oral, and passed on. These unofficial stories and images take their place beside Duliani's "true human chronicle" (3) and become part of the dynamic of our collective memory. This emotional baggage can be a genuine force in some people's lives. The collective impact of this emotional residue was what prompted a group of Italian Canadians to act and it manifested itself in the campaign for redress spearheaded by the National Congress of Italian Canadians (NCIC). As Duliani himself put it: "[W]hat we suffer most ... is memory itself"; so how are we to move forward toward a meaningful understanding of these events, in themselves and in relation to the current social and political climate?

Melucci's ideas about collective identity and social action are useful here in considering both internment and the campaign for redress. He talks about collective identity not as a reality but as a tool for better understanding reality, and, like Antonio Gramsci, points to the central role of culture and symbolic production as agents of social change. Collective actors, Melucci asserts, "are neither historical heroes nor villains ... they are not 'subjects' that act with unity of purpose ... they are always plural, ambivalent, often contradictory" (78). He suggests that the time and conditions in which collective action occurs have a profound impact. Previously collective actors were deeply rooted in specific, shared social conditions — a working class background, organized in the structures of everyday life; there was a solidarity that shaped the identity of the group and grounded it in the material and cultural conditions of the everyday. (A description that could be applied to the Italian Canadian internees as a collective.) By contrast, today we see social movements which do not relate to specific social conditions (as in the case of the movement among those Italian Canadians who pursued the campaign for redress.) Whereas those interned had a greater sense of collective identity which sprang from their common material and cultural conditions, the Italian Canadian community today represents a much more diverse group. Consequently, because it is less homogeneous, it struggles to maintain a sense of collective identity. One way to do this is by recalling the events of the past in which Italian Canadians were wronged and trying to act in solidarity in response to those events. So, viewed from one perspective, the movement for redress is a means of trying to approximate the level of cohesion that existed then, but which the Italian Canadian community today has lost.

We have come to accept that our identities are works in progress, constantly evolving and reacting to our experiences; but it is equally true that our identity is also always about the past (which is fixed) and memory (which is not fixed but shifts over time). Similarly, identity is always positioned somewhere between the self — me as "I", and the group — me as one of "Us". These are unresolvable contradictions and our interpretation of specific events, such as internment, takes place in the gap between the fixed nature of the past and the dynamic nature of memory; between the impulse to maintain an integrated and dynamic sense of self (as individual), and to the need to identify with others with whom we share a common bond, to be part of a community. In the post-911 era Canadians find themselves facing difficult issues around ethnic profiling once again; Italian Canadians recall their own collective history and experience as victims of powerful legislation, policies and security measures that were, and remain for some, the cause of so much hardship, shame and suffering. Melucci suggests that "[m]ore than in any previous culture identity today is in need of a relationship to the past. Such a relationship is created by the necessity of retaining something while changing, of maintaining roots, of reconstructing our history without which there is no possibility of progress" (85).

In a culture like ours, where speed is championed and the speed of change in our lives is constantly accelerating, texts like this one serve to slow us down. Duliani's text makes me pause and reflect on how the Italian Canadian community was perceived and treated, how it is perceived today, and the relation between the two. *The City Without Women* plays an important role in creating a sense of collective identity for the Italian Canadian community because, as a text, it stands as a singular and unique written record of significant historical events, and also because the Italian Canadian community continues to invest in internment as meaningful to its self-definition as an ethnic community. "What we suffer most is memory itself" — but suffering need not be pointless or meaningless. As Duliani points out, suffering can build character and stiffen the resolve of the afflicted to overcome adversity. It can also move us to focus on the plight of others. So too, reflecting back on the internment of Italian Canadians through Duliani's *The City Without Women* can move us to better understand how ethnic communities are affected by historical memory. This exercise can help us respond to difficult social issues such as immigration, national security, and ethnic profiling. The internment of Italian Canadians, and Mario Duliani's compelling account of it, demonstrate how sometimes a glance in our rear view mirror can help us to navigate the difficult road ahead.

- **Note: The differences between *La ville sans femmes* and *Città senza donne* are examined in Fabiana Fusco's essay, appearing in this publication.**

Endnotes

1. Other accounts of the internments, such as the one in Kenneth Bagnell's *Canadese* (Chapter 4 "Days of Darkness, Days of Despair") emphasize the incredulity of the Italian Canadian community at what was happening and the

sense of injustice; still there is a strong sense that Italian Canadians were powerless to resist these events, given the legislation enacted in Parliament (under the Defense of Canada Regulations (DOCR) in September 1939), the tide of public opinion against them, and the relative lack of influence they had in terms of their collective social status.

2. The focus of this campaign seems now to have shifted from one seeking redress (including financial compensation) to one that has as its central objective the recording of an "official" apology, delivered in the House of Commons of Canada's Parliament. See: "Political Apologies: a delicate art" *Globe and Mail*, 4/24/10.

3. The debate on this issues is best illustrated by the opposing views of, on the one hand, Bruno Ramirez, whose article "Ethnicity on Trial"(1988) is sharply critical of the actions taken against those interned; and, on the other hand, Roberto Perin, who is far less willing to accept the claims of innocence made by and on behalf of Duliani and others interned. Perin's article offers a detailed scholarly investigation into Duliani's political involvement and activities, in an attempt to establish whether or not he was involved with fascist organizations in Canada and abroad prior to his arrest.

4. In his analysis, Perin suggests: "Whatever the book's literary merits, the problem is how to approach it. Is this a novel or a historical document? [It] can be read either way, provided the critics define their objectives at the outset" (313). He suggests "a literary method seems most appropriate for stylistic or broadly thematic analysis " (313), but he cautions that, in their enthusiasm for the text, literary critics have not exercised sufficient care in

scrutinizing the historical materials: "Ironically, although Duliani revivalists are trained in literature, they fail to substantiate their ambitious claims concerning the book's literary merits. Instead they establish his importance as a writer by exploiting the politics of internment" (313).

5. For example, present day security concerns, prompted by terrorist attacks, have fueled debate about the legitimacy of ethnic profiling. In October 2001 a legal scholar noted that, with the recent introduction of Bill C-36 before Parliament, "ethnic and racial profiling ... [had] burst onto the national agenda" and "attained renewed prominence" (Choudhry 367). Considering the impact and the constitutionality of ethnic profiling, Professor Choudhry suggested that "the harm to human dignity — what transforms the use of stereotypes into discrimination — is that doing so has the effect of stigmatizing all the members of that group, by promoting the view that they are somehow less worthy of respect and consideration, because they all possess the undesirable trait in question" (371). These concerns have prompted many Canadians to debate sensitive issues — balancing human rights and civil liberties against the need to ensure the safety and security of citizens. Many in the Italian Canadian community remember the events of June 1940 and recognize the terrible symptoms of ethnic profiling that Choudhry describes.

6. The "Note About the Author" in Mazza's translation of *The City Without Women* notes that Duliani was "[b]orn on September 26, 1885, in Istria (north-eastern region of the Kingdom of Italy which became part of the Yugoslavian Republic of Croatia following the Second World War)"

(158). So his birthplace was part of Italy when he was born, but it later became part of another country. For many people now ethnicity is not reducible simply to "country of origin" but will be retained as ethnic heritage that may be traced through multiple migrations and through multiple, mixed ethnic heritages. Consequently, ethnicity becomes more complex — a hybrid — as opposed to its former strict association with a "country of origin."

7. Although journalism was his livelihood, Duliani's passion was theatre; he is credited as being a major figure in "the birth of professional French theatre in Canada" (Salvatore 64). His contribution to the performing arts was recognized in 1961 when he became the first Italian-Canadian to be appointed to the Conseil des Artes du Quebec (65). There is a not so subtle irony in the fact that a man once regarded as an "enemy alien" and a threat to national security could later be celebrated as a pillar of the arts community and a champion of French Canadian theatre. Apparently, whatever his political indiscretions might have been in the 1930s, Duliani had been fully and completely "rehabilitated" by 1961. Viewed from another perspective, however, this fact might be taken as evidence of the rehabilitation of Canadian society, and the diminishment of prejudice against Italian Canadians.

8. Curiously, these issues seem to recede from view as concerns surrounding the interpretation of the English version of his text. They are not taken up by Mazza, Bagnell, or in a review in the *Globe and Mail* by Mark Thompson.

9. Michael Del Balso, at Dawson College (Montreal), provided useful information about the Italian edition: it

was published in 1946 by Gustavo D'Errico, Editore. It included a preface which, Del Balso notes, was "specifically written for the Italian edition in which [Duliani] implies the French edition had some impact." Details of publication are noted in the Italian text as follows: "Di questo libro sono stati tirati cinquanti esemplari, numerate da 1 a 50 su carta byroni, e 5,000 esemplari su carta delle cartiere rolland che costituiscono l'edizione originale ..." The Italian edition also lists Duliani's previous publications, theatre works and books in Italian and French, of which the earliest are published in 1906 in Milan.

10. Professor Frank Davey offered useful comments on this matter. He noted that the idea of the rehabilitation of Italian Canadians after the War must be contextualized within the rehabilitation of Italy that began in 1944. This project involved efforts on many fronts. From late 1944 on, Italy was characterized in the Allied media as a friendly country being liberated, not an enemy one being conquered. This view was disseminated widely in Canada after the war by Churchill's popular 6-volume history of the war, as well as by Hollywood films that depicted the Italian campaign only in terms of a German enemy, and the entry of Allied troops into Rome as being greeted by crowds of flower-bearing Italians.

11. Italian Canadian writer Nino Ricci makes a passing reference to internment in his novel *In A Glass House* (1993); his character Victor speculates that issues arising from the war, including internment, contributed to Italians withdrawing from public life in Canada for a long time after the war (271).

12. Salvatore provides a brief sketch of Duliani's professional involvement in Canada after he arrived in Montreal in 1936. He was employed as a journalist for French language publications including *La Presse* and *L'Illustration nouvelle*, and the Italian language weekly newspaper *La Verità* (64). Salvatore suggests that Duliani had "an easy pen and a brilliant mind" and consequently "his common, everyday French enjoyed mass appeal" (65). It seems natural then that he would gravitate toward the language in which he felt most comfortable for his account of internment.
13. Census stats confirm this. (At that time, a census was completed only every 10 years in Canada, in 1941 and 1951.) In 1941 there were 9,195 people living in Quebec whose place of birth was Italy. Of these 5,935 were literate in both French and English, 1,419 were literate in French only, and 1,324 were literate in English only. Fully 80% then of Quebecers born in Italy could have read the French text. I am indebted to Professor Don Kerr for pointing out that during the war years demographers have noted that ethnicity was typically under reported or not reported accurately. He suggested that at this time Italians living in Quebec likely spoke Italian in the home and French in the workplace; affinities between the two languages would have made this a relatively easy adjustment.
14. Publication information indicates that 5,000 copies were printed of the Italian text, but there are no records of sales or distribution of the text. In 1951 there were 24,619 people living in Quebec whose mother tongue was Italian. Some 20,619 of them resided in Montreal. Census data indicate that a relatively small number of Italian-born residents of Quebec could not read either French or English.

15. In researching Duliani's language proficiency I consulted Professor Roberto Perin at York University. He noted (in e-mail correspondence): "I can only infer that Duliani spoke no English." Perin suggested that Duliani's contacts in Montreal were only with French speakers. The Montreal Repertory Theatre had an English-speaking section with which Duliani seemed to have no contacts. Perin had no information about the book's popular reception in Quebec in the '50s and '60s, although he noted that historians were aware of its existence. According to him, detailing the popular response to the text moves into "largely uncharted waters". Salvatore provides a comprehensive list of his publications, including works in progress that were never completed; no English titles appear. He adds that "Duliani's last years were spent in solitude, in bad health, and destitution" (72).
16. The translation of Duliani's text into English can be seen as part of a process that Tejswani Nataranjan cites as the use of translation in re-writing that leads to deterritorialization. For a full discussion of translation and its deterritorializing function in postcolonial texts see Nataranjan's *Siting Translation* (1992).
17. Frank Davey notes that the post-war shame of Italian Canadians is very complex. It involves matters other than internment, for example, if individuals had supported Mussolini or anti-semitism. Also, post-war shame was experienced not only by Italians but also by Germans, Austrians, Hungarians and members of other ethnic groups.

Works Cited

Bagnell, Kenneth. *Canadese: A Portrait of the Italian Canadians.* Toronto: Macmillan, 1989.

Bruti Liberati, Luigi. "The Internment of Italian Canadians." Trans. Gabriele Scardellato. In Iacovetta et al. 76-98.

Duliani, Mario. *The City Without Women: a chronicle of internment life in Canada during the Second World War.* Trans. Antonino Mazza. Oakville: Mosaic, 1994.

Harrison, Trevor, and John Friesen. *Canadian Society in the Twenty-First Century.* 2nd Ed. Toronto: Canadian Scholars' Press, 2010.

Iacovetta, Franca, Roberto Perin, and Angelo Principe. Eds. *Enemies Within: Italian and other Internees in Canada and Abroad.* Toronto: UT Press, 2000.

Iannucci, Susan. "Contemporary Italo-Canadian Literature." *Arrangiarsi: The Italian Immigration Experience in Canada.* Eds. Roberto Perin and Franc Sturino. Montreal: Guernica, 1989.

Perin, Roberto. "Actor or Victim? Mario Duliani and His Internment Narrative." in Iacovetta et al. 312-334.

Mazza, Antonino. Introduction. *The City Without Women.* Oakville: Mosaic, 1994.

Melucci, Alberto. *Challenging Codes: Collective Action in the Information Age.* Cambridge, NY: Cambridge UP, 1996.

Nataranjan, Tejaswini. *Siting Translation: History, Poststructuralism and the Colonial Context.* Berkley: U California Press, 1992.

Pivato, Joseph. *Echo: Essays on Other Literatures*. Toronto: Guernica, 1994.

Ricci, Nino. *In A Glass House*. Toronto: McClelland & Stewart, 1993

Ramirez, Bruno. "Ethnicity on Trial: The Italians of Montreal and the Second World War." *On Guard for Thee*. Ed. Norman Hillmer, *et al*. Ottawa: Cdn. Committee for Second WW, 1988. 71-84.

Salvatore, Filippo. *Ancient Memories, Modern Identities: Italian Roots in Contemporary Canadian Authors*. Trans. Domenic Cusmano. Toronto: Guernica, 1999.

Stellin, Monica. "*Città senza donne* and the Italian Literature of Migration." Quaderni d'Italianistica Vol XVII, No.2, Autunno 1996. 125-132.

Thompson, Mark. "The Lamentable Internment of Italian Canadians." Rev. of *The City Without Women*. trans. Antonino Mazza. *The Globe and Mail* 11 April 1994: C19.

Ventresca, Robert and Franca Iacovetta. "Redress, Collective Memory and the Politics of History." Iacovetta et al. 379-405.

FABIANA FUSCO
(Translated by GIULIA DE GASPERI)

From Imprisonment to Writing:
The Case of Mario Duliani's
La ville sans femmes/Città senza donne

The aim of this essay is to bring to light an account, the only one written by an Italian inside a Canadian internment camp, of important historical-literary significance. The account is Mario Duliani's *La ville sans femmes* written while he was a prisoner in the internment camps of Petawawa (Northern Ontario) and Fredericton (New Brunswick) from June 1940 to October 1943. He was there with other Italian and German, as well as English and French internees. These individuals were not charged with any offence but were considered possible threats.[1] This "fictional documentary," as Duliani himself described it, was published after his release (1945) and was followed by the Italian translation done by Duliani himself in 1946.[2]

Duliani was born in Pisino, Istria in 1885 and moved when quite young to Milan. There he devoted himself to journalism and the theatre. He then moved to Paris where he worked as a correspondent for several Italian newspapers, while writing successful plays in French. During the 1930s he met Eugène Berthiaume, at that time the Canadian consul in Paris, and following his invitation (or, as some say, with his help), he moved to Montréal in 1936 to run a new Italian-language newspaper. At the same time he contributed to the improvement of the city's theatrical scene, thanks to the experience he had gained in Europe. He also successfully ran the French section of the *Montréal Repertory*

Theatre. When Mussolini declared war against Great Britain, France and Canada, the Canadian government reacted by invoking the War Measures Act to intern "enemy aliens" without having to bring specific criminal charges. Duliani, although a leading figure in the journalistic and theatrical scenes of Montréal, was among those interned. The experience may have proved distressing but, on his release, Duliani soon resumed his life as a journalist and playwright. He died in 1964, three years after being appointed to the *Conseil des Arts du Québec*. With his death, *La ville sans femmes* faded into oblivion. It was only during the 1980s that the book was re-evaluated and seen as a historical source on the condition of Italian immigrants and as an invaluable account of the birth of an Italian-Canadian cultural identity. The 1980s were also the years during which the National Congress of Italian-Canadians began its tenacious battle against the federal government of Canada to push for the recognition of the wrongful action taken against Italian Canadians accused of representing a possible threat to the country's national security. On November 4 1990, in front of an emotional audience (but not in Parliament), Prime Minister Brian Mulroney expressed, on behalf of the government and of the Canadian people, his full and sincere apologies to his fellow citizens of Italian origin subjected to arbitrary internment.

The work by Duliani, as mentioned earlier, focuses on the drama of the internment in Camp Petawawa. However, the two texts, the original in French and the Italian translation, show some structural differences. The Italian version has a subtitle, *Il libro degli italiani d'America*, and also an extra chapter, chapter XIII (CD, 243-50), entitled "Gli italiani d'America," for a total of 270 pages. According to the author, this section should have helped shed some light on the social and historical framework within which the narration is set, as well as providing some criticism towards the Italian government and its representatives in Canada. As he does in other parts of the novel, Duliani explains the drama of emigration through the voices of individuals (voices that remain anonymous) caught up in a reconstructed passionate dialogue. On the other hand, the French text has 316 pages and 'Annexes' (VF, 301-316) that Duliani consciously chooses to omit in the Italian version. Other important aspects emerge by comparing the two versions: the language of the Italian translation shows characteristics that are not found in the original text. There are interferences between Italian and French that, as is known, constitute a quite common experience among bilingual speakers, as well as the borrowing of words from English that are not present in the original text and that provide the Italian reader with a sense of realism and local context. In the Italian version there are also frequent explanatory additions that at times overshadow the poetic components. The impression the reader has is that Duliani wanted to permeate the Italian version with an excessive realism cutting down, in some parts, the emotional elements. The author of this journal is however able to create an authentic document where historical and life events alternate with dramatic and lyrical aspects.

The Italian translation, dedicated, as is the original French, to Duliani's wife (Henryette Gaultier Duliani), is made up of sixteen chapters, two of which, more specifically the second (*La nostra città*) and the tenth (*La città senza donne*), recall the title of the work itself. Duliani's decision to define his place of imprisonment as a "city" can be explained in relation to the layout of the camp itself which was made up of twelve large wooden barracks where the internees were lodged, as well as barracks that housed a kitchen, a hospital, a pharmacy, recreational quarters, and a prison. All of these buildings were lined up in two irregular rows facing each other, separated by a wide strip of land that the Italians of Montreal had jokingly christened "rue Sainte-Catherine" (VF, p. 38 e CD, p. 46), a tribute to one of the city's main thoroughfares. This image is definitely ironic when compared to the sad functions these buildings had. In fact, in the introductory chapter, Duliani recalls the distress during his very first night in the new "city" where the dark and gloomy majesty of the Canadian boreal forest adds one more element to the sinister image of the barbed wire and of the lights mounted on it. The "city" that housed Duliani and his companions in misfortune is mentioned also in some excerpts in the second chapter:

> Un camp d'internés au Canada ressemble à une petite ville ou, mieux, à une grosse bourgade. Dans les deux camps où j'ai vécu, en effet, la population atteignit par moment presque mille âmes. C'est une population! Certes, de temps en temps, il s'est produit des migrations massives qui ont bouleversé, temporairement, le fonctionnement normal de la vie collective (VF, 35).

> Un campo d'internamento nel Canada rassomiglia ad una piccola città, o, meglio, ad una grande borgata. Nei due campi dove ho vissuto, infatti, la popolazione ha raggiunto, ad alcuni momenti, più di mille anime ... Ma queste anime inquiete, erano piuttosto fluttuanti ... Avvenivano di tanto in tanto migrazioni in massa, arrivi e partenze collettive, sgretolamenti progressivi a causa di 'rilasci' o di liberazioni individuali. Tutto ciò accadeva per la misteriosa volontà degli 'uffici' che dirigevano le operazioni dell'internamento, la cui logica naturalmente sfuggiva alla nostra competenza. Un caricaturista tedesco del Campo fece un disegno a colori che ebbe molto successo. Vi si vedeva un vasto autocarro carico d'internati,

> scortati da soldati, che filava a tutta velocità sulla strada ... E sotto, questa leggenda: - Se volete visitare il Canada, fatevi internare! ... Ma tutto questo andirivieni aveva per effetto di provocare frequenti squilibri nell'organizzazione della vita diremo così cittadina del campo (CD, 41).

One can see immediately that the Italian text clearly is longer than the French. Duliani rewrites this section to highlight the unavoidability of the situation while taking the liberty of being ironic. The account of the everyday life of hundreds of individuals unrolls through a series of episodes like the one described above; some sad, some funny (many of which appear only in the Italian version) representing Duliani's sharp but also humanly forceful nature. The absolute silence of the night spent inside the double-locked wooden barracks with barred windows sadly brings the prisoners back to the past. Duliani remembers and travels through his memories, often using representational direct speech and thus providing the reader with the historical background wherein his journal is set:

> En tout cas, ce serait une "sale histoire" pour tous ceux qui, habitant le Canada, avaient manifesté une sympathie idéologique ou platonique envers le fascisme, car ils se trouveraient à devenir ipso facto des ennemis! «Que deviendrons-nous? se demandaient ces Italiens auxquels, évidemment, on ne pouvait faire grief de ce que déciderait le Gouvernement de Rome. Des amis, gens bien intentionnés ou bien renseignés, avaient pris le soin de les prévenir: «Prenez garde à vous! Si Mussolini déclare la guerre, vous courrez le risque d'être internés». Les Italiens répondaient: «Pourquoi le serions-nous, puisque nous n'avons rien fait contre le Canada, que nous avons créé une famille ici, dans le pays ...» (VF, 26).

•••

> Ma quel che era certo si era che tutto ciò stava per diventare "una faccenda complicata" per coloro che, residenti nel Canada, avevano manifestato una simpatia ideologica o platonica per il fascismo, perchè ipso facto si sarebbero trovati ad essere considerati come nemici. Nemici del Canada? Nemici dell'America? Ma era mai possibile? «E allora, che cosa diventeremo?» si domandavano non senza un'ansia viva questi italiani. Alcuni amici — bene intenzionati o bene informati — avevano preso cura di avvertirli: «State attenti! Se Mussolini dichiara la guerra, correte rischio di essere internati». E quelli di rimando: «Ma perchè lo saremmo? ... Perchè ci si dovrebbe far carico di quello che si deciderà a Roma?...E poi, noi non abbiamo mai fatto nulla contro il Canada ... Abbiamo fondato una famiglia in questo paese ...» (CD, 32-33).

Several times, Duliani, giving license to his characters and also to himself to use direct speech, adds to, or better, rewrites in the Italian, some short dialogues found in the French version:

> Mais dans l'obscurité de la baraque où nous sommes cadenassés pour la nuit, voici qu'un jeune homme marié depuis quelques mois, couché à côté de moi, me confie à voix basse: — Je pense à elle. Que fait-elle, à cette minute précise? Elle qui, tous les soirs, se blotissait contre moi, comme un petit enfant qui veut se mettre à l'abri des mauvais rêves. Dort-elles ou pense-t-elle à moi comme je pense à elle? Je suis sûr qu'elle ne dort pas ... (VF, 22).

> Ma nell'oscurità della baracca dove siamo chiusi a lucchetto per la notte, un giovanotto sposato da qualche mese solt-

anto, mi s'avvicina e mi domanda: - Dormi? — No — Io non posso dormire! ... Penso a lei ... — A chi? — A mia moglie! ... Siamo sposati da poche settimane, ma aveva già l'abitudine di rannicchiarsi nelle mie braccia come un bimbo che vuol mettersi al riparo dei cattivi sogni ... Che cosa fa in questo momento preciso? Dorme, o fa come me, e pensa a me com'io penso a lei? E dopo un breve silenzio, egli accentua la sua convinzione con voce più viva: — No, no! ... Sono sicuro! ... Non dorme! (CD, 28-29).

The text translated by Duliani seems to aim at making the reader participate in the suffering felt by Duliani and his companions, suffering caused by the abrupt separation from their loved ones, through a sort of dialogical "staging," only slightly delineated in the original text. This painful deprivation explains the lyrical inspiration present in the text that gives coherence and cohesion to the novel whose plot is not developed through a chronological line, but along a series of alternating remembrances of the internment period. The passages dedicated to the suffering experienced by those who have been taken away from their loved ones, without a chance for defense, and imprisoned, without a time-limit, are the most touching ones. Duliani becomes, on those occasions, the spokesperson for all those Italian Canadians who, through no fault of theirs, were in the "city without women." Among those are the memories of both young and old prisoners, who are tormenting themselves about what has happened and seem unable to find peace:

> Peu à peu, insensiblement, on égraine le rosaire des confidences et l'on s'abandonne à l'angoissant rappel des choses du passé (VF, 37).

•••

> E poco a poco, insensibilmente — dopo aver esaurito tutti i 'si dice' sulle prossime 'liberazioni in massa' — si comincia a sgranare il rosario delle confidenze, ci si abbandona all' angosciosa rievocazione del passato.
>
> - Un giorno mia moglie mi disse ...
>
> - Una volta, mio figlio maggiore, tornato a casa dalla scuola ...
>
> - Mi ricordo di una bella ragazza che abitava poco lontano da casa mia ...
>
> E così di seguito... Finchè l'emozione sale alla gola. E, nessuno dice più niente. Perché nessuno può più parlare! (CD, 45)

Here too, the Italian version is longer than the French one, since memory is here recalled using the reconstruction of the representational direct speech aiming, once again, at underlining the suffering of the prisoners, unjustly deprived of the comfort of their loved ones. The stress on the figure of the woman and on the lack of love gives the author the opportunity to introduce other important themes of the novel, that of the arrests and of the internments. Being physically deprived of their loved ones' affection and of freedom acquires an even more serious meaning since it represents, for the prisoners, the tangible proof of the suspicion of being traitors to their own country. The political situation makes the prisoners feel anxious from a moral stand point; an even more difficult position to bear since they know they are innocent victims:

> Les derniers «journaux parlés» de la nuit, aux postes radiophoniques, laissaient prévoir comme imminente une décision de l'Italie. Pendant la matinée du lundi, les derniers espoirs

s'évanouissaient un à un. A midi, l'irréparable était accompli! Dans un geste de folie, le Gouvernement de Rome venait de déclarer la guerre à la France et à la Grande-Bretagne. Le sort en était jeté. A Montréal, commença la râfle ... Ceux qui étaient désignés devaient être arrêtés. Et ils le furent tous (VF, 27).

Gli ultimi "giornali parlanti" della notte, ai Posti della Radio, avevano lasciato prevedere imminente una decisione dell'Italia. Durante la mattinata del lunedì le ultime speranze di tutti coloro — ed era l'immensa maggioranza degl'italiani d'America — che volevano veder l'Italia fuori dal conflitto, vanivano una ad una. A mezzogiorno l'irreparabile era compiuto! In un gesto di follia, il Governo di Roma aveva dichiarato la guerra alla Francia ed all'Inghilterra. Il dado era gettato! A Montreal comincia la "retata" ... Coloro che era già stati designati dovevano essere arrestati. E lo furono tutti. Molti si presentarono anzi spontaneamente, come me, per esempio (CD, 33-34).

Thanks to his lively personality and a spirit full of initiative and self-denial, Duliani takes on the task of nurse in the hospital camp. Through his position, he becomes the repository of intimate life stories, stories of physical and moral sufferings. The author wants to emphasize the civil behavior the internees have, a behavior that is respected by the authorities running the camp who, in turn, try to meet the internees' requests and needs:

> Chaque heure de travail était suivie d'un smoking time, dix minutes de repos qui nous permettaient d'en griller une. Les soldats et nous, couchés par terre, échangions des propos aimables. Aucune allusion à la guerre. Les officiers avaient

donné cette consigne aux soldats. Et nous prenions garde de ne pas mettre dans l'embarras ceux qui avaient la charge de nous accompagner (VF, 41).

Ogni ora era seguita da dieci minuti di riposo, lo "smoking time" che ci permettevano di fumare una sigaretta. Allora i soldati facevano altrettanto, e, fra una buffata e l'altra scambiavamo qualche parola ed anche qualche scherzo amichevole.

Fu così che un giovanotto — partito poi per il fronte — mi confessò:
  - Dapprincipio non osavamo parlarvi ...
  - Perchè mai?
  - Perchè ci avevano detto che eravate tutti 'uomini molto pericolosi'.

Naturalmente nessuna allusione alla guerra. Gli ufficiali avevano data la consegna ai soldati. E noi prendevamo ben cura di non metter nell'imbarazzo coloro che avevano l'incarico di sorvegliarci (CD, 51).

In this passage the change is quite evident since a short dialogue is inserted. The author, aware of the duality of the historical and literary components of his work, wants to make the reader aware of the civil behavior he and his companions have. In order to prove the injustice they suffered, Duliani lets a soldier speak of the foolishness of the charges that the Canadian government brought against them.

In the remaining pages and chapters of *Città senza donne*, despite the injustice he and his companions have suffered, Duliani maintains an admirable serenity of spirit and a balance in his reasoning that bring him — through touching and sincere pages, closer to a rewriting than a translation — to an understanding of the behaviour the Canadians displayed towards the European immigrants. It also reaffirms his sentiment of belonging to this new and young nation that did not show any generosity or sensibility towards him. In the *Preface* Duliani, explaining why he wrote the book, does not condemn, as one would expect, the firmness of the nation in its enforcement of the law on its foreign citizens, but expresses a timid opinion that tends to be conciliatory in the hope of "dissipating the last doubts, of clarifying the last misunderstandings" (CD, 24).

Endnotes

1. M. Duliani, *La ville sans femmes*, Montréal, les Éditions Pascal, 1945 and *Città senza donne*, Montreale (Montréal), Gustavo D'Errico, 1946 (shortened as VF and CD). In 1994 the English translation was published, *The City without Women: A Chronicle of Internment Life in Canada during the Second World War* and included a preface by Antonino Mazza, Oakville, Mosaic Press. In 2003 Cosmo Iannone Editore published a re-print of the Italian translation with an introduction by Filippo Salvatore.
2. This essay draws upon themes discussed in other works by the same author, cited here also for biographical purposes: *Da La ville sans femmes a Città senza donne di Mario Duliani*, in *Itinerranze e transcodificazioni. Scrittori migranti dal Friuli Venezia Giulia al Canada*, a cura di A. Ferraro e A.P. De Luca, Udine, Forum, 2008, 51-74; *Le migrazioni linguistiche e l'autotraduzione di Mario Duliani*, in «Oltreoceano» 5 (2011), 15-30 [monographical issue entitled *L'autotraduzione nelle letterature migranti*, edited by A. Ferraro]; *Francese e italiano a confronto: La ville sans femmes e Città senza donne di Mario Duliani*, in *Comparatio*

delectat. Akten der VI. Internationalen Arbeitstagung zum romanisch-deutschen und innerromanischen Sprachvergleich (Innsbruck, 3-5 September 2008), hrsg. E. Lavric, W. Pöckl, F. Schallart, Frankfurt am Main, P. Lang, 2011, 831-847.

Venera Fazio

City of a Perilous Legacy

On June 10, 1940, and in the months following, while Canada was at war against Italy, hundreds of Italian Canadian men across the country were arrested by virtue of the War Measures Act. Terrified men, some as young as eighteen and others in their seventies, were whisked away to internment camps in the Canadian bush to serve a sentence as "enemy aliens"; yet they were never formally charged with any crime.

A first-hand account of these events of Orwellian magnitude is *La ville sans femmes* by Mario Duliani, published in French in 1945 and translated into English as *The City Without Women* by Antonino Mazza in 1994.

"Imagine," says Antonino Mazza from his home in Ottawa, "you do not know what you have done wrong or for how long you will be punished ... you live in suspension, in limbo ... you experience a huge torment of being alive and great anxiety." With Mazza's translation of Mario Duliani's text, renewed attention was focused on the trauma and injustice inflicted on these Canadian-born or naturalized citizens.

The events that began on June 10, 1940, would have far-reaching consequences, not only for the internees, but also for their families and for the fabric of Italian Canadian culture. They also foreshadowed the racial profiling of today, as we wage yet another global war — the war on terrorism.

Mazza, poet and award-winning translator, knew about the internment long before he translated Duliani's book. "In the Italian community where I grew up, people knew about the camps," he explains. "They would whisper about it, but not talk openly. They tried to keep it a secret. There was a lot of shame surrounding the subject."

Mario Duliani, who died in Montreal in 1964 at the age of 79, served a forty-month sentence, first in Camp Petawawa near Ottawa and then in Gagetown, New Brunswick. A year after the publication of *La ville sans femmes*, Duliani published *La città senza donne*, an Italian translation of his original account. Few paid attention to his chronicle, and those who did dismissed it by maligning the author. "[Discrediting Duliani] was a total red-herring," says Mazza, his voice rising. "He was a well-respected journalist, playwright, and a prominent leader in the literary and artistic communities of Montreal. People focused on his political leanings, on whether or not he was a fascist, instead of paying attention to what he wrote about."

The City Without Women is a documentary infused with poetic language. To maintain the privacy of his fellow inmates, Duliani does not mention anyone by name or dwell in depth on any one individual. Instead, he provides an overview of life within the camps. The men lived in stark physical surroundings. Both camps were set up in isolated locations surrounded by miles of forest. The barracks did not have electricity and the prisoners slept on iron bunk beds. There were bars on the windows, and barbed wire circled the camps.

A number of the men were members of the Fascio, the Canadian branch of Mussolini's fascist Party, but the majority had been arrested because of their visibility within their Italian communities. They were leaders, professional men of importance, businessmen, members of Italian social clubs, and participants in parades organized by the Italian Consulate. "Their greatest crime was to show emotional loyalty to their country of origin," emphasizes Mazza.

They were arrested for no reason other than their ethnic heritage. Duliani reports that one man did not even know, until he arrived at the camp, that Italy had declared war on the Allies.

Every profession and trade was represented, including a member of parliament, doctors, lawyers, engineers, musicians, farmers, gangsters, labourers, students, ministers, and a Catholic priest. Some were able to practice their trades within the camps, but most helped build roads, cleared brush, or cut timber to fire the camp's furnaces and stoves. Those unsuitable for hard labour worked at lighter chores, such as kitchen duties. Others who had been mentally fragile before they were interned suffered relapses and had to be transferred to mental institutions. Almost all of the internees endured bouts of depression and anxiety.

Duliani writes: "The value of the past radically increased ... At moments the nostalgia for a landscape, for a face, a voice, bursts in our hearts and ... chokes us ... Our collective temperament is dictated by the loss of our women." Men over fifty who were close to reaching the high point of their careers "feared the inadvertent crumbling of the edifices they had built with the dedicated patience, hard work, and the sacrifices of a lifetime."

Duliani was one of the lucky ones. He resumed his pre-internment life. "Many others did not," says Mazza. "[Because of the stigma,] they changed their names. Some moved to other cities. They developed strategies to disappear within their communities."

During the internment, the Italian communities across Canada collapsed, their leaders no longer there, and their social clubs and organizations erased. Health care deteriorated with the forced exile of Italian-speaking doctors. The communities were rife with confusion, discouragement, and resentment. Italian Canadians began to hide their ethnicity. Later, those who had immigrated before the Second World War distanced themselves from the postwar Italian immigrants.

"They were too Italian for their taste," states Mazza. "They considered them uncivilized and called them nicknames like 'greenhorn.' The established Italians wanted the newcomers to shut down their cultural volume." Post-war immigrants, hoping for a helping hand from their countrymen, had to look elsewhere. It took decades for the Italian-Canadian communities to re-establish themselves.

Now, more than seventy years from the start of the internment, our country is once again grappling with racial profiling, this time ensnaring Arabs and Muslims. "We are moving towards total bigotry," emphasizes Mazza. "[The passing of Canada's anti-terrorism laws, Bills C-36, C-22, C-35, and C-42] is the most vile suppression of civil rights yet, far worse than the War Measures Act. In a sweeping fashion, Bill C-36 obliterates the Charter of Rights and Freedoms." It represents a precarious balance between civil rights and national security. The anti-terrorism laws allow the government to arrest without warrants, hold secret trials based on secret evidence, and convict without proof of criminal intent. "Because trials can be conducted in secrecy," Mazza continues, "no one knows what is going on ..."

Rocco Galati, a constitutional lawyer from Toronto, is familiar with "secret" trials. In a speech to the Justice Committee on November 6, 2001, he stated, "... there are approximately 800 illegal detentions in this country currently going on in the correctional centres ... Muslims and Arabs have been directed not to be able to phone their lawyers, see their lawyers, phone their families ... I see it in jails everyday."

"We have a militaristic approach to solving problems," protests Mazza. "We seem to take a concentration camp approach." It's a paradox that our country turns against its own, and chooses to trample on the rights of citizens in order to protect itself from predators. "All immigrants are here by invitation," Mazza adds. "We ask them to come, yet we do not create a safe environment for them ... I think Trudeau got it right with his Charter of Rights and Freedoms."

In his introductory essay to Duliani's book, Mazza quotes the Mayan proverb, "Those who do not know their history cannot predict their own future." By translating *The City Without Women*, Mazza makes sure that the history of the Italian internment will not be forgotten. He also forces us to think about how we and our children might remember the profiling and internment of Muslims and Arabs sixty years from now.

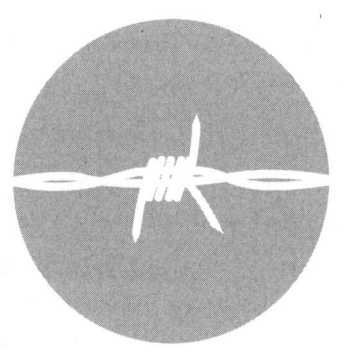

Sam Migliore

Painful Memories of a Forgotten Past

NOTE: This is a revised version of a paper I published as "War Wounds: Painful Memories of a Forgotten Past." In Shantz, Jeff, ed. 2010. *Racial Profiling and Borders: International, Interdisciplinary Perspectives*, pp. 175-201. Lake Mary, Florida: Vandeplas Publishing. The paper is based, in part, on research I conducted for: Migliore, Sam, and A. Evo DiPierro, eds. 1999. *Italian Lives, Cape Breton Memories*. Sydney, Nova Scotia: University College of Cape Breton.

Introduction

In 1989, during a casual conversation with a new male acquaintance, I happened to mention that I was of Sicilian background. The man surprised me by stopping to say: "I thought you were *white*!" From what I know of the man, I don't believe that he meant the statement in a derogatory way. His statement, however, did raise questions in my mind as to my place in Canadian society. Having light hair, fair skin, and blue eyes does not necessarily make me "white." I learned this a long time ago, although it had never been spoken so clearly. As a child, I emigrated to Canada with my parents from Sicily. Before I had a chance to learn English, several boys my age wanted to fight with me because I was "strange." My grade eight teacher suggested that I take a two-year high school diploma program, so I could join the other Italian boys as a construction worker or machine shop operator. He didn't think I could complete a regular high school program, let alone go on to university. Even today, when I meet people for the first time, it is not uncommon to experience a joke or two about the "Mafia." *Whiteness*, I learned, is a cultural concept that goes well beyond physical features. It depends not only on who you are or how you look, but also on how people are prepared to view and act towards you.

Although Canada has been ranked by the United Nations as "the best place in the world to live" on a number of occasions since 1992, Canadian history has not been free of prejudice and discrimination. A number of ethnic and racial groups have experienced some form of discrimination at one point or another, while others (such as the various First Nations) have had to deal with this reality over an extended period of time.[1] For Italian Canadians, the prejudice and discrimination directed towards them reached its peak during the Second World War. When Mussolini declared war on Britain and France on June 10, 1940, Italians residing in Canada suddenly became "the enemy within". The Federal Government made use of the War Measures Act to force thousands of Italians to report their whereabouts to the RCMP (Royal Canadian Mounted Police) on a regular basis, to arrest approximately 6,000 people, and eventually intern some 700 individuals.[2] This was not the first, or last, time the War Measures Act was used in this way. During the First World War, more than 80,000 people were registered as "enemy aliens," and some 6,000 Ukrainian Canadians were interned (*Freedom Had A Price*, 1996; Swyripa, 2000). Later, when Japan entered the Second World War, virtually the entire Japanese Canadian population, including women and children, was removed from Canada's Pacific coast and isolated in camps (mostly in the Interior of British Columbia), while their property and assets were confiscated (see Adachi, 1991; Kogawa, 1981; Omatsu, 1992).

Compared to some minorities in Canada today, the Italians have become much more accepted and, in many respects, allowed to become part of mainstream Canadian society. There are prominent politicians, professors, doctors, lawyers, etc. that have made both a name for themselves, and important contributions to life in Canada. Italians as a group, if not individually, have achieved *a degree of whiteness*. Painful memories from the past, however, are not easily forgotten. The image of Italians as "enemy aliens," as the "fifth column," in Mussolini's struggles with Canada, Britain, and the world, may have little significance in Canadian society today. The institutional racism that allowed for the internment of Italian Canadians may have disappeared from collective memory. But, the wounds these actions left behind have not healed completely.

In this paper, I make use of both archival and interview statements to present some of these painful memories. My aim is to address an aspect of Canadian history, and the Italian Canadian experience in particular, that has not received sufficient public or scholarly attention. To achieve my aim, I will make use of examples primarily, although not exclusively, from the experiences of Italian Canadians from Cape Breton Island, Nova Scotia. Understanding of the past, in my view, is essential to ensure that similar mistakes are not repeated in the future. This point takes on added significance in this post 9/11 period, a period when people of Middle Eastern descent or Islamic religion are experiencing racial profiling and other negative consequences throughout much of Europe and North America.

The Italian Experience in Cape Breton

Although certain individuals may have arrived earlier, Italian settlement in Cape Breton began in the second half of the 19th century (Migliore and DiPierro, 1999). By 1941, the Italian population of the island numbered 1,762, with "cultural enclaves" in Sydney (Whitney Pier), Dominion, and New Waterford (Census Canada, 1944). The vast majority were men who worked in either the steel plant or the coal mines, but a significant number had established families in Cape Breton. These Italian communities were, in many respects, self-sufficient — planting gardens, raising animals, establishing shops and providing various services for one another.

The War Years and the Internment of Italians

When Italy entered the Second World War in 1940, Prime Minister W.L. MacKenzie King made the following public statement: "The Minister of Justice has authorized the Royal Canadian Mounted Police to take steps to intern all residents of Italian origin whose activities have ground for the belief or reasonable suspicion that they might, in time of war, endanger the safety of the State, or engage in activities prejudicial to the prosecution of the war...." The RCMP, which had already compiled a list of names to target in the various Italian communities across the country, began to arrest people immediately. In Cape Breton, those arrested tended to reside within the larger Italian enclaves in the Industrial areas of the island.

The Arrests. One of the men I interviewed from Dominion recalled how the RCMP picked up his father as he arrived home from work at the local coal mine:

> Dad walked home from the station, and the Mounties were there, waiting for him ... He didn't even have time to have his

supper ... Nothing at all! ... For days after, I didn't even know that they had taken him to the Sydney jail. There was no explanation as to why they had taken him. They just said, "You are a member of the Italian Hall, the treasurer, we have orders to arrest you."

They were happy times, if we had been left alone. But, the fact that Mussolini sided with the Germans killed the whole thing. Bang, we were hit. It had nothing to do with people here. My father came to Canada as a young fella. What I think is that the Canadian Government panicked. They grabbed everybody, and made it look like there was, what did they call it, a "Fifth Column" within Canada. It was unreal. They rounded them up like a bunch of cattle. Look at what happened to the Japanese people too. They took their properties, confiscated their money, and shipped entire families inland (Migliore, 1999: 110).

Annie, who as a young girl in Whitney Pier witnessed her father taken away in handcuffs by the RCMP, recalled returning home one day and finding the house empty. She became agitated and began to yell for her mother, afraid the police had returned and taken her away, as well. Fortunately, the mother was nearby and was able to comfort and reassure her that things were going to be okay. As these statements indicate, the arrests were traumatic for not only the men involved but also for their family members.

Memories of the Internment. One of the individuals arrested on June 10, 1940 was Dominic Nardocchio of Sydney.

Well on June the 10th ... about two o'clock in the afternoon ... the RCMP came into my shop and said: "Are you Dominic

Nardocchio?" I said: "Yes sir." [pause] And he said to me: "You are under arrest." I said: "What have I done?" "Well," he said, "you know Italy declared war on England." "What's that got to do with me?" "Well," he said, "the orders come from Ottawa that I have you arrested [pause] ..." He was a man ... doing his duty. There was nothing you could do, so I ... went with him ... [to] the city lockup ... The next morning, they ... took us away by car. Well, four or five of [the Italians] had black eyes ... They took us to Truro and from Truro they put us on the train ... [to] Petawawa ...[3]

While in the camp, the men were put to work. Romano Scattolon of Dominion recalls:

> The camp at Petawawa was just like a prison with high walls and barbed wire, soldiers and guns. There were interns from all over Canada, of different nationalities. Most were German and Italian. Life there was not too bad. The food was good, there was no violence or beatings and of course we had to work. Each day I was taken to the brush, under guard, and I cut wood for two years and three months. I still had no correspondence with my family ... (Migliore, 1999: 111-112).

Although the internees were not mistreated in the camp, they faced the mental strain and concern of not knowing what was happening to their families.

> I thought I would forget it, so in the camp, this is dated November 1940, I bought a scribbler and took the covers off, and the whole story of the arrest is here. [Reading from the scribbler] "In a few seconds we were away leaving behind our

families in despair without protection or sympathy from anyone. Without knowing where the next meal would come ..." This is what I wrote in the concentration camp. And I had to take it out in a shoe, because I know that we were not allowed to take it out. See, we were censored; everything we did: we were not allowed to read newspapers; my wife's letter to me was censored, whatever I wrote was censored (Dominic Nardocchio).[4]

When finally released, the internees faced new problems.

> The authorities paid my train fare home. I was happy to be with my family, but I did not have a job. A coal company official explained to me that if I were rehired there could very possibly be an outbreak of hostilities among the non-Italian citizens. There was a strong resentment against people like myself... Also, my wife and family were discriminated against during my internment and after my release (Romano Scattolon, in Migliore, 1999: 112).

"Enemy Aliens" — Labelling and Its Consequences

In terms of numbers, only a small proportion of the Italian population of Cape Breton (and Canada in general) was interned during the war years. The label of "enemy alien," however, had consequences for a relatively large portion of the Italian population across Canada. Many individuals were forced to report to the RCMP (or their local police force) weekly, and later on a monthly basis. People lost their jobs or were prevented from carrying out their work duties, while others faced violence or discrimination of one form or another. Those who were not directly affected by the internment often experienced the fear of what might happen to them, or their loved ones, in uncertain times. These fears had dramatic effects on people of all age groups — including fear of acknowledging, expressing or revealing one's cultural identity.

> I was nine years old when the war started ... My mother wouldn't let me have my ears pierced. She said it would make me look "Italian" ... "That's for Italian girls," she would say. "You are Canadian ..." She would also say: "When the other girls ask what you had for lunch, don't say spaghetti or pasta." That, of course, would give away my Italian culture ... My father ... was not interned [but he was] so afraid of what was happening ... that he removed everything from our home that denoted being Italian ... Everything! Any pictures (even one of the Pope), ornaments, or mementos from the homeland were gone. And his homemade wine! I remember my mother ... insisted that the police would not arrest him just because he made some wine, but he poured it all out anyway (Migliore, 1999: 114).[5]

The fears that many Italians experienced during this period were not unfounded. In Dominion and New Waterford, for example, non-Italian miners refused to work with their Italian counterparts (individuals that they had often known and worked with, without trouble, for years).

> It was the time the War was on they done that. That was the silliest thing I ever heard. I was born in New Waterford, and it was a hell of a good man I was, and I lost my job because I might have "done something" to the War. I forgive but I can't forget, you know. Really, the fellas that I worked with said that to me! And I worked right in Waterford, worked all

my life in the coal mine, and I lost my job. And me with five children (James Nemis, in deRoche, 1999: 99; see also Bagnell, 1989).

We were scared that time, you know. A few men were taken to the internment camp... They were taken away for nothing! And we were scared too. The Italian miners were off work for six months. And, when they went back, some of the English people would throw rocks at the train taking them in to work. Back then, we were getting nothing. [No relief was provided during the initial period.] Not even a dollar. No! Then, after a while, I guess they felt some shame and gave us something like 75 cents for a child, and a $1.50 per woman and man. Per week. Welfare ... [How would you manage?] Well, we had the chickens, a pig, we made bread, and we had the garden. We made it anyhow. But, if it had gone longer ... When the men went back to work, they were put on back shift. They were away all night, and we were scared ... [Families were harassed at night, while the men were away.] Hard, hard, hard (Amalia Zorzi of Dominion, in Migliore, 1999a: 105).

Denying miners the right to work created a great deal of hardship, fear, and further uncertainty for entire families. It is fair to say that, in one way or another, everyone was affected by the actions taken by both individuals and the Canadian Government towards specific members of the Italian communities of Cape Breton.

Friend or Enemy: The Ambiguities of War

The Italian Canadian experience(s) during the Second World War cannot be understood in simple terms. At the very same moment that certain individuals were interned, lost their jobs, or were mistreated in some way, other Italian Canadians (sometimes from the same family) served with the Canadian Forces in the combat zones.

> They said it wasn't safe to work [in the mines] with the Italians. My brother-in-law had two sons in the army ... Was it fair for [them] to serve in the Canadian Army, when [their] father couldn't go to work? (Giovanni Antonello, Dominion, in CBC Radio, 1977)[6]

> On June 10, 1940, the RCMP arrested Michael [Martinello] without any explanation to the family. Before the evening was over, the family discovered that Frank Martinello and a cousin, Felix (Felice) Martinello along with a number of other Cape Breton Italian men had been [arrested, and later put on a train for Camp Petawawa]... The internment years were very hard on Michael's wife. She became ill during this time, probably because of the stress ... The irony was that [her son] Eddy Martinello was serving in the Canadian Army at the same time that his father was in a Canadian internment camp ... Eddy was not the only son of an interned Canadian of Italian-descent who served in the Canadian military forces. Frank Martinello, who also was imprisoned at Camp Petawawa, had two sons and a daughter serving in the Canadian Armed Forces during World War Two. One of Frank's sons, Harry, even served with the Canadian Forces in Italy ... (Anna Martinello, in Marshall and Diekelmann,1999: 92-93).

Paradoxically, in a sense, Italian Canadians were treated as both "enemy aliens" and "friends of the nation" during this period. The situation becomes even more complex when one considers that, in some cases, individuals released from the internment camps were sometimes called up for Canadian military service. Benny Ferri of Hamilton, Ontario, for example, found himself in precisely this position just two weeks after his release from the camp at Petawawa.

> I said to myself: "One time I am dangerous ... and another time I am a good soldier. What makes me?" And sometimes, if you think about it, it's complicated, because you are in a position, "how can you be an enemy today, and tomorrow, you know, friendship enemy is one thing, but war enemy is another thing." That's the way I see it; I could be wrong.⁷

The End of Internment and the Lingering Effects

As the war came to an end, the last of the Italian Canadian internees were released. None of these individuals was ever charged or prosecuted for a crime against Canada. Upon their return home, however, they often faced new problems — unwelcoming communities; loss of previous employment; difficulty finding new jobs; threats to leave the area or be "burned out"; and, among other things, the lingering suspicion in the minds of others that they must have done something wrong, or they would not have been interned.

> My wife would walk on the main streets. She'd see people walking towards her; first they were friends, then they would walk on the street and not talk to her. It's unbelievable. You destroy a family's morale and character, financially, but then you don't restore that. No money can buy that. Even today, some people think: "[O]h, the government has something on him." They had nothing on us, absolutely nothing (Dominic Nardocchio, Sydney).⁸

The final phrase in Dominic Nardocchio's statement is significant. One of the features consistent in the narratives of Italian Canadian internees is the espousal of innocence (see Duliani, 1994; *Barbed Wire and Mandolins*, 1997; and Migliore and DiPierro, 1999).

In Search of Redress

In 1988, the Government of Canada reached a settlement with Japanese Canadians to provide redress for the mistreatment and internment they experienced during the war years. The settlement, among other things, included both an apology and a compensation package that would pay $21,000 to survivors of the internment process (see Daniels, 1991; Omatsu, 1992). "Inspired by the settlement awarded Japanese Canadians for their wartime sufferings, the National Congress of Italian Canadians (NCIC) launched its redress campaign in January of 1990" (Iacovetta and Ventresca, 2000: 379).[9] The internees' espousal of innocence served as a key feature of the NCIC redress campaign.

Several months later, on November 4, 1990, Prime Minister Brian Mulroney publicly apologized to Italian Canadians:

> What happened to many Italian Canadians is deeply offensive to the simple notion of respect for human dignity and the presumption of innocence. The brutal injustice was inflicted arbitrarily, not only on individuals suspected of being security risks but also on individuals whose only crime was being of Italian origin ... None of the 700 internees was ever charged with an offence and no judicial proceedings were launched. It was often, in the simplest terms, an act of prejudice — organized and carried out under law, but prejudice nevertheless ... Forty-five years of silence about these wrongs is a shameful part of our history ... On behalf of the government and the

people of Canada, I offer a full and unqualified apology for the wrongs done to our fellow Canadians of Italian origin during World War II.[10]

The statement, however, was not made in Parliament; therefore, it did not constitute an official apology and provided no basis for compensation. "Since the settlement of the Japanese Canadian Redress Claim ... the Canadian Government adopted a de facto 'closed door' policy on any dialogue or consideration of redress and reparations for historical injustices" (Canadian Race Relations Foundation, ND).

The redress issue, however, would not disappear. Finally, on November 12, 2005, Prime Minister Paul Martin signed an agreement-in-principle with various Italian Canadian associations (including the NCIC) to set aside an initial $2.5 million for educational purposes.

> The Government of Canada and the Italian Canadian Community have developed this agreement-in-principle, premised on the principles of "no compensation" and "no apology." This is a first step in articulating their shared vision for the acknowledgement, commemoration and education of Canadians on the historic experience of Italians in Canada who were designated as enemy aliens and some of which, as well as some persons of Italian origin, were interned. It also highlights the contributions that the Italian Canadian Community has made to building Canada. It is the intention of both parties that a final agreement, including additional funding and an appropriate acknowledgement by the Government of Canada of national internment operations, will be concluded as soon as possible (Persichilli, 2005).

There was some indication that the final figure could reach as much as $12.5 million by the end of the program (Persichilli, 2005). The announcement, however, was made in an Italian neighbourhood of Montreal a couple of months before the Federal election of January 23, 2006. The new Conservative Government raised the total for the agreement to $5 million, but insisted that the $12.5 million the Liberals had proposed was merely a campaign promise (Grasser, 2008).

In 2009, Massimo Pacetti, the Liberal MP for St-Leonard/St-Michel, introduced Bill C-302 to Parliament, as a private member's bill, with the aim of addressing the injustices that occurred during the Second World War. A year later, the House of Commons passed the bill as the Italian-Canadian Recognition and Restitution Act. The Bill was supported by all parties except the Conservatives. The Act clearly states:

> The Parliament of Canada hereby acknowledges the unjust treatment received by persons of Italian origins as a result of their designation as "enemy aliens", their registration and internment and other infringements of their rights during the Second World War, and apologizes on behalf of Parliament, the Government of Canada and the Canadian people of earlier times and of today for the suffering that this treatment caused.

In terms of restitution, Bill C-302 indicated that funding would be channelled towards the "production of educational materials that will provide information on Italian-Canadian history and promote ethnic and racial harmony, and the distribution of those materials ..." Unfortunately, the bill did not become law. The passing of C-302 was delayed in the Conservative-dominated Senate, and quietly disappeared after the Conservative victory in the federal election of May 2011. The Harper Government, however, has provided some funding for educational purposes to address the issues surrounding the internment of Italians. No arrangements have been put in place to provide for any direct compensation for internees and their families.

The Case of Osvaldo Giacomelli

Osvaldo Giacomelli was one of the last Italian Canadian internees to be released in 1945. "Born in Hamilton, he had left for Italy as a child with his parents — only to return to Canada on the eve of the war" (Cumbo, 2000: 112; see also Scardellato, 2000). Although not a member of any Fascio (fascist group), he spent close to five years in the internment camps — first in Petawawa, and later in New Brunswick. According to Carmela Fragomeni (2005), "Giacomelli, tired of waiting years for compensation, filed a $750,000 lawsuit in December 2004 against Ottawa."

The lawsuit was based on allegations that the Federal Government's "refusal to offer compensation [for the internment] was discriminatory and contrary to the freedoms and liberties of the [Canadian] Charter [of Rights and Freedoms] ..." (Yach, 2008: 6). The Government of Canada failed in its attempt to have the lawsuit dismissed, but Osvaldo Giacomelli passed away on March 4, 2006. The Attorney General's Office then argued that Giacomelli's estate should not be able to pursue the lawsuit, and the Court of Appeal for Ontario agreed. On June 18, 2008, the Supreme Court of Canada supported the Ontario decision to bring the case to an end. The following statement appears as part of the summary to the Supreme Court decision:

> The Applicant was a Canadian citizen of Italian origin who brought a claim against the Respondent [the Government

of Canada] after having been wrongfully arrested and detained in 1940 under the Defence of Canada Regulations, 1940 made pursuant to the *War Measures* Act, R.S.C. 1927, c. 206. The claim alleged violations of ss. 7 and 15 of the *Canadian Charter of Rights and Freedoms*. The Respondent sought to strike the statement of claim as disclosing no reasonable cause of action, but its motion was unsuccessful. The Applicant died on March 4, 2006 and the proceeding was stayed in accordance with the Rules of Civil Procedure pending an Order to Continue, which was obtained by the trustees of the Applicant's estate on July 13, 2006. Following the Supreme Court of Canada's decision in *Hislop*, the Respondent brought a motion to vary the Order to Continue. The Respondent asked that the order be varied so that any Charter claims could not be continued by the estate. The motion was granted. The Applicant's subsequent appeal was dismissed (Supreme Court of Canada).

Osvaldo Giacomelli did not receive an apology, and his estate will not receive compensation. With the failure of Bill C-302 to pass into law, the family may have run out of options in its search for compensation.

Setting the Record Straight

In 2000, Franca Iacovetta, Roberto Perin, and Angelo Principe produced an edited volume titled *Enemies Within: Italian and Other Internees in Canada and Abroad*. One of the aims of the volume is to help set the record straight by moving away from simplistic perspectives on the internment of Italian Canadians (and others). Franca Iacovetta and Roberto Perin, for example, state in their introduction:

In contrast to the first, and still important, Canadian collection on internment during the Second World War, On Guard for Thee: War, Ethnicity and the Canadian State, 1939-1945, where most contributors shared the same perspective, this volume includes scholars who do not always agree with each other. It also offers a challenge to the central thesis of On Guard for Thee, which was that the internment of Canada's ethnic minorities constituted a "war against ethnicity." According to this view, the Canadian government caved in to wartime hysteria and xenophobia by arbitrarily incarcerating people on the basis of incomplete information hastily scraped together. By contrast, the authors here present differing assessments of government officials and security forces inside and outside Canada. While criticism of state authorities is much in evidence, as is a certain sympathy for the innocent victims of internment, many authors argue for the reasonableness of wartime policy intended to suppress suspected Nazi and Fascist activists (Iacovetta and Perin, 2000: 5; see also Hillmer, Kordan, and Luciuk, 1988; Marsh 2008).

The book also makes a notable contribution to the study of the internment and the Italian Canadian experience by addressing social and gender issues, the role of the Italian media in Canada, fascist and anti-fascist activities in the pre-war years, and the process and politics of redress.

One of the key points repeated in several of the articles is the suggestion of "reasonableness" to the Canadian Government's "wartime policy." This suggestion is based on: 1) the presence of an Italian fascist movement in Canada; 2) the relatively small number of individuals of Italian background interned (unlike the large-scale internment of Japanese Canadians); and, 3) the establishment of a review process that led to the release of internees after varying periods of time. Given the historical information available to us, it is difficult for anyone to deny the validity of these three points.

At the same time, I feel that the volume sets in motion a potentially dangerous argument with respect to notions of human rights. Although the three points listed above ring true in-and-of themselves, they do not necessarily lead to the conclusion that the Canadian Government was justified in interning approximately 700 Italian Canadians. This becomes even more troubling when specific authors suggest that at least some of those interned may have been less than innocent, because of their links to Italian fascism (see Principe 2000; Pennacchio 2000; Bruti Liberati 2000, Perin 2000, Scardellato 2000, and Iacovetta and Ventresca 2000). In certain articles of *Enemies Within*, the focus of attention has shifted. Fascism itself becomes the "crime" that warrants internment. As Angelo Principe (2000: 36; see also 1999) states: "Canada's internment of Italian-Canadian Fascists was politically sound and necessary. In the ideologically charged clash of the Second World War, allowing self-declared Fascists to move freely about the country would have been a security risk."

Not all of those interned were fascists, and some fascists were not interned. It is true, however, that a number of the internees were in one way or another linked to Italian fascist associations or clubs in the pre-war years, and that some of them were committed fascists. Yet, this was not a crime in the years leading up to the Second World War:

> Where was the sin of being a Fascist when Senator Lawrence A. Wilson gave the money to paint Mussolini, mounted on his horse, on the dome of the most beautiful Italian church, *La Madonna della Difesa*, in Montreal? Authorities in power accepted invitations to Fascist feasts in Canada. Winston

Churchill, the spirit of the war against Nazism had publicly declared in Rome that if he were an Italian, he would be a Fascist and that Italy was fortunate to have Mussolini as its leader. When R.B. Bennett was prime minister of Canada, his minister of justice, the Hon. Hugh Guthrie, flatly refused a delegation of Italian anti-fascists who urged him to imitate the United States and prohibit any Fascist organization in Canada. His argument was that the Italian government was a friendly government and that the Italians in Canada were justified in wearing black shirts and marching in military formation on public streets ... (Spada 1969: 126-127; see also Principe 1999).

One of the internees I interviewed in Hamilton, Ontario — a prominent figure in an Italian fascist organization — stated emphatically that he was a fascist, and that he wore a black shirt. At the same time, he added that his children were born in Canada, and that he would never have done anything to hurt Canada.

My aim is not to defend fascism. The preceding internee statement, however, leads me to believe that "fascism" — as both an organizational entity and a political philosophy — not only had different levels of commitment within Italian Canadian communities, but also had different meanings for different people. Principe's fascinating work on fascism and the Italian media tells us a great deal about the role of the Italian Government in promoting Italy and fascism, and the propaganda generated through the media. As Gabriele Scardellato (1999: 12-13) states in his introduction to Principe's *The Darkest Side of the Fascist Years*:

> Principe amasses a wealth of evidence, drawn in particular from the three principal fascist newspapers of the inter-war period, for fascist propagandising and organizing activity

across the country. His concerns therefore, are not necessarily with the consequences of Italian-Canadian fascist activity in Canada — that is, the internments themselves and the hostility toward Italian Canadians that they provoked — but rather with the environment which fascist propagandising helped to create and with the very vehicle that helped to create it. In these concerns, a reader can detect a desire on Principe's part to address his inability to understand the internees themselves and to challenge those who have allowed themselves to be deceived by them. In short, through his analysis of the history of the black-shirt press and its agents and promoters and proprietors, and in particular of the issues that its various newspapers attacked or defended, Principe silences the often-heard claim of naivety and innocence on the part of many who were interned, and those who have written about them, with numerous detailed examples of the proliferation and attempted dissemination of fascist ideology in Canada amongst Italian Canadians in particular.

By concentrating on written materials and official records, Principe is not in a position to understand the point of view of those who were interned. He cannot tell us what specific individuals were thinking as they frequented the "After Hours" clubs or paraded on the streets. He cannot tell us if those interned read these newspaper articles and, if they did, what influence, if any, the articles may have had on them. A similar argument can be applied to Gabriele Scardellato's (2000) article in *Enemies Within*. Some of the photos taken at the internment camps clearly show the presence of fascist symbols. A study of the symbols alone, however, does not tell us why internees displayed the symbols, nor does it tell us what the symbols meant to the individuals in the photographs. Do the symbols indicate guilt? Do they indicate that these individuals posed a danger to Canada? Or, do they suggest pride in Italy, resentment for their internment, or a variety of other possibilities? Although Scardellato's article is a welcome addition to the study of the Italian Canadian experience during the Second World War, the questions I pose cannot be answered from an analysis of the symbols themselves.

From my perspective, concepts (including fascism) and symbols of any kind are human constructions that have no meaning in-and-of themselves. It is people who give meaning to concepts and symbols in specific contexts, and these meanings are open to interpretation. I also argue that meaning, because it involves interpretation, renders our concepts and symbols much more vague, ambiguous, variable, and prone to change than we may intend (see Migliore 1997; 2001). What is needed, in my view, is an understanding of the meanings people attach to various concepts and symbols as part of their everyday life experiences — and, how people construct, deconstruct, and reconstruct these meanings over time. I believe that it is irresponsible to question the validity of internee statements based on studies that privilege media and propaganda statements, official reports, and other documents. Rather than treat internee narratives as "truth" or "lies," it would be more appropriate to examine the meanings and messages people attempted to construct and communicate through their statements. The statements of those who experienced internment, directly or indirectly, are not simply "self-serving," they are rich in communicating feelings, memories, and how people view reality (see also Salvatore 1998). We also have to remember that media reports, official documents, and other archival materials are not necessarily a reflection of the "truth". They too are statements created by people who had their own points of view, bias, and experiences.

My role here is not to judge individual internees, nor to comment on their innocence or guilt. Were some fascists? Yes. But, for me this is not the key question. What is important to ask is: Did they commit acts of espionage or sabotage? Were they guilty of some politically related crime against the nation? The answers to these questions is clear; it is no. A number of Italian Canadians were incarcerated, some for extended periods of time, without charge. They were denied what we call basic human rights. The issue is not whether they were or were not fascists, but rather how the Canadian Government suspended civil liberties for certain individuals, and in the process caused hardship for those individuals and their families (as well as many other Italian Canadians who were not touched directly by the internments).

Conclusion

Canada, as an imagined nation, has been constructed in terms of metaphors and images of masculinity and whiteness (see Strong-Boag et al., 1998). Within this context, it is not surprising to find a long history of discrimination towards Aboriginal Peoples and members of various minority groups. Italian Canadians faced acts of discrimination and hostility both before and after the Second World War. The most severe cases, however, occurred during the emotionally charged war years. Although Italian Canadians are now accepted, and sometimes well-positioned, in mainstream Canadian society, news reports during the Second World War (and earlier) often represented Italians (and others) as not only "enemy aliens" but racialized others who were a threat to the very fabric of Canadian society (Smolash 2007). Canadian Government officials were not immune to these representations, and sometimes helped to create or reinforce negative images of Italians.

The application of the label of "enemy aliens" to Italian Canadians and other groups created a great deal of hardship for certain segments of Canada's overall population.

Italian Canadians did not experience the same treatment as Japanese Canadians in the 1940s. The total number of Italian Canadians interned was relatively small, approximately 700 individuals, when compared to the mass internment of Japanese Canadian families. These individuals, however, were denied their civil liberties — imprisoned for varying periods of time without trial or conviction, while their families (and many other Italian Canadians) were exposed to hostility and discrimination of various kinds. Had those interned been charged with some crime, had there been any evidence of wrong doing or disloyalty, the actions of the Canadian authorities would be more understandable and acceptable. This, however, was not the case. None of the individuals interned was ever charged with a crime or offence against the nation.

Canada also has a history of attempting to make amends for violations of human rights — in some cases through apologies, financial redress or, as in recent years, through cash payments for educational purposes in lieu of official apology and compensation. Yet, institutionalised discrimination, the suspension of civil liberties, and/or the failure of the Canadian Government to protect its people continue to take place.

Italian Canadians, as a group, are not prone to the same visible and sustained forms of discrimination that people experienced during the war years. Although I personally have experienced discrimination at certain times, I cannot say that discrimination is currently a significant factor in my life. The situation has changed radically for most Italian Canadians. Canada's First Nations, however, are still engaged in a struggle over their rights and claims.

Today, people of Middle Eastern or Islamic background face racial profiling as they attempt to cross international borders. The Maher Arar case for example illustrates that civil liberties continue to be violated, causing a great deal of physical and mental distress for individuals and their families (see maherarar.ca; Arar Commission, 2006). It is as if we have learned very little from our history, continuously repeating similar mistakes and abuses. It is important to break free from this cycle, and to begin to breakdown the fears, prejudices, and stereotypes that fuel acts of individual and institutionalised discrimination.

The painful memories expressed by internees and others are not simply oral histories that can be analysed to determine "truth value." We are dealing with emotionally charged, powerful statements that serve to challenge the official record, a record often left behind by those in positions of power. They are also statements that express traumatic life experiences, and attempt to reassert people's right to dignity and respect. As the famous Sicilian writer, Leonardo Sciascia, stated:

> Quando un popolo, un paese, una collettività grande o piccolo che sia, non è disposta a perdere la memoria, vuol dire che non è disposta nemmeno a perdere la libertà.[11]

> When a people, a nation, a social community (whether large or small) is unwilling to lose its collective memory, it means that it is unwilling to lose its liberty [my translation].

The very fabric, the very freedom(s) we desire in Canadian society depends on recognition of past (and current) injustices to various minority groups, and an attempt to ensure that these injustices do not recur.

Endnotes

1. See, for example, Ken Adachi (1991), Isabelle Knockwood (1992), Peter Li (2008), J.R. Miller (1996), Jennifer J. Nelson (2008), and Veronica Strong-Boag et. al (1998).
2. It is difficult to determine the exact number of Italian Canadians interned during the war years. The figure may have been as low as 500, to as many as 750 or more individuals. In a letter to M.M. Mahoney (Canadian Legation, Washington, D.C.), dated February 18, 1941, N.A. Robertson (Acting Under-Secretary of State for External Affairs) states that: "The total number of Italians interned in Canada is now about 850." We know that roughly 100 of these individuals were Italian Merchant Marines held as prisoners in Canada, but it is not clear if this is an approximation or an accurate figure. A further complication in addressing the exact number of Italian Canadians interned is the fact that certain individuals may have been released by February of 1941, and that others may have been interned after that date.
3. T2214, Dominic Nardocchio, "Internment of Italians," Beaton Institute, University College of Cape Breton, 1986 — the interviewer is not identified, but the recording may have been done for a local CBC Radio program. See also "A Talk with Dominic Nardocchio," *Cape Breton's Magazine*, no. 53, January 1990.
4. From *Barbed Wire and Mandolins*, directed by Nicola Zavaglia, National Film Board of Canada, 1997. My transcription.
5. Other Italian Canadian communities also experienced problems. For a detailed discussion of the negative effects

experienced by both individuals and the Italian community of Hamilton, Ontario as a whole, see Enrico Carlson Cumbo (2000).
6. Quote from T941, The Italian Community of Dominion, Beaton Institute, Cape Breton University. Interview taped for "Cape Breton: The Hidden Identity," CBC Radio, Sydney, Nova Scotia, September 27, 1977. Wendy O'Conner (research) and Bill Doyle (producer).
7. From *Barbed Wire and Mandolins*, my transcription.
8. From *Barbed Wire and Mandolins*, my transcription.
9. See also National Congress of Italian Canadians, *A National Shame: Redress, World War II and the Internment of Italian Canadians*, http://www.ncic.ca/campaigns/nshame.html (accessed July 16, 2009).
10. Excerpts from "Notes for an Address" by Prime Minister Brian Mulroney to the National Congress of Italian Canadians and the Canadian Italian Business Professional Association. Toronto, November 4, 1990. The speech was obtained courtesy of the Department of Foreign Affairs and International Trade.
11. Leonardo Sciascia made this statement in Racalmuto, Sicily, during the inauguration of an art exhibit titled "Ritratti racalmutesi 800" (on June 27, 1981). The statement now appears on a plaque in front of the doors of Racalmuto's Town Hall.

References Cited

Adachi, Ken. 1991. *The Enemy that Never Was: A History of the Japanese Canadians*, Toronto: McClelland and Stewart Inc.
Arar Commission. 2006. Press release from the Commission of Inquiry into the Actions of Canadian Officials in Relation

to Maher Arar. Ottawa, December 12, 2006. http://www.redress.org/news/Arar%20Commission%20recommends%20a%20new%20review%20agency.pdf. Accessed July 31, 2009.

Bagnell, Kenneth. 1989. *Canadese: A Portrait of the Italian Canadians*, Toronto: Macmillan.

Barbed Wire and Mandolins. 1997. Nicola Zavaglia, director. Ottawa: National Film Board of Canada.

Bruti Liberati, Luigi. 2000. "The Internment of Italian Canadians." In Franca Iacovetta, Roberto Perin, and Angelo Principe, eds., *Enemies Within: Italian and Other Internees in Canada and Abroad*, Toronto: University of Toronto Press, pp. 76-98.

Canadian Race Relations Foundation. N.D. "Claims Within the Canadian Context." http://www.crr.ca/index2.php?option=com_content&do_pdf=1&id=312, accessed July 16, 2009.

Cape Breton's Magazine. 1990. "A Talk with Dominic Nardocchio." Number 53, January 1990.

CBC Radio. 1977. "Cape Breton: The Hidden Identity," CBC Radio, Sydney, Nova Scotia, September 27, 1977. Archival source: T941, The Italian Community of Dominion, Beaton Institute, Cape Breton University.

Census Canada. 1944. *Eighth Census of Canada, 1941: Volume II, Population by Local Subdivisions*. Ottawa: Edmond Cloutier, the King's Printer, pp. 324-339.

Citizenship & Immigration Canada. 2010. News Release: The Government of Canada funds Italian-Canadian educational project — Columbus Centre project will commemorate WWII internment of Italian-Canadians. http://www.cic.gc.ca/english/department/media/releases/2010/2010-07-29.asp. Accessed October 13, 2010.

Cumbo, Enrico Carlson. 2000. "'Uneasy Neighbour': Internment and Hamilton's Italians." In Franca Iacovetta, Roberto Perin, and Angelo Principe, eds. *Enemies Within: Italian and Other Internees in Canada and Abroad,* Toronto: University of Toronto Press, pp. 99-119.

Daniels, Roger. 1991. "Afterword: The Struggle for Redress." In Ken Adachi, *The Enemy that Never Was: A History of the Japanese Canadians.* Toronto: McClelland and Stewart Inc., pp. 371-377.

deRoche, John. 1999. "Remembering the Pain of 1940". In Sam Migliore and A. Evo DiPierro, eds. *Italian Lives, Cape Breton Memories,* Sydney, Nova Scotia: University College of Cape Breton Press.

Duliani, Mario. 1994. *The City Without Women,* translated by Antonino Mazza. Oakville: Mosaic Press.

Fragomeni, Carmela. 2005. "PM's deal won't derail internment lawsuit: Victim's Lawyer." *Hamilton Spectator,* November 16, 2005.

Freedom Had a Price. 1996. Film by Yurij Luhovy, produced by La Maison de Montage Luhovy Inc., in association with the National Film Board of Canada.

Government of Canada. 2010. Bill C-302, the *Italian-Canadian Recognition and Restitution Act.* Ottawa, Ontario: Publishing and Depository Services, Public Works and Government Services Canada. Also available at http://www.parl.gc.ca/HousePublications/Publication.aspx?DocId=4477133&Language=e&Mode=1&File=24#1. Accessed July 3, 2011.

Grasser, Keely. 2008. "Rivals spar over redress for Italian-Canadians." http://www.yorkregion.com/printarticle/82605. October 9, 2008. Accessed July 19, 2009.

Hillmer, Norman, Bohdan Kordan, and Lubomyr Luciuk, eds. 1988. *On Guard for Thee: War, Ethnicity and the Canadian State, 1939-1945*. Ottawa: Canadian Committee for the History of the Second World War.

Iacovetta, Franca, and Roberto Perin. 2000. "Introduction — Italians and Wartime Internment: Comparative Perspectives on Public Policy, Historical Memory, and Daily Life." In Franca Iacovetta, Roberto Perin, and Angelo Principe, eds. *Enemies Within: Italian and Other Internees in Canada and Abroad*, Toronto: University of Toronto Press, pp. 3-21.

Iacovetta, Franca, Roberto Perin, and Angelo Principe, eds. *Enemies Within: Italian and Other Internees in Canada and Abroad*, Toronto: University of Toronto Press, 2000.

Iacovetta, Franca, and Robert Ventresca. 2000. "Redress, Collective Memory, and the Politics of History." In Franca Iacovetta, Roberto Perin, and Angelo Principe, eds., *Enemies Within: Italian and Other Internees in Canada and Abroad*, Toronto: University of Toronto Press, pp. 379-412.

Internment of Italians. 1986. "T2214, Dominic Nardocchio." Sydney, Nova Scotia: Beaton Institute, University College of Cape Breton.

Knockwood, Isabelle. 1992. *Out of the Depths: The Experience of Mi'Kmaw Children at the Indian Residential School at Shubenacadie, Nova Scotia*, Lockeport, Nova Scotia: Roseway.

Kogawa, Joy. 1981. *Obasan*, Toronto: Penguin Books.

Li, Peter. 2008. "Reconciling with History: The Chinese-Canadian Head Tax Redress," in *Journal of Chinese Overseas* 4 (1): 127-140.

MacKenzie King, W.L. 1940. *Canada and the War: New Situations and Responsibilities: (1) Canada's War Effort*

Viewed in Relation to the War Effort of the Allied Powers; (2) Italy's Entry into the War. Broadcasts: Friday, 7 June and Monday, 10 June 1940. Ottawa: King's Printer, 18 pp.

MAHERARAR.CA. 2009. "We all have a right to the truth." http://www.maherarar.ca/ (accessed July 30, 2009.

Marsh, Patrick. 2008. *Oral History in Cape Breton: An Italian Internment History.* BA Thesis, Department of History. Sydney, N.S.: Cape Breton University.

Marshall, Margaret, and Paul Dickelmann. 1999. "All They Ever Wanted Was a New Life and an Apology: One Italian Family's Experience." In Sam Migliore and A. Evo DiPierro, eds. *Italian Lives, Cape Breton Memories,* Sydney, Nova Scotia: University College of Cape Breton Press, pp. 92-94.

Migliore, Sam. 2001. "From Illness Narratives to Social Commentary: A Pirandellian Approach to 'Nerves'," in *Medical Anthropology Quarterly* 15 (1): 100-125.

Migliore, Sam. 1999. "From Internment to Military Service: An Historical Paradox". In Sam Migliore and A. Evo DiPierro, eds. *Italian Lives, Cape Breton Memories,* Sydney, Nova Scotia: University College of Cape Breton Press.

Migliore, Sam. 1999a. "Three Women of Dominion". In Sam Migliore and A. Evo DiPierro, eds. *Italian Lives, Cape Breton Memories,* Sydney, Nova Scotia: University College of Cape Breton Press.

Migliore, Sam. 1997. *Mal'uocchiu: Evil Eye, Ambiguity, and the Language of Distress,* Toronto: University of Toronto Press.

Migliore, Sam, and A. Evo DiPierro, eds. 1999. *Italian Lives, Cape Breton Memories.* Sydney, Nova Scotia: University College of Cape Breton Press.

Miller, J.R. 1996. *Shingwauk's Vision: A History of Native Residential Schools.* Toronto: University of Toronto Press.

Mulroney, Brian. 1990. Excerpts from "Notes for an Address" by Prime Minister Brian Mulroney to the National Congress of Italian Canadians and the Canadian Italian Business Professional Association. Toronto, November 4, 1990.

National Congress of Italian Canadians. N.D. *A National Shame: Redress, World War II and the Internment of Italian Canadians*, http://www.ncic.ca/campaigns/nshame.html (accessed July 16, 2009).

Nelson, Jennifer J. 2008. *Razing Africville: A Geography of Racism*. Toronto: University of Toronto Press.

Omatsu, Maryka. 1992. *Bittersweet Passage: Redress and the Japanese Canadian Experience*, Toronto: Between the Lines.

Pennacchio, Luigi G. 2000. "Exporting Fascism to Canada: Toronto's Little Italy." In Franca Iacovetta, Roberto Perin, and Angelo Principe, eds., *Enemies Within: Italian and Other Internees in Canada and Abroad*, Toronto: University of Toronto Press, pp. 52-75.

Perin, Roberto. 2000. "Actor or Victim? Mario Duliani and His Internment Narrative." In Franca Iacovetta, Roberto Perin, and Angelo Principe, eds., *Enemies Within: Italian and Other Internees in Canada and Abroad*, Toronto: University of Toronto Press, pp. 312-334.

Persichilli, Angelo. 2005. "Ottawa announces $2.5 million for internment 'fund', but offers no apologies." http://www.tandemnews.com/viewstory.php?storyid=5754. November 20, 2005. Accessed July 19, 2009.

Principe, Angelo. 2000. "A Tangled Knot: Prelude to 10 June 1940." In Franca Iacovetta, Roberto Perin, and Angelo Principe, eds., *Enemies Within: Italian and Other Internees in Canada and Abroad*, Toronto: University of Toronto Press, pp. 27-51.

Principe, Angelo. 1999. *The Darkest Side of the Fascist Years — The Italian-Canadian Press: 1920-1942*, Toronto: Guernica.

Salvatore, Filippo. 1998. *Fascism and the Italians of Montreal — An Oral History: 1922-1945*. Translated by George Tombs. Toronto: Guernica.

Scardellato, Gabriele. 2000. "Images of Internment." In Franca Iacovetta, Roberto Perin, and Angelo Principe, eds., *Enemies Within: Italian and Other Internees in Canada and Abroad*, Toronto: University of Toronto Press, pp. 335-354.

Scardellato, Gabriele. 1999. "Introduction," in Angelo Principe, *The Darkest Side of the Fascist Years — The Italian-Canadian Press: 1920-1942*, Toronto: Guernica, 1999, pp. 9-18.

Smolash, Naava. 2007. "News and the World Wars: A Geneology (sic) of Canadian Discourse about the 'Enemy Within'." *Narratives of Citizenship 2007*, Conference paper. http://www.nofcit.com/papers/Essay_N.%20Smolash.pdf (accessed July 30, 2009).

Spada, A.V. 1969. *The Italians in Canada*, Canada Ethnica VI, Ottawa & Montreal: Rivieraj.

Strong-Boag, Veronica, Sherrill Grace, Avigail Eisenberg, and Joan Anderson. 1998. *Painting the Maple: Essays on Race, Gender, and the Construction of Canada*. Vancouver: UBC Press.

Supreme Court of Canada. Case Information: Summary to Case #32690. http://www.scc-csc.gc.ca/case-dossier/cms-sgd/sum-som-eng.aspx?cas=32690. Accessed July 19, 2009.

Swyripa, Frances. 2000. "The Politics of Redress: The Contemporary Ukrainian-Canadian Campaign." In Franca Iacovetta, Roberto Perin, and Angelo Principe, eds.,

Enemies Within: Italian and Other Internees in Canada and Abroad, Toronto: University of Toronto Press, pp. 355-378.

Villa Charities Inc. 2011. *Columbus Centre: Italian Canadians as Enemy Aliens: Memories of World War II.* http://www.villacharities.com/ICWW2/main.asp?View=Home. Accessed on July 3, 2011.

Yach, Melanie A. 2008. "Ontario Court of Appeal Confirms an Estate Cannot Continue a Claim based upon the *Charter*: *Giamomelli* (sic) *v. Canada (Attorney General)* [2008] O.J. No. 1687, 292 D.L.R. (4th) 379, 236 O.A.C. 212 (Ont.C.A.)." In *Deadbeat* (Ontario Bar Association), volume 27, number 2, pp. 5-6.

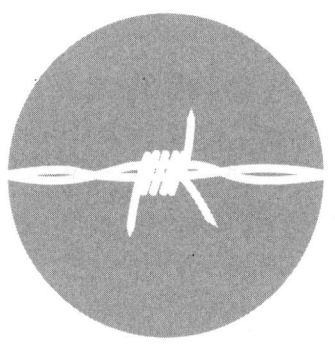

Contributors' Biographies

Antonio Calcagno

Antonio Calcagno is Associate Professor of Philosophy at King's University College at The University of Western Ontario. He works in the areas of contemporary European philosophy, medieval and Renaissance philosophy, as well as social and political thought. He is the author of *Giordano Bruno and the Logic of Coincidence*, *The Philosophy of Edith Stein, Badiou and Derrida: Politics, Events and their Time*. He is the editor of *Symposium: Canadian Journal of Continental Philosophy / Revue canadienne de philosophie continentale*.

Licia Canton

Licia Canton is the author of *Almond Wine and Fertility* (2008) — stories for women and their men. She is also a literary critic and translator, and the editor-in-chief of *Accenti* — the Canadian magazine for lovers of all things Italian. As editor she has published several collections, including *The Dynamics of Cultural Exchange*, *Adjacencies: Minority Writing in Canada*, and *Reflections on Culture*. A member of the Writers' Union of Canada, she is currently President of the Association of Italian Canadian Writers. She holds a Ph.D. from Université de Montréal. She lives in Montreal with her husband and three children.

Vittorina Cecchetto

Vittorina Cecchetto (recently retired) has a Ph.D. in Italian Language and Linguistics and for many years taught Italian and Linguistics at McMaster University in Hamilton, Ontario. Her research interests include the genesis of immigrant contact languages in a multicultural society, the linguistic and identity problems of first and second generation immigrants, didactic stereotyping in second language instruction and language attrition in aging immigrants. She is the author of numerous articles and has co-edited a number of books, among which *The International Classroom: Challenging the Notion* and *Exile, Language and Identity*.

Raymond Culos

Raymond Culos is recognized as a foremost chronicler of the social history of Vancouver's Italian community. Inspired by his Italian-born father Marino Culos, he contributed a regular column to *L'Eco d'Italia* in 1978/79. Following retirement from *The Vancouver Sun* and *The Province* in 1993, Culos wrote a three-volume series entitled *Vancouver's Society of Italians*. In 2009, he launched *Vancouver's Shoeshine Boys*, the story of Italians who worked the local shoeshine stand concessions circa 1900-1975. This latest publication represents a definitive history of BC's Italian enemy aliens during the Second World War.

Domenic Cusmano

Domenic Cusmano is a Montreal publisher, writer and communications consultant. He is the co-founder and publisher of *Accenti Magazine*, an English-language national quarterly whose mission is to give expression to Canada's Italian heritage. He is also the founder of Longbridge Books, a publishing house launched in 2007 whose mandate is to promote fiction and non-fiction that convey Canada's multicultural character.
www.accenti.ca   www.longbridgebooks.com

Lucy Di Pietro

Lucy Di Pietro (B.A. Honours, M.MSt.) has over a decade of experience in various areas of museum work including research and archival work, collections management, exhibition planning and production, digitization and web technologies, oral history collections, and program development and delivery. Having worked at the Royal Ontario Museum, Canada's largest museum, she is currently the Project Director for *Italian Canadians as Enemy Aliens: Memories of World War II,* a project of Columbus Centre of Toronto.

Adriana A. Davies

Adriana A. Davies, CM, Ph.D., was born in Italy and grew up in Canada. She received B.A. and M.A. degrees from the University of Alberta, and a Ph.D. from the University of London, England. She has worked as a researcher, writer, editor, lecturer, executive director and curator for more than 35 years in England and Canada. Professional accomplishments include: Science and Technology Editor, *The Canadian Encyclopedia*; Executive Director, Alberta Museums Association; and creator and editor-in-chief of the *Alberta Online Encyclopedia* — www.albertasource.ca. In 2009, the 81-multimedia websites were gifted to the University of Alberta. Dr. Davies is a recipient of the Order of Canada.

Giulia De Gasperi

Giulia De Gasperi is originally from Treviso. She now lives in Scotland, making frequent visits to Canada, the USA and Italy. She currently holds a Postdoctoral Fellowship in Ethnology at the Department of Celtic and Scottish Studies, Edinburgh University. Her research interests are the diasporic Italian communities, with a particular focus on the Italian community of Dominion, Cape Breton Island, Canada, and collecting and documenting farming life in the Treviso province in the North of Italy. She received her Ph.D. from Ca' Foscari University (Venice) in 2007 and was a recipient of a Government of Canada Award in 2004-2005. www.apanera.com

Antonella Fanella

Antonella Fanella was born in Milan, Italy, and raised in Calgary, Alberta. She is a graduate of the University of Calgary where she earned a B.A. and an M.A. in History. She is the author of numerous articles and has published two books. An archivist, historian and writer, Antonella Fanella lives in Calgary with her husband and daughter. She is inspired by the strength and courage demonstrated by Angelina Rebaudengo during the Second World War.

Venera Fazio

Venera Fazio was born in Sicily and now lives in Bright's Grove, Ontario. Before dedicating herself to writing and editing, she worked as a social worker (MSW). Altogether she has co-edited six anthologies relating to her culture of origin, including the recent *Descant* 154 issue: *Sicily, Land of Forgotten Dreams*. Her poetry and prose have been published in literary magazines in North America and Italy. She is past president of the AICW.

Fabiana Fusco

Fabiana Fusco is Associate Professor of Linguistics and Translation Studies at the University of Udine. In addition to self-translation, her research interests include Italian and French sociolinguistics (youth language, language and gender, language for special purposes), languages in contact and audiovisual translation. She has published widely in these areas. She is also vice-director of the "Centro Internazionale sul Plurilinguismo" at the same university.

Frank Giorno

Frank Giorno was born in Montalto Uffugo, Calabria, Italy, and grew up in Toronto. He now lives in Timmins, Ontario, where he worked on energy conservation for three First Nations. He recently started the Timmins Voices Reading Series. He has worked as a journalist, environmental activist and government communicator. Frank Giorno graduated with an Honours B.A. from York University and a journalism degree from Ryerson University. He is a past editor of the AICW Newsletter. He has written two books of poetry: *Elvis in America* (2006) and *Arrivederci! Plastic-Covered Couch* (2008), published by Lyricalmyrical Press. He has two children, Sophie and Giancarlo.

Patrick Marsh

Patrick Marsh hails from Sydney, Nova Scotia, where he first took an interest in history studies in high school at Sydney Academy. After receiving a B.A. degree in History and English from Cape Breton University in 2008, Marsh received his Masters in History from the University of New Brunswick in 2010. His primary focus is writing Atlantic Canadian history but is also passionate about the political history of Canada, labour history, Cape Breton history, and the history of professional hockey.

James McCreath

James McCreath was born in Toronto in June 1948. He is the eldest of four children born to Ralph McCreath and Myrtle Franceschini. James was educated at St. Andrew's College, York Mills Collegiate and the University of Toronto. His business career has been primarily in real estate, but he has also spent time in the sports, entertainment and publishing fields. James McCreath is the author of the novel, *Renaldo*. He is married with four children and three grandchildren.

Sam Migliore

Sam Migliore is a medical and visual anthropologist at Kwantlen Polytechnic University in Surrey, British Columbia. He has worked extensively with Italian Canadians, and has also travelled to Italy for additional research. His research has led to the publication of numerous articles, several ethnographic films, and two books. Sam recently served as the principal investigator of a SSHRC-funded research project addressing issues of culture and well-being among Italian Canadians in Cape Breton, southern Ontario, and the lower mainland of British Columbia.

Michael Mirolla

Novelist, short story writer, poet and playwright, Michael Mirolla's publications include two novels, *Berlin* (F.G. Bressani Literary Prize winner and finalist for the Indie Book and National Best Books Awards) and *The Facility*, which features among other things, a string of cloned Mussolinis; a novella, *The Ballad of Martin B.*; two short story collections, *The Formal Logic of Emotion* and *Hothouse Loves & Other Tales*; and two collections of poetry, the English-Italian bilingual *Interstellar Distances/Distanze Interstellari* and *Light And Time*. Along with partner Connie McParland, Michael Mirolla runs Guernica Editions, a Canadian literary publishing house.

Joyce Pillarella

Joyce Pillarella is an oral historian whose research focusses on Italians in Montreal. Her MA thesis, which is under the direction of Dr. Steven High at Concordia University, is based on the oral history of the Italians who immigrated to Ville Emard, which was an industrial working class neighbourhood in Montreal. Pillarella has lectured, organized oral history projects in the community and has involved high school students in her research and presentations. In 2011, for the Canadian Historical Recognition Program, she interviewed families of the internees for the *Italian*

Canadians as Enemy Aliens: Memories of World War II national archive at Toronto's Columbus Centre.

Joseph Pivato

Joseph Pivato, professor of Literary Studies at Athabasca University (Edmonton), has focussed his research and writing on Italian-Canadian writing. His publications include: *Contrasts: Comparative Essays on Italian-Canadian Writing* (1985 & 1991), *Echo: Essays on Other Literatures* (1994 & 2003), *The Anthology of Italian-Canadian Writing* (Guernica, 1998), *F.G. Paci: Essays on His Works* (2003), *Caterina Edwards: Essays on Her Works* (2000), *Literatures of Lesser Diffusion* (1990), *Mary di Michele: Essays on Her Works* (2007), *Pier Giorgio Di Cicco: Essays on His Works* (2011). He was born in Italy, lived in Toronto, and has a Ph.D. from the University of Alberta.

John Potestio

John Potestio was born in Grimaldi, Italy, in 1939, and came to Canada with his family in 1953. He is a graduate of the University of Western Ontario (B.A.) and Lakehead University (M.A.) and was a teacher of history in Thunder Bay until his retirement in 1996. He is the author of several books, including *In Search of a Better Life: Emigration to Thunder Bay from a Small Town in Calabria* (2000), *The Memoirs of Giovanni Veltri* (1987), *The Italians of Thunder Bay* (2005). He also co-edited *The Italian Immigrant Experience* and *Thunder Bay's People* with Antonio Pucci.

Angelo Principe

Angelo Principe has a Ph.D. from the University of Toronto. He published widely about the Italian Canadian experience and fascism in Italian, Canadian and American journals. He is the author of *The Darkest Side of the Fascist Years* (Toronto: Guernica, 1999) and co-author of two books. About Italian Canadian women, he wrote, "Glimpse of Lives in Canada's Shadow: Insiders, Outsiders, and Female Activism in the Fascist Era" which is found in *Women, Gender, and Transnational Lives* (Edited by Donna Garbaccia and Franca Iacovetta).

Filippo Salvatore

Filippo Salvatore, Ph.D. Harvard, Cavaliere della Repubblica Italiana, is associate professor of Italian and Italian/Canadian Studies at Concordia University in Montreal and editor-in-chief of the bimestrial trilingual magazine *PanoramItalia*. The Italian presence in Canada is one of the fields of his scholarly interests. He is the author of many books; among them are *La Fresque de Mussolini* (1989), *Le Fascisme et les Italiens à Montréal* (1995), *Le Cinéma de Paul Tana, parcours critiques* (with Anna Gural, 1997), *Ancient Memories, Modern Identities: Italian Roots in Contemporary Canadian Authors* (1999), *Referendum 1995* (2010), *Il Littorio e il Fiordaliso: Il fascismo e gli italiani del Quebec* (2012, forthcoming).

Travis Tomchuk

Travis Tomchuk completed his Ph.D. in History at Queen's University in the fall of 2010. His dissertation, "Transnational Radicals: Italian Anarchist Networks in Southern Ontario and the Northeastern United States, 1915-1940," explored the formation of the Italian anarchist movement in North America through the migration of activists from Italy. This work also examined the movement's political culture and cross-border organizing. Travis

Tomchuk also worked as researcher/writer for the *Italian Canadians as Enemy Aliens: Memories of World War II* (ICEA) project based at Columbus Centre, Toronto. It was while conducting his research for ICEA that he learned of interesting individuals such as Augusto Bersani.

Jim Zucchero

Jim Zucchero grew up in Toronto and now lives in London, Ontario. He teaches Canadian Studies and works as an academic counsellor at King's University College at the University of Western Ontario. He earned a Ph.D. in English at UWO and has published creative non-fiction and essays on Italian-Canadian writers and Canada's National War Memorial. In 2010 he co-edited *Reflections on Culture* (with Licia Canton and Venera Fazio).

Founded in 1986, the **Association of Italian Canadian Writers** is a nonprofit organization that brings together a community of writers, critics, academics, and other artists and promotes Italian Canadian literature and culture within an ethnoculturally diverse society. To learn more, please visit www.aicw.ca

Opened in 1980, **Columbus Centre**, an affiliate of the nonprofit organization Villa Charities, is the largest Italian Canadian cultural centre in Canada. Located in Toronto, the centre provides extensive educational, athletic and cultural programs and special events, and houses the renowned Joseph D. Carrier Art Gallery. With more than 100,000 visitors each year, Columbus Centre is the *piazza* and heart of the community. Visit www.villacharities.com/ICWW2

Since 1978, **Guernica Editions** has published over 400 titles and 500 authors from around the world. Many of its fiction and nonfiction books deal in one way or another with the pleasurable understanding of different cultures. Visit www.guernicaeditions.com

Founded in 2002, **Accenti Magazine** brings together readers and writers around the idea of shared cultural experience and heritage, to encourage creative expression and celebrate common cultural values. An independent voice, *Accenti* provides a platform for aspiring writers and photographers.
Visit Accenti Online at www.accenti.ca.

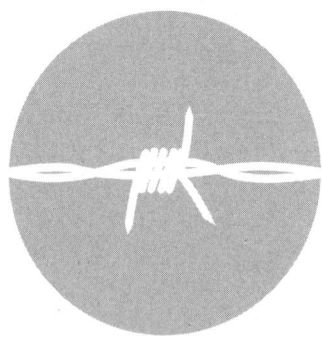

Printed on Rolland Enviro100, which contains 100% recycled post-consumer fibre, is EcoLogo, Processed Chlorine Free and FSC ® Recycled certified and manufactured using biogas energy.